The Economics of Productivity in Asia and Australia

To Navarani

The Economics of Productivity in Asia and Australia

Renuka Mahadevan

The University of Queensland

Edward Elgar
Cheltenham, UK • Northampton, MA, USA

Published by
Edward Elgar Publishing Limited
Glensanda House
Montpellier Parade
Cheltenham
Glos GL50 1UA
UK

Edward Elgar Publishing, Inc.
136 West Street
Suite 202
Northampton
Massachusetts 01060
USA

A catalogue record for this book
is available from the British Library

Library of Congress Cataloguing in Publication Data
Mahadevan, Renuka.
The economics of productivity in Asia and Australia / by Renuka Mahadevan.
p. cm.
Includes bibliographical references and index.
1. Industrial productivity—Asia. 2. Industrial productivity—Australia. 3. Industrial efficiency—Asia—Measurement. 4. Industrial efficiency—Australia—Measurement. I. Title.

HC79.I52M34 2004
338.4'5'094—dc22

2003056458

ISBN 1 84064 961 5

Printed and bound in Great Britain by MPG Books Ltd, Bodmin, Cornwall

Contents

Figures

Tables

Appendices

Abbreviations

DEA	Data Envelopment Analysis
FDI	Foreign Direct Investment
GLS	Generalised Least Squares
MLE	Maximum Likelihood Estimation
MNCs	Multinational Companies
NIEs	Newly Industrializing Economies
OLS	Ordinary Least Squares
R&D	Research and Development
TFP	Total Factor Productivity
TE	Technical Efficiency
TP	Technological Progress

Acknowledgements

My initial interest in productivity growth analysis was triggered by the hot debate and discussions on the East Asian miracle economies as it was a sexy topic when I first started my PhD in 1995 (and still is). I must admit that having only scratched the surface of this research area, I decided quite bravely to venture into writing a book to share my empirical findings, and to consolidate my understanding, thoughts, doubts and even confusion, on what I had learnt so far. In the event, I very quickly realized how much more there was to do but I am glad that I finished this project as it has given me direction and focus in learning and writing in this field.

To this end, I am greatly indebted to Professor Kali Kalirajan of the National Graduate Institute for Policy Studies in Tokyo, who was instrumental in the development of my interest and progress in this area of research. He has been an excellent mentor to me in more ways than one. I am also most grateful for the wonderful support and friendship of John Asafu-Adjaye and Robert Jackson who have gone to great lengths to read my work carefully and have contributed significantly to how the book reads today.

Lastly, I am grateful for the permission granted for material drawn from some of my published work in journals such as *Applied Economics*, *Empirical Economics*, *Journal of Economic Studies* and *Atlantic Economic Journal*.

PART I

Productivity and Efficiency Measures

1 Introduction

1.1 INTRODUCTION

Productivity growth has long been recognized by both economists and non-economists as being necessary for all economies aspiring to raise their standard of living. But since the 1990s, it has also become a rather fashionable buzzword for politicians and policymakers in the Asia-Pacific region. Among researchers, the concept of total factor productivity (TFP) gained importance when it was recognized that output growth could not be sustained by input growth as the latter was subject to diminishing returns in the long run. Thus, TFP growth has become synonymous with long-run growth as it reflects the potential for growth. This spurred great interest in trying to obtain improved and more accurate TFP growth estimates. However, just how important TFP is has been a matter of ongoing controversy since the birth of the TFP concept in Tinbergen (1942). While one source of controversy arises from the sins of omission rather than commission in the estimation of TFP growth measure, the other part of the controversy is about methods and assumptions in the estimation techniques as well as the interpretation of TFP growth in empirical analyses.

The basic motivation for writing this book is an empirical one and the aims of this book are twofold. Firstly, to highlight the conceptual differences and advantages and disadvantages of the various TFP measures and suggest ways and strategies for choosing the best technique. Information on econometric software packages available for use is also provided. Secondly, to guide readers to interpret empirical results from the six case studies presented in this book. The analysis on the selected Asia Pacific economies is not only informative but also allows for variety in issues concerning productivity analysis.

In addition, sector and industry-level data on the manufacturing and services sectors as well as firm-level data on the banking sector have been used to cover analysis at various levels of aggregation and disaggregation. All the case studies' analyses used panel data and this allowed the simultaneous investigation of efficiency change among industries or firms as well as efficiency change over time.

It must, however, be stressed that the interest is in the measurement and interpretation rather than causation (although two case studies are devoted to this) not because such an exercise is deemed unimportant but because uncovering the pattern of productivity and efficiency performance comes first and the analysis of the causal factors is just an extension of the first exercise. An attempt is, however, made to explain the results, as Sherlock Holmes said, 'by getting into the region where we balance probabilities and choose the most likely. It is the scientific use of the imagination, but we have always some material basis on which to start our speculations.'

The book is divided into three parts. Part I consists of three chapters that explain the theoretical concepts underlying productivity analysis, and discusses the various approaches to productivity and technical efficiency measures. Part II comprises three chapters – each is a case study using a different technique of productivity measurement. Part III presents three more case studies that extend productivity analysis by linking it with other aspects in the economy such as trade liberalization and industrial policy as well as other microeconomic and macroeconomic policies. Thus Parts II and III are interpretative in the sense that they attempt to probe behind the numerical figures obtained from the empirical results.

The book has an applied focus with policy orientation and is thus intended as reference material for economists, researchers in industry and government, and graduate students who are interested in productivity analysis. Although the underlying theoretical framework is deliberately kept simple without excessive notation, an understanding of an undergraduate level of economics and some knowledge of basic econometrics is required. But to narrow the gap for those unfamiliar with these aspects, there are relevant references provided for supplementary reading as and where necessary.

1.2 THE CONCEPT OF PRODUCTIVITY AND EFFICIENCY

This section provides definitions and explanations of the concepts underlying the various productivity and efficiency measures. These include:

- Partial productivity
- Total factor productivity (TFP)
- Multifactor/total productivity

- Productive/economic efficiency
- Technical efficiency
- Allocative efficiency
- Scale economies.

1.2.1 Types of Productivity Measures

Productivity refers to the relationship between outputs and inputs in real terms and is often measured as a partial measure, a TFP measure, or a multifactor productivity measure.

The partial measure is calculated as labour or capital productivity, that is, net or gross output per unit of the respective input. It is given by:

$$\text{Labour productivity} = Q/L \qquad \text{Capital productivity} = Q/K$$

where Q, K and L are the aggregate level of output, capital and labour respectively.

But this measure only considers the use of a single input and ignores all other inputs, thereby causing misleading analyses. Thus the partial measure does not measure overall changes in productive capacity since it is affected by changes in the composition of inputs. For instance, improvements in labour productivity could be due to capital substitution or changes in scale economies, both of which may be unrelated to the more efficient use of labour. However, Kendrick (1991) maintains that these measures are useful in showing the savings achieved over time in the use of the input per unit of output. Sargent and Rodriguez (2000) advocate the use of labour productivity to examine trends over a period that is less than a decade given the biases in estimating capital stock to obtain TFP growth. From the welfare point of view, Norsworthy and Jang (1992) explain that labour productivity which is linked to output per capita by labour force participation and the age structure of the population, ultimately limits per capita consumption. Therefore, this partial measure retains a role in the family of productivity measures relevant to national economic policy. Typically, labour productivity moves in the same direction as TFP but grows at a somewhat faster rate reflecting the influence of capital deepening.

Unlike the partial measure, the multifactor and TFP measures consider the joint use of the inputs in production and mitigate the impact of factor substitution and scale economies. They are given by:

$$\text{TFP index} = Q_1 / (aL + bK)$$

$$\text{Multifactor productivity index} = Q_2 / (aL + bK + cM)$$

where Q_1 is value added output, Q_2 is gross output, M is intermediate inputs, and a, b, and c are weights given by input shares.

These measures are the ratio of output to the weighted average of inputs. The distinction between TFP and multifactor productivity is that the latter includes the joint productivity of labour, capital and intermediate inputs, and the former considers the joint productivity of labour and capital only. Intermediate inputs comprise of materials, supplies, energy and other purchased services and value added is defined as gross output less intermediate inputs. The multifactor productivity measure may also include other inputs such as land and other natural resources used in the production process.

1.2.2 Types of Efficiency Measures

While more often than not, productivity measures are incorrectly or loosely called efficiency measures, productivity growth can generally be thought of as consisting of various types of efficiencies. Here, a distinction is made between some of these concepts.

Consider a simple production process in which a single input (x) is used to produce a single output (y) in Figure 1.1. The line $0F$ represents a 'production frontier' that defines the relationship between the input and the output and represents the maximum output attainable from each input level, reflecting the current state of technology in the industry. In other words, it is the locus of all the efficient input–output combinations. Firms in that industry operate either on that frontier if they are technically efficient or beneath the frontier if they are not technically efficient. Point A is inefficient because technically it could increase output to the level associated with the point B without requiring more input and thus the distance AB represents technical inefficiency. 'Technical efficiency', which is represented by a movement towards the frontier, refers to the efficient use of inputs due to the accumulation of knowledge in the learning-by-doing process, diffusion of new technology, improved managerial practice and so on.

To illustrate the distinction between technical efficiency and productivity, we use a ray through the origin to measure productivity at a particular data point in Figure 1.1. The slope of this ray is y/x and hence provides a measure of productivity. If the firm operating at point A were to move to the technically efficient point B, the slope of the ray would be greater, implying higher productivity at point B. However, by moving to the point C, the ray from the origin is at a tangent to the production frontier and hence defines the point of maximum possible productivity. This latter movement is an example of exploiting scale economies. The point *C* is the point of (technically) optimal scale and operation at any other point on the production frontier results in lower productivity. Thus a firm may be technically efficient but may still be able to improve its productivity by exploiting scale economies. Given that changing the scale of operations of a firm can often be difficult to achieve quickly, technical efficiency and productivity can be given short-run and long-run interpretations.

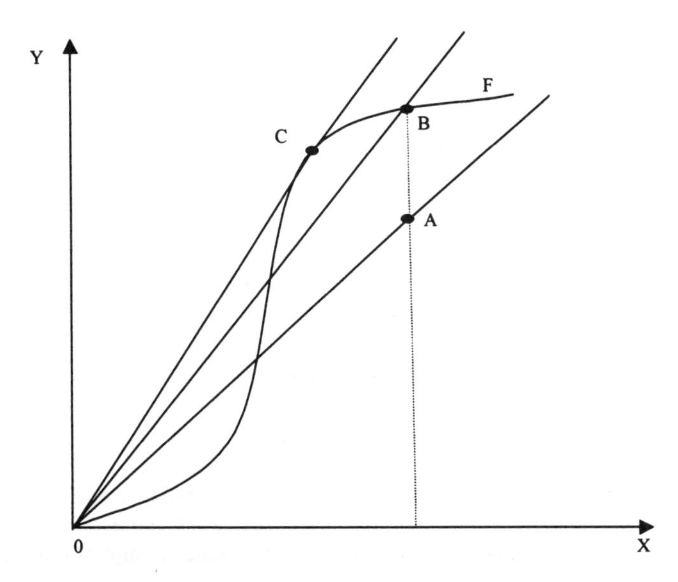

Figure 1.1 Productivity, technical efficiency and scale economies

When a firm increases its productivity from one period to the next, the improvement may have been due to technical change or the exploitation of scale economies, or from some combination of these factors.

Now we move away from the discussion involving physical quantities and technical relationships to issues such as costs or profits. With information on cost of production, prices of output and input, and behavioural assumptions of cost minimization or profit maximization, allocative efficiency can be considered in addition to technical efficiency. 'Allocative efficiency' (in input mix)[1] involves selecting that mix of inputs which produce a given quantity of output at minimum cost at the prevailing input prices. Figure 1.2 illustrates allocative and technical efficiency from the cost perspective of a single-output producing firm using two inputs, X_1 and X_2.

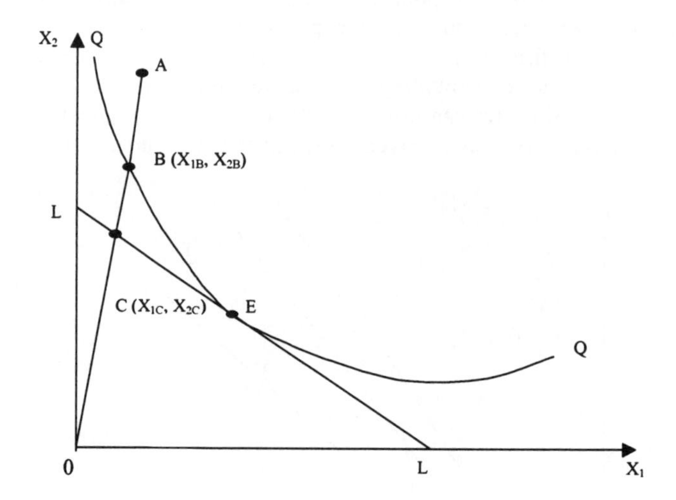

Figure 1.2 Allocative and technical efficiency

An efficient isoquant *QQ* shows all possible input mixes of X_1 and X_2 that would produce the same output. The isocost line *LL* shows all possible combination of inputs of X_1 and X_2 given the input prices and a fixed budget. If the firm is producing at point *A*, then the distance *AB* represents the amount by which input use could be reduced to produce the same amount of output.

$$\text{Technical efficiency} = \frac{OB}{OA}$$

But point *B* is allocatively inefficient since costs of using input mix (X_{1B}, X_{2B}) is above the isocost line *LL*. To produce the same amount of output, the input mix (X_{1C}, X_{2C}) can be used, as the cost of production at point *C* is lower than that at point *B*.

$$\text{Allocative efficiency} = \frac{OC}{OB}$$

The above measure gives the increase in costs solely attributable to a suboptimal input mix. The distance *CB* represents the reduction in costs if production were to move to take place at the allocatively and technically efficient point *E*, instead of at point *B* which is technically efficient but allocatively inefficient.

$$\text{Total economic efficiency} = \frac{OC}{OA} = \frac{OB}{OA} \text{X} \frac{OC}{OB}$$

$$= \text{Technical efficiency X Allocative efficiency}$$

Thus, allocative and technical efficiency combine to provide an overall economic efficiency measure or what is sometimes called 'productive efficiency'. Leibenstein and Maital (1992) also refer to this as *X*-efficiency. As these efficiency measures are ratios, they range from zero to one.

1.2.3 Why Study Productivity Growth?

In the study of productivity growth and efficiency, the first component comprising measurement techniques to date are reasonably well developed. But this does not answer the most interesting and important question of why productivity and efficiency rates have changed over time. This second equally important component concerns the incorporation of exogenous variables which are neither inputs to the production process nor outputs of it, but nonetheless exert an influence on producer performance. Figure 1.3 shows the broad category of factors and the various determinants in each category.

It must be noted that government policies (implicitly stated as national policy) do play a key role in influencing other factors within the economy. Quite inevitably, factors in one category are related to (by causing or being affected by) other factors in another category. For obvious reasons, management decision pertaining to investment in plant and equipment is affected by external factors such as investment tax credits as well as internal factors such as worker behaviour or response to upgrading machinery. Appropriate data are often used to proxy the measurement of the above factors to be used in empirical investigation to draw out policy options for enhancing productivity and efficiency.

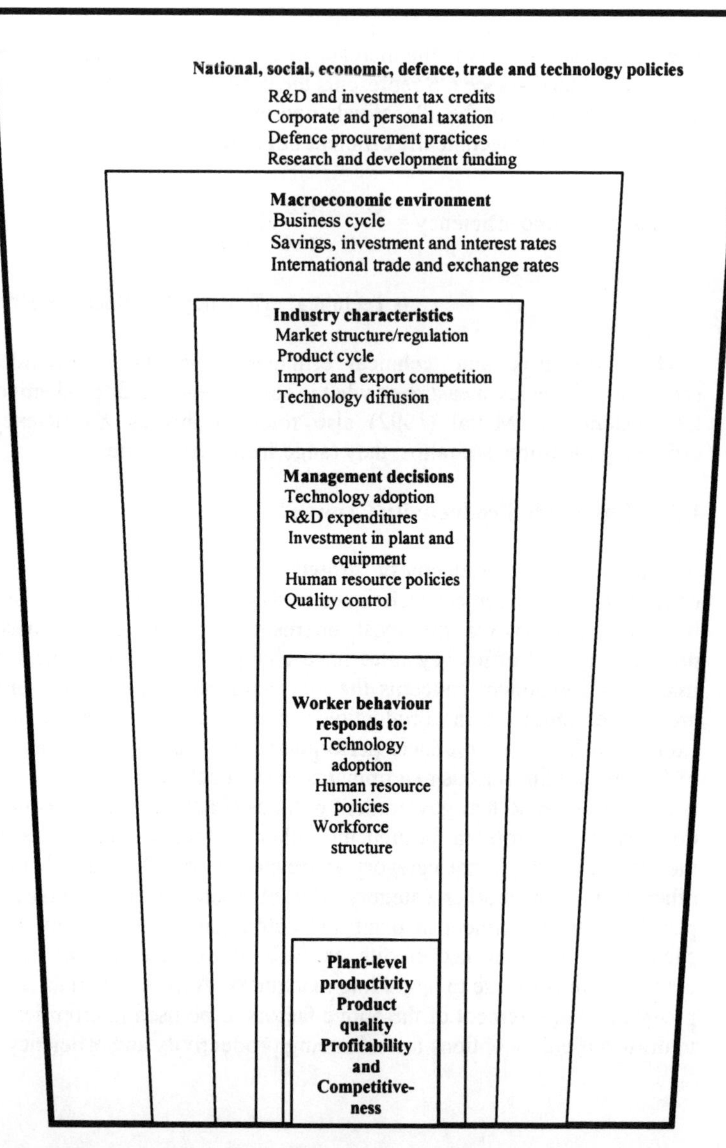

Source: Adapted from Norsworthy and Jang (1992).

Figure 1.3 Determinants of productivity and efficiency measures

1.3 OUTLINE OF CHAPTERS

Part I of this book is theoretical as it explains the theories underlying the various approaches to measuring TFP growth and technical efficiency. Allocative and scale efficiencies are not discussed at length as there is less controversy regarding their measure and if there is a problem, it lies with the availability and reliability of price data rather than the analytical and empirical measurement technique used for measurement. The measurement of technical efficiency has, however, proven to be difficult and complex and thus one chapter is devoted to it. The approaches to the TFP growth and technical efficiency measures are broadly categorized into frontier and non-frontier before explaining the parametric and non-parametric estimation techniques under each approach. Chapters 2 and 3 in Part I are quite technical so as to give the more interested reader a brief introduction to the models, but the less inclined reader is not left in the dark as the content is covered in a general sense and thus kept easy to follow. The models are then detailed in Part II, which comprises three chapters on case studies of various economies using real data as a numerical example of some of the methods described in Part I. In particular, the translog-divisa index, the average production function, the stochastic production and stochastic cost frontiers as well as the data envelopment analysis are the methods used for illustration. The empirical results are then analysed to draw policy implications for each of the economies concerned. Part III covers three chapters which are extensions to the productivity analysis using more case studies.

It must, however, be noted that since all but one case study uses the non-parametric frontier approach, the theoretical Chapters 2 and 3 deal with the parametric frontier techniques in reasonable detail. Such a choice also reflects the fact that I am an applied economist and thus I apologize that the traditional DEA and various other non-parametric frontier models which are based in the operations research school of thought are neglected in this book. Besides, it would be an impossible task to do a thorough job with such a twin-focus in mind. The outline of the subsequent chapters is presented below.

Chapter 2: Total factor productivity growth estimation

This chapter first provides an overview of the broad web of approaches that have been spun over the years in obtaining TFP measures. Then both parametric and non-parametric techniques under each of the frontier and non-frontier approaches are discussed, and information on econometric software packages available for estimation is included. The chapter concludes with a discussion: (1) on the advantages and disadvantages of various methods and suggests ways of choosing the best technique, (2) on the measurement issues related to output and inputs, and (3) on some issues regarding the relevance and use of productivity estimations in an attempt to address some of the controversies surrounding TFP growth.

Chapter 3: The measurement of technical efficiency in production frontier models

This chapter is laid out in a similar fashion to Chapter 2. With the help of a flowchart, readers are guided through the core techniques of measuring technical efficiency from various types of frontier and non-frontier models.

Chapter 4: The non-frontier approach – case study: Hong Kong's manufacturing sector

First, the theoretical framework underlying both the parametric and non-parametric techniques of the non-frontier approach is discussed. These refer to the translog-divisia index, and the Cobb-Douglas average production function. Second, using aggregate manufacturing sector level data from 1984 to 1999, output growth is decomposed to obtain input growth and TFP growth using these approaches. The results are interpreted with supporting evidence drawn from the literature.

Chapter 5: The stochastic production frontier approach – case study: Singapore's services sector

Here, the theoretical model of the parallel and non-parallel shifting stochastic frontiers are set out to parametrically estimate the Cobb-Douglas production function for Singapore's services sector. Using industry-level data comprising 17 types of service from 1975 to 1994, the output growth is first decomposed to input growth and TFP growth, and then TFP growth is further decomposed to technical change and technological progress. The empirical analyses from both these models are compared to draw appropriate policy implications for long-run growth.

Chapter 6: The data envelopment analysis (DEA) approach – case study: Korea's banking sector

The non-parametric frontier technique of data envelopment analysis (DEA) is first described and discussed. Then using the Malmquist output-orientated production index, this chapter studies the productivity and efficiency performance of the Korean banking industry with firm-level data comprising 15 Korean banks from 1981 to 1996. With measures of scale efficiency, technical efficiency and technological progress, analysis is undertaken in the light of evaluating Korean financial deregulation efforts of the 1980s.

Chapter 7: How technically efficient are Singapore's manufacturing industries?

This chapter identifies and tests for factors affecting the technical efficiency of Singapore's manufacturing industries using 28 manufacturing industries from 1975 to 1994. Here, a parallel shifting production frontier is estimated and specific microeconomic policy measures for improvements in attaining potential output are considered.

Chapter 8: Trade liberalization and productivity growth in Australia's manufacturing industries

This chapter first obtains the productivity and efficiency measures for Australia's manufacturing sector by using industry-level data from eight manufacturing industries for 1968/69 to 1994/95 and parametrically estimating the non-parallel shifting production frontier. It then goes on to analyse whether trade liberalization had any significant effect on its productivity and efficiency measures. This was done using the ordinary least squares estimation to empirically test for a host of factors including the effective rate of protection. This analysis sheds some light upon, and potentially adds to, the ongoing debate of trade effects on productivity.

Chapter 9: Looking beyond obtaining the 'real' TFP growth for Malaysia's manufacturing sector

Using data on 28 manufacturing industries from 1981 to 1996, this chapter compares the results of the productivity performance of the Malaysian manufacturing sector using the non-parametric DEA model as well as two parametric models of the production frontier approach. Drawing on the robustness of the results, strategies for improving TFP growth in this sector are discussed.

NOTE

1. See Kumbhakar and Lovell (2000) for measurement of output allocative efficiency.

2 Total factor productivity growth estimation

2.1 INTRODUCTION

This chapter provides a review of the various methods (both parametric and non-parametric) under the broad frontier and non-frontier approaches which can be used to measure TFP growth. In particular, these techniques are traced by linking their underlying theoretical and empirical aspects before drawing out their differences. As the literature to date is inconclusive on the issue of which method to use, this chapter also provides suggestions on how best to choose the appropriate estimation method. Information on econometric software packages available for use as well as measurement issues related to output and inputs are briefly discussed before the relevance of TFP growth estimation is questioned by reviewing some of the controversies plaguing the use of this measure.

Depending on the reader's background, this chapter may or may not seem technical, but it hopes to be general enough to engage most readers. While it is deliberately kept simple without a large dose of mathematical and technical detail, sufficient readings are referenced to complement the material for those who want more out of it. The detailed theoretical framework and discussion on the models are set out in the case studies of the chapters that follow. As the directions taken by productivity analysis are not easy to summarize in a unified way, here a modest attempt is made to offer some structure to the development of these measures without making any pretence of being an exhaustive survey.

2.2 APPROACHES TO TFP MEASUREMENT

The concept of TFP growth dates back to the works of Tinbergen (1942),[1] Abramotivz (1956), Solow (1957) and Griliches and Jorgenson (1966) among many others. While these and a significant number of studies after them have often focused on the non-frontier approach of calculating TFP growth, the frontier approach to TFP measurement was first initiated by Farrell (1957) but it was not until the late 1970s that this approach was formalized and used for empirical investigation. The flowchart in Figure 2.1 is used to map out the main TFP measuring methods under the frontier and non-frontier approach.

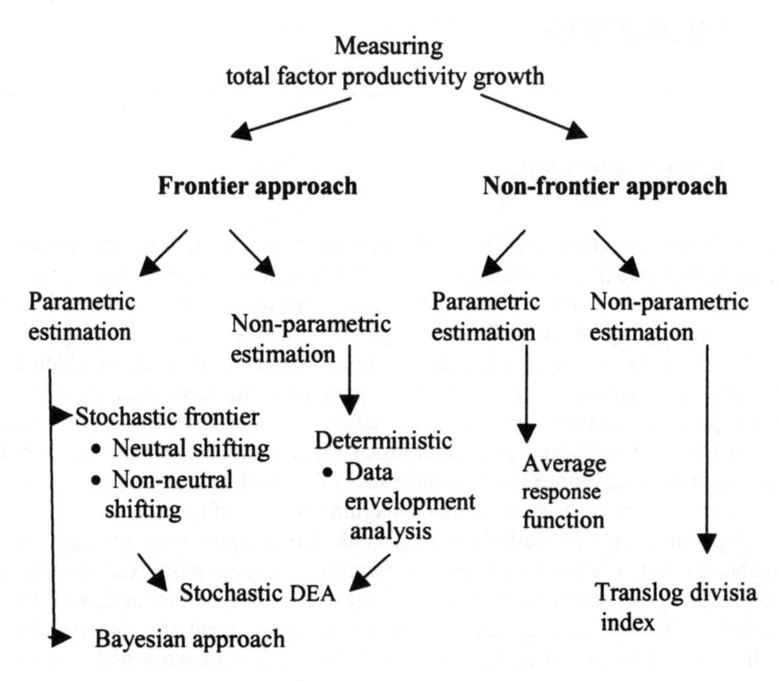

Figure 2.1 Total factor productivity estimation methods

The crucial distinction between these approaches lies in the very definition of the word 'frontier'. A frontier refers to a bounding function or, more appropriately, a set of best obtainable positions. Thus a production frontier traces the set of maximum outputs obtainable from a given set of inputs and technology, and a cost frontier traces the minimum achievable cost given input prices and output. The production frontier is an unobservable function that is said to represent the 'best practice' function as it is a function bounding or enveloping the sample data. This is different from the average function, which is often estimated by the ordinary least square (OLS) regression as a line of best fit through the sample data.

The frontier and non-frontier categorization is of methodological importance since the frontier approach identifies the role of technical efficiency in overall firm performance while the non-frontier approach assumes that firms are technically efficient. Technical efficiency which is represented by a movement towards the frontier, refers to the efficient use of inputs and technology due to the accumulation of knowledge in the learning-by-doing process, diffusion of new technology, improved managerial practice and so on. The frontier TFP growth measure consists of outward shifts of the production function resulting from technological progress due to technological improvements incorporated in inputs, as well as technical efficiency related to movements towards the production frontier. The non-frontier approach on the other hand only considers technological progress as a measure of TFP growth.

Kalirajan and Shand (1994) relate this absence of technical inefficiency in the non-frontier approach to an implicit assumption of long-run equilibrium behaviour. Following Schultz (1975), they argue that the short-run disequilibrium is a more usual condition, and understanding how firms or industries proceed to equilibrium over time depends both on their efficiency in responding to any given disequilibrium, and on the costs and returns of the sequence of adjustments available to them.

Another difference between the frontier and non-frontier approach is that the former is best suited to describe industry or firm behaviour. This is due to the benchmarking characteristic of the frontier approach, whereby a firm's actual performance is compared with its own maximum potential performance or as defined by the best-practice efficient firm in the sample.[2] Benchmarking has little place in the non-frontier approach which was first used to obtain estimates of aggregate TFP growth measure for the entire economy and then was progressively used for various sectors or industry-level analysis when disaggregated data became more widely available. The parametric non-frontier approach which is typically statistical, is characterized as a central tendency approach and it evaluates firms relative to an average producer.

One feature shared by the frontier and non-frontier approaches is that they can both be estimated using either the parametric or the non-parametric method. The parametric technique is an econometric estimation of a specific model and since it is based on the statistical properties of the error terms, it allows for statistical testing and hence validation of the chosen model. However, the choice of the functional form is crucial for modelling the data as different model specifications can give rise to very different results. The non-parametric technique, on the other hand, does not impose any functional form on the model but has the drawback that no direct statistical tests can be carried out for validation. A more thorough discussion on the advantages and disadvantages of both techniques follows later.

2.3 THE NON-FRONTIER APPROACH

The non-frontier approach uses the standard growth accounting framework which separates the growth of real output into an input component and a productivity component. It is given as:

$$\text{Output growth} = \text{Input growth} + \text{TFP growth} \tag{2.1}$$

$$\Rightarrow \text{TFP growth} = \text{Output growth} - \text{Input growth} \tag{2.2}$$

where input growth consists of the sum of the increases in the use of all factors purchased for production.

Here, output is seen to increase by the increased use of inputs and/or increases in productivity. This framework is able to provide the contribution to output growth of each of the inputs used. Since real data on output and input are available, TFP growth in equation (2.2) is estimated as a residual measuring 'everything and anything' of output growth that is not accounted for by input growth. And because the determinants of TFP growth are yet to be proved, this measure is often called a 'measure of ignorance' (Abramovitz 1956) since it is nothing more than a measure of what we do not know. In fact, Jorgenson and Griliches (1967) advanced the hypothesis that careful measurement of the relevant input variables should cause this residual to disappear.

But growth accounting is a step towards a reconciliation of the economic balance sheet, as it provides a filing system that is complete in the sense that all phenomena that affect economic growth must do so through input factor qualities and relative factor intensities (Nadiri 1972). In spite of its limitations, the results from growth accounting have proven to be useful policy parameters, and the residual has provided the theory to guide a considerable body of economic measurement.

We first briefly discuss the non-parametric index number method and then move on to the parametric average response function to measure TFP growth. The details of the measurement techniques are, however, laid out in Chapter 4.

2.3.1 The Translog-Divisia Index

The most commonly used index for productivity measurement is the Theil-Tornqvist index or the Translog-Divisia index that is defined for two time periods *s* and *t*:

$$Ln \frac{TFP_t}{TFP_s} = Ln\ TFP_t - Ln\ TFP_s$$

$$= \frac{1}{2}\sum_{i=1}^{N}(w_{is} + w_{it})(Ln\ y_{it} - Ln\ y_{is}) -$$

$$\frac{1}{2}\sum_{j=1}^{K}(\gamma_{js} + \gamma_{jt})(Ln\ x_{jt} - Ln\ x_{js}) \tag{2.3}$$

where the y's and x's represent the value of output and input, and the w's and γ's represent value shares of outputs and inputs respectively.

For the labour input, γ is the labour income as given by salaries paid out to workers, and for the capital input, the share is given by income earned by capital. The above index is easy to compute and can be calculated with just two data points, but it is appropriate only under the assumption of constant returns to scale with the imposition of the marginal productivity conditions where each input is assumed to be paid the value of its marginal product. However, unlike the parametric estimation, the index number does not assume constant weights as the periodic variations in factor shares given by the γ's are directly taken into account. The breakdown of the above index into its price and quantity indices is discussed in Chapter 4, while section 2.5 in this chapter explains the measurements of the price and quantity indices of inputs.

Index numbers[3] are expected to satisfy a number of desirable properties:

1. The identity test: the comparison in which prices and quantities do not change implies that the index is 1.
2. The commensurability test: implies that the index is not sensitive to the units of measurement for quantities or prices.
3. The determinateness test: the index number is not zero, unbounded or indeterminate when individual quantities become zero.
4. The proportionality test: if inputs are scaled up by some constant, the value of the index is that scaling constant.

5. The point reversal test: $z_f^{f'} = \frac{1}{z_{f'}^{f}}$

6. The circularity (or transitivity) test: $z_f^{f'} = z_f^{f''} \; X \; z_{f''}^{f'}$

where z can either refer to input, output or TFP indices and, f, f', f'' refer to the observations for different firms, time periods, or combination of the two in panel data applications.

The widely used Tornqvist index is said to satisfy all but the transitivity and point reversal properties. It has, however, been shown in the literature that the failure of the index on the point reversal test is by only a small order (Theil 1973) and the transitivity issue (which is not necessary for temporal comparisons) can be solved using the techniques of Eleto-Koves (1964) and Szulc (1964) as shown by Coelli et al. (1998).

The SHAZAM econometric package has an INDEX command to calculate the Tornqvist indices automatically. TFPIP[4] is another software that computes this index with an additional feature generating indices allowing for transitivity.

2.3.2 The Average Response Production and Cost Function

The non-frontier parametric estimation takes the form of the average response function using data from the production or cost side. By far the most important aspect of this method is the selection of an appropriate functional form, which ranges from the simple Cobb-Douglas to the more flexible translog form.[5] Although a flexible functional form would result in more generalized estimates, Kopp and Smith (1980) found that overly flexible forms result in a loss in statistical efficiency. Berndt and Christensen (1973) and Caves and Barton (1990) too raise theoretical objections to the translog function because it need not be well behaved for every possible combination of inputs; output need not increase monotonically with all inputs, and the isoquant need not be convex everywhere. Afriat (1972) remarks that the widespread use of the translog form in the parametric framework is due more to its analytical and technical convenience as the properties of the functions 'are not deliberate empirical hypotheses but are accidental'. However, with the Cobb-Douglas production function, Rodrik (1997) warns that if the sum of the true elasticity of output with respect to inputs is below one, then capital deepening would cause the factor share of capital to fall over time and the true TFP growth would increase correspondingly. And similar to the index number method, the constant returns to scale condition is a strong assumption underlying the Cobb-Douglas function. More is said about the estimation of the average production function in Chapter 4.

However, it is necessary to note that an often ignored problem in the OLS estimation of the production function is that of simultaneity biases.[6] This arises because the right-side variables containing the inputs are chosen in some optimal way by producers themselves and thus are not exogenous. However, Zellner et al. (1966) used the example of agriculture to assert that, while much of what was random (such as weather and pets) was unanticipated by farmers, most of the resources used were largely predetermined. This position has often been adopted on the premise that producers maximize expected profit or assume profit maximization *ex ante* or *ex post*. But Griliches and Mairesse (1997) argue that this story is especially inapplicable to industrial data, and even with agriculture, the random term can contain expected permanent components such as land quality. To get around this problem of endogeneity, some studies have attempted to use instrumental variables estimation but this has met with mixed success.[7] As obtaining appropriate instruments is not easy, it is not common practice for most empirical work to consider this form of estimation.

Sometimes, instead of the primal approach of the production function, the dual approach of the cost function is estimated. The above mentioned endogeneity problem does not arise because the right-side variables of the cost function are factor prices and output of a production function. The cost function is appropriate when prices and output are exogenous and input demands are endogenous. Furthermore, input cost share equations and the cost function together form a system that provides more information than the single-equation methodology used in the primal approach of the production function. For example, price-induced technological input bias as well as 'own' and 'cross' price elasticities of inputs can only be obtained from the cost function. The estimation of the cost function is, however, more demanding as it requires accurate input price data which are difficult to obtain.

2.4 THE FRONTIER APPROACH

Although the measurement of technical efficiency is the main motivation for the study of frontiers, this chapter concentrates on the frontier approaches that have primarily focused on TFP growth.

Unlike the non-frontier approach, the frontier approach is able to decompose output growth into not just input growth and TFP growth, but goes a step further to decompose TFP growth into various efficiency components. For instance, with the estimation of the production frontier, TFP growth can be decomposed into technical progress and gains in technical efficiency using the theoretical framework popularized by Nishimizu and Page (1982). The estimation of the cost frontier, on the other hand, enables TFP growth decomposition to provide information on technical progress, technical efficiency and allocative efficiency and the nature of returns to scale. Such a decompositional analysis is important for more accurate policy prescriptions based on the various sources of TFP growth. Often studies have regressed a host of factors on TFP growth to draw out policy implications, but such analysis is misguided as the components of TFP growth are conceptually different and may move in opposite directions, thereby calling for different policies.

We first discuss the parametric method of the parallel and non-parallel versions of the stochastic production frontier followed by the non-parametric estimation using data envelopment analysis (DEA). One attractive feature of DEA over the stochastic frontier is that, unlike the latter, it is able to handle multiple output and this is crucial for firms with heterogeneous products. Although Bauer (1990) argues that parametric estimations of cost, revenue and profit functions[8] can also deal with multiple output, empirical applications of this nature are very rare.

The parametric and non-parametric approaches use different techniques to envelope data more or less tightly in different ways. In so doing, they make different accommodations for random noise and for flexibility in the structure of the production technology. It is these two different accommodations that generate the strengths and weaknesses of the approaches. While I am of the opinion that neither approach strictly dominates the other, not everyone agrees with this.

2.4.1 The Stochastic Production Frontier

The stochastic frontier defined here has two error components; that is, $\varepsilon = u + v$.[9] This composed error model was independently considered by Aigner, Lovell and Schmidt (1977) and Meeusen and Van den Broeck (1977).

The following Cobb-Douglas stochastic production function provides an illustration:

$$Ln\,Y = A' + \alpha\, Ln\,K + \beta\, Ln\,L + u + v \tag{2.4}$$

where Y is value added output;
K is capital expenditure;
L is number of workers employed; and
$u \sim N(\mu, \sigma_u^2)$ and $v \sim N(0, \sigma_v^2)$

The error term u measures technical inefficiency and is the combined outcome of non-price and organizational factors that constrain firms from achieving the maximum possible output from their given set of inputs and technology. This error term is one-sided and non-negative since technical inefficiency is defined to be greater than zero. The error term v, on the other hand, represents all statistical random disturbance terms that are not within the control of the firm such as weather, strikes, luck and so on. The above model is often estimated using maximum likelihood or generalized least squares technique. However, much debate surrounds the assumed distribution for u and many studies have experimented with u taking on various distributions.[10] However, it is not unreasonable to question the expectation of statistical noise to satisfy specific distributional assumptions chosen for their statistical attractiveness and not based on theoretical reasoning. Furthermore, different specifications of the parametric frontier provide different results and this is considered a serious methodological problem.

For some time, the stochastic frontier models also assumed that u was time-invariant until Cornwell et al. (1990) attempted to relax this rigidity without assuming a specific distribution for u. This was a big improvement, as production coefficients were allowed to vary both cross-sectionally and over time. But the underlying assumption in all the above models was that the production frontier only considered parallel shifts (where innovation improves the marginal productivity of all inputs equally) over time which is based on the assumption that Hicks-neutral technology underlies the shift in the production frontier. This is similar to the production coefficients of the average response function of the non-frontier approach that remain constant with the exception of the intercept term.

Relaxing this assumption allows for non-neutral shifts in the production frontier such that the marginal rate of technical substitution at any input combination changes over time. This follows from Kalirajan and Shand's (1994) argument that with the same level of inputs, different levels of output are obtained by following different methods of applications. Kalirajan and Shand further explain that this would be misleading as one aspect of the distinguishing between the frontier and non-frontier methods lies with the fact that the former method models observation-specific production behaviour and thus would shift the frontier function non-neutrally from the realized production frontier. While a neutral shift is a special case, the more general case is a non-neutral shift. The value of this concept was first appreciated by Nerlove (1965) who found it appropriate to treat elasticities of output with respect to inputs as random variables, differing from firm to firm. This random coefficients approach was later popularized by Swamy (1970) and based on this, Kalirajan and Shand (1994) propose the stochastic varying coefficients frontier approach while Huang and Liu (1994) incorporate non-neutrality by including factors besides inputs and interacting these non-factor inputs with the inputs as regressors.

For Kalirajan and Shand's (1994) non-neutral-shifting model, the Fortran-written TERAN program could be easily obtained for use.[11] Other ready-to-use stochastic frontier estimation routines are available in the LIMDEP software as well as the FRONTIER software program of Coelli (1996a). Alternatively, one could use the numerical optimization routine in statistical software such as SAS or GAUSS, or one could code the methods directly using a computing language such as C or Fortran.

2.4.2 The Bayesian Approach to Stochastic Frontier Modelling

This approach, which is a relatively recent development to productivity growth analysis, provides robustness to model and parameter uncertainty thus guarding against drawing strong conclusions from weak evidence. Koop (2001) explains that this can be done by focusing on any quantity of interest and deriving its full posterior distribution and in particular, the distribution of any individual efficiency or function of efficiencies. This allows standard deviations and hence statistical differences between the performance of the units in question to be compared. This advantage distinguishes the Bayesian approach from the classical parametric stochastic frontier models.

The second advantage with the Bayesian approach is that Bayes factor or posterior odds can be used as a criterion to test, compare and decide on which of the various distributions for the efficiency term has the highest probability of being correct. And any uncertainty can then be resolved by mixing over a number of contending efficiency distribution based on these probabilities. The third advantage of the Bayesian application to frontier has been the development of a more structural approach to specifying the model (Koop et al. 1999, 2000). For instance, if human capital is believed to affect labour, and investment in equipment is thought to affect capital, then 'effective-factors correction' for inputs is undertaken as Koop argues that frontier output depends on effective factors and not observed factors. Thus observed inputs are transformed into effective inputs by 'adjustment factors' which are then parametrized into the stochastic frontier model which takes a bilinear form. The fourth advantage is that unlike most econometric models, the Bayesian model enables the investigation of the conditional distribution of the frontier output given the inputs and the various factors that are believed to have an effect on these inputs. Koop et al. (1999) explain that the Bayesian model can be also modified to consider the joint distribution of the frontier output and the inputs.

However, the Bayesian approach is not without its limitations. First, it can be computationally burdensome and one needs to be well versed with other techniques such as Monte Carlo integration to analyse some complex problems. Second, if informative priors are used, the basis of the choice can be questionable and if non-informative priors are used (such as the sampling theory estimators as is often the case), then one might ask, why bother with the Bayesian estimates? Third, Koop et al. (2000) also note that although a proper prior ensures the existence of a posterior distribution, it does not guarantee the existence of posterior moments and thus direct statistical inferences may not always be possible.

2.4.3 The Deterministic Approach

The non-parametric method initiated as data envelopment analysis (DEA) by Charnes et al. (1978) builds upon Farrell's (1957) concept of frontier by extending the efficiency analysis to multi-output situations using linear programming methods. This provides piecewise flexible linear approximations to tightly envelop the data to model the 'best practice' reference technology without imposing a specific functional form on either technology or deviations from it. Thus the programming framework lends itself naturally to the construction of frontier technology without requiring the assumption of cost minimization or profit maximization. There are also numerous types of DEA models which differ in their orientation (input-orientation, output-orientation, additive, multiplicative), disposability (strong, weak), diversification and returns to scale, type of measure (radial, non-radial, hyberbolic) and so on. While the DEA models are often convex, the freely disposable hull models (Deprins et al. 1984) do not require that convex combinations of every observed production plan be included in the production set.

Unlike the parametric estimation, the deterministic estimation has a single one-sided error component where $u \geq 0$ represents technical inefficiency. As the deterministic method does not account for statistical errors, all deviations from the frontier constitute technical inefficiency. Thus it can be expected that TFP growth from non-parametric estimation would be lower than that estimated parametrically.

Importantly, recent work in DEA has opened the ways to exploring the statistical properties of its non-parametric estimators for sensitivity analysis. Grosskopf (1996) provides an excellent survey on the various methods of sampling techniques such as jackknifing and bootstrapping, the application of semi-parametric methods and the use of chance-constrained programming techniques. Although bootstrapping has seen much in the way of improvements

(Simar and Wilson 2000), there still remain concerns about small sample problems, the incidental parameters problem (Banker 1993), consistency and finite sample properties of bootstrap distributions such as convergence of efficiency measures. While the bootstrap might provide a solution, it may not necessarily be a good one and in such a situation one has to decide if a poor solution is better than no solution. More importantly, empirical work in productivity analysis using the bootstrap technique or other non-parametric statistical techniques have yet to fully catch on. In fact, they are mostly understood and undertaken by a selected group of people who publish in the field of operations research. One reason for this is the lack of computational and programming skills on the part of the applied economists and until this technique becomes more accessible for use, it would unfortunately remain underutilized in productivity analysis.

2.4.4 Which Approach or Technique to Use?

It is quite clear that no one technique is perfect in its TFP calculation, as typically there is no unique measure of TFP that is necessarily the best measure for all analytical uses. As the empirical results are model dependent, there is always a model selection problem but simulation studies using Monte Carlo experiments which may help improve our understanding of the properties of the different models and facilitate model choice have yet to be satisfactorily undertaken. Until then, a choice depending on the case under consideration has to be made by weighing the advantages and disadvantages of the methods. The alternative ways of studying productivity do not necessarily yield contradictory or identical results. Even if alternative models seem compatible at the root, differences will remain due to reasons such as variations in the methods of aggregation or differences in the statistical estimation methods employed.

Although ignoring technical inefficiency conceptually flaws the non-frontier approach, this approach is still being used for its ability to provide detailed information on the contribution of each of the inputs to output growth using the growth accounting framework. This sheds light on various input intensities in production. In addition, if the empirical question is to find out, on average, how much output has been obtained from a given set of inputs, then the average response function estimation by ordinary least squares (OLS) would be a better choice than the index number or frontier approach. The non-frontier method still remains popular for studying aggregate economies' TFP growth over time as well as in inter-country comparison studies, partly because the frontier approaches are less suitable for economy-wide data.

However, to answer questions on maximum productive or best practice output levels given the input structure of each firm, the frontier approach would be the appropriate method. This is because, with firm-level data, the stochastic frontier reflects firms' catch-up behaviour with respect to its maximum potential, while the deterministic DEA allows for the study of the performance of each firm relative to efficient firms in the sample. Also, for the study on the sources of TFP growth, the decompositional analysis of TFP growth into various efficiency components under the frontier approach is necessary for more accurate and specific policy implications. However, if the researcher simply wants to know if output growth is TFP or input-driven growth, then the non-frontier approach would suffice.

One limitation of the decomposition framework of the frontier models is that it does not explain or study the path which the firm or industry takes. For instance, the interaction or dynamics between technical progress and technical efficiency in one period, and hence its effect on the resulting technical progress or technical efficiency in the next period is unknown. Modelling efforts towards incorporating this interaction (while dealing or econometrically handling the resulting exogeneity or endogeneity issues) of technical progress or technical efficiency have yet to be undertaken.

Once the choice of the frontier approach has been made, one then has to decide on the parametric or non-parametric technique to be used. Again, this depends upon the application. For example, for analysis of the agricultural sector where measurement error is related to inaccuracy in data due to poor quality of data or the way data are generated, and where weather is likely to play a significant role, then the assumption that all deviations from the frontier constitute technical inefficiency would be grossly inaccurate. Hence the parametric stochastic frontier method is highly recommended in this context. Additional information about the type of activity under study must also be drawn upon before deciding on the best approach. For instance, information about scale and substitution properties is best handled within a parametric approach.

However, Wan (1995) explains that the idea of technological change that can only be reflected in varying values of the estimates from the parametric frontiers is rather restrictive and unrealistic, as there is no reason to rule out the possibility that production technologies for two firms in the same period or one firm in different time periods may differ. Thus, when our knowledge of underlying technologies is weak, it is best to use the non-parametric DEA which does not impose unwarranted structure on the frontier.

In addition, where production involves multiple outputs as is often the case in service industries such as banks, schools, hospitals, hotels and public sector enterprises, the use of DEA is more appropriate. The construction of an aggregate output measure in these cases is cumbersome or almost impossible because these output measures are likely to be in different units. Thus DEA provides a solution to the common complaint of the difficulties in measuring intangible service output which has resulted in service sector productivity analysis lagging behind the analysis of the manufacturing sector for many years. For frontier estimation of non-profit and regulated sectors in both manufacturing and services sectors, DEA is again a better choice as it is not based on optimizing conditions. Also, if price data are difficult to obtain (which is true of most services), then DEA which does not require price data and still provides information on allocative efficiency, is more appealing than the stochastic frontier. Lastly, as argued in Gong and Sickles (1992), DEA is more compelling than the econometric model as inefficiency is likely to be correlated with the inputs.

A less obvious advantage of DEA is its ability to model undesirable outputs such as pollution, and the use of slack variables to consider congestion inefficiency due to the costly disposal of inputs and outputs. Also, Sengupta (1989) claims that often in empirical investigations, resources or technology constraints are ignored, but these can be easily formulated into the linear programming problem of DEA. However, as more of such environmental variables are included (that is, the number of constraints in the linear programs increase) or when more inputs and outputs are defined, the model is said to suffer from inflated efficiency scores and thereby fails to discriminate between the relative productive performance of firms. This is a direct result of the dimensionality of the input or output space relative to the number of firms (Seiford and Thrall 1990) as more of the firms tend to get an efficiency rating of one as they become too specialized to be evaluated with respect to the other firms. Other drawbacks of DEA are as follows.

First, DEA is not ideal for small samples as the corner points (for which one of the inputs or the outputs is very small or very large) often get erroneously classified as efficient when there are not an adequate number of reference points to compare with.[12] Second, as the number of time periods increase, the effect of statistical noise on DEA efficiency measurement is mitigated. Third, DEA results are extremely susceptible to outliers, and Burgess and Wilson (1993) explain that when two or more outliers are present, one can mask the effect of another. Although Burgess and Wilson (1993) and Wilson (1995) provide some suggestions to detect and overcome this problem, they are not all that easy to implement in practice.

However, of late, theoretical developments have been drawing the parametric and non-parametric techniques of the frontier approach closer. Varian's (1990) goodness-of-fit measures for non-parametric estimation as well as attempts by Li (1998) and Sengupta (1990, 1998) to undertake stochastic DEA have allowed the marriage of the strengths of these techniques. But it is lamentable that this type of model which promises to combine the ability to handle statistical noise with the functional form flexibility that non-parametric methods offer, has yet to catch on in empirical applications of productivity growth analysis although it has been quite widely applied in efficiency studies.

2.5 MEASUREMENT ISSUES

2.5.1 Value Added Versus Gross Output Measure

Often two types of output measures can be used to calculate TFP growth. One is the value added output, which is gross output corrected for purchases of intermediate inputs, and the other measure is gross output. For value added output, single deflation is appropriate and for gross output, double deflation has to be used because there are two components to deflate in gross output. Diewert (2000) notes that for comparing TFP growth at the industry level, it is best to use value added output rather than gross output as the latter includes the purchase on intermediate inputs which may very greatly among the industries. In addition, Bernolak (1980) comments that value added is best used for primary production and for comparing enterprises that produce different product mixes that are vertically integrated to different degrees, or produce outputs of different quality. Ark (1996) explains that the value added remains a useful concept particularly for international comparisons of productivity because it is simple, avoids the need for estimates of intra-industry transactions, and bears closer resemblance to primary statistics such as production census and representative firm data.

On the other hand, Norsworthy and Jang (1992) and Oulton and O'Mahony (1994) maintain that using value added distorts technology in estimating TFP growth because all raw and semi-finished materials, subassemblies, energy and purchased services are omitted from measured inputs. Often TFP growth from the value added measure is greater than that of the gross output measure due to the upward bias created by the omission of these intermediate goods and services. Also, if the growth rates of value added output and gross output differed greatly, this would magnify the TFP growth distortion even more. If the ratio of inputs to gross output remained constant, then Star (1974) notes that any bias from the omission of material inputs can be corrected as the growth of the TFP residual from the gross output measure will be a fraction of the TFP measure obtained from the value added measure, the fraction being the share of receipts going to all non-material inputs. Domar (1961), on the other hand, showed that the TFP measure of the value added measure would exceed that of the gross output measure by a factor equal to the ratio of gross output to value added. But the choice between gross output and value added output can be easily determined by testing for the separability conditions for a value added approach[13] which means that the intermediate inputs must be weakly separable from the other inputs, that is, the marginal rate of substitution between capital and labour must be independent of the level of intermediate inputs.

2.5.2 Measurement of Output

One of the biggest problems in output measurement is that of product mix. Hardly any firm produces one homogenous product as firms often change their product mix over time and differences in output characteristics will affect the number and type of inputs required. Unless output differences are controlled, different input requirements must be accommodated. The problem is compounded when making inter-industry or international comparisons. When Caves et al. (1987) investigated the effects of output characteristics on productivity performance in the airline industry, it was found that productivity differences can in part be explained by differences in output mix.

Any index of real output also has to account for quality. Market prices in the base period are often taken to reflect relative values that capture quality differences, but when quality changes are not associated with increases in production costs (and hence market prices), productivity will be underestimated. Griliches and Mairesse (1997) point out that using a single price deflator of the industry output is based on the simplistic assumption that the law of one price holds whereby all firms in an industry charge the same price and that all prices move in unison over time.

With services, the output measure is fraught with more problems than with industrial output.[14] An example that draws attention to the analytical significance of the distinction between a good and a service is, a movie on a cassette if purchased is a good but it is a service when rented. Levitan (1985) states that to some extent, the determination of what is a service and what is not, is a statistical artefact. This is particularly pronounced with the development of computer and information technology, and the growth of producer services. The term 'services' is often used loosely to mean an intangible good, or defined as all economic activities that are not agriculture, mining or manufacturing. There is no universally acceptable definition or classification of 'services' and there are almost as many answers as there are researchers that have written on the subject.

The measurement of service outcomes is also especially intractable. For instance, there is very little information on the contribution of services to health, learning or utility. Health outcomes from developments are not included in the output of the health care industry even when changes in health status are clearly the result of resources devoted to and actions taken by that industry. As with government services, the difficult problem of valuation has led to a largely underestimated measure of output in these areas by the common use of the cost of inputs that go into the production of such services. The uniqueness of services also makes aggregation of output more difficult. As discussed earlier, the problem of considering quality changes is more pronounced in service output. For example, how do you take into account faster transport, a more effective communication system and an increased array of financial services?

2.5.3 Measuring Intermediate Goods and Services

These refer to material inputs, energy (electricity and fuel) and non-energy inputs, as well as business or producer services that enter the production of the final good. To deflate this component of intermediate consumption, some studies use the producer price index for manufacturing while others compute separate price deflators for intermediate materials and services. This is done by first using the input–output tables to obtain weights of each individual material or service from the aggregate intermediate materials and services in the industries. Then using the producer price indices of these inputs, the weighted average price deflator can be calculated.

2.5.4 Measurement of Labour Input

The common way to measure the quantity of labour is to use number of hours worked or number of workers employed. Often, the former is preferred to the latter as it accounts more accurately for part-time and full-time employees in terms of actual hours worked. However, even total number of hours worked is not a satisfactory measure if a mix of skilled and unskilled workers are employed. Hours of work contributed by highly skilled workers generally contribute more to production than the unskilled workers. Thus to incorporate quality into labour input, and employment matrices cross-classified by sex, education, employment status and, in some cases, regional status of workers are constructed.

To obtain the price of labour, using wage rate alone is not accurate. Estimates of labour compensation based on wage, employer's contribution to workers' benefits, year-end bonuses and payments in kind is more reflective of the workers' worth as these affect workers' productivity. Ideally speaking, labour payments should also be cross-classified as above.

2.5.5 Measurement of Capital Input

> 'The measurement of capital is one of the nastiest job economists have set to statisticians.' (Hicks, 1981: 204)

Measurement of capital services is said to be less straightforward than labour services because the employer of a capital service is usually also the supplier of the service. As such, data on values of transactions in capital services are recorded only in the internal accounts of economic units, and to extract the required information it is necessary to begin not with transactions in capital services but with transactions in investment goods. These values must first be separated into price and quantity.

The production function $Q = F(K, L)$ is conventionally interpreted as a relationship between the flow of output and the flow of inputs' services. But as no data on the flow of capital services are available, the easiest option is to assume that capital flows are proportional to net capital stock after depreciation. The other aspect to capital measurement is the valuation of the capital input given by the rental price of capital services. These concepts are discussed below.

Capital services represent the quantity of capital input measures for depreciable assets derived by representing capital stock at each point in time as a weighted sum of past investments. The weights correspond to the relative efficiencies of capital goods of different ages. The perpetual inventory equation to measure capital services can then be written in two ways (with a constant geometric depreciation of δ) as:

$$K_t = I_t + (1\text{-}\delta)\, I_{t-1} + \ldots + (1\text{-}\delta)^{t-v} I_v + (1\text{-}\delta)^{t-v+1} K_{v-1} \qquad (2.5)$$

that is, the capital stock at time t is the efficiency-weighted sum of investment back to year v plus the remaining efficiency of the capital stock at time v-1 or

$$K_t = (1\text{-}\delta)\, K_{t-1} + I_t \qquad (2.6)$$

where K_t is capital at time t and I is gross investment.

It must be noted that since capital is bought or hired in anticipation of a certain level of activity and on long-term contract, actual factor payments do not reflect their marginal products except in the case of perfect foresight and only in the long run.

The dual to the perpetual inventory method is based on the relationship between the price of an investment good at a point in time, and rental prices of capital services from that point onwards. Each rental price of capital services involves a nominal rate of return, rates of depreciation, and capital loss or gain for the type of asset, and variables incorporating the tax structure. The rental price of capital (ignoring tax terms) is given as:

$$P_{Kk}(T) = P_{Ik}(T-1)\, r(T) + \delta_k P_{Ik}(T) - [P_{Ik}(T) - P_{Ik}(T-1)] \qquad (2.7)$$

where P_{Ik} denotes the investment price of capital good k;

$r(T)$ is the nominal post-tax rate of return between periods T and $T-1$;

δ_k is the depreciation rate of capital asset k; and

$P_{Ik}(T)-P_{Ik}(T-1)$ is the capital loss or gain of capital good k.

There are basically two ways of measuring the rate of return. One is to set it equal to an external market rate such as yield on long-term bonds (Oulton and O'Mahony, 1994). The other is to use an internal measure which equates the marginal product of aggregate capital in an industry to the realized profits in that industry, that is,

$$r = \frac{\Pi - \sum_k \delta_k P_{Ik}(T) + \sum_k \{P_{Ik}(T) - P_{Ik}(T-1)\} A_k(T)}{\sum_k P_{Ik}(T-1) A_k(T)}$$

$$= \text{[Gross profits} - \text{Depreciation} + \text{Capital gains] / Value of capital} \qquad (2.8)$$

where Π represents gross profits and $A_k(T)$ is capital stock of asset k.

Depending on the availability of data, sometimes, instead of gross profits, total property compensation after property taxes is used. If tax structure is to be considered, it might be appropriate to use the data on property compensation by legal form of organization (see Jorgenson et al. 1987).

Often capital stock is decomposed into asset categories such as land and buildings for non-residential purposes, transport equipment and machinery equipment. The former is deflated by the property price index and the latter two deflated by the gross domestic fixed capital formation deflator if no capital asset specific deflator is available.

In reality, as capital input is not used with a constant intensity over time, it should be adjusted for capital utilization since the use of capital is subject to cyclical factors such as in a recession or boom. If excess capacity is understated, then the residual TFP growth will be understated. In a way, utilization rates are seen as a means of converting capital stocks to flows. The intuitively appealing practice of multiplying the capital stock by a utilization rate to obtain 'real' capital input is a way of addressing the inadequacy of the equilibrium-based neoclassical theory of production to take into account the slow adjustment of capital in the short run. In a not quite useful manner (since data on capital flow is unavailable), capital utilization is often defined as:

Capital utilization ratio = Ratio of flow to the stock of capital

This ratio can be expected to vary considerably on a year-to-year basis and this is consistent with profit maximization. Winston (1974) notes that transaction costs, lumpiness and shift wage differentials imply valid reasons why the capital flow may be less than capital stock, thus providing a less than one value for the above ratio. However, in the long run, cyclical fluctuations in the flow of services average out and one can take the ratio of the capital service flow to the capital stock to be constant and this allows the use of the perpetual inventory equation.

In some early studies, Okun (1962) expressed the relative utilization rate in terms of the labour unemployment rate,[15] while Jorgenson and Griliches (1967) used fluctuations in electricity use as a measure of utilization since it captures what is used in the actual production process. But since the early 1970s, the US Federal Reserve Board has published average (Wharton) capacity utilization indices for as far back as 1948 and these have been widely used. While such indices have progressively seen improvements for empirical use for the USA and other developed nations also devising similar estimates, those for the developing economies are non-existent.

One way around the problem of obtaining capital utilization rates is to adopt the approach in temporary or short-run equilibrium and interpret the production function as a relationship between the flow of output and a flow of variable labour inputs applied to a quasi-fixed stock of capital, since capital stock is fixed in the short run. Thus short-run adjustments to output can only be accommodated by changes in the amount of labour used. To avoid detailing the attempts in the literature on the measure of the capital utilization ratio, readers are referred to Berndt and Fuss's (1986) solution to this measure in a static optimization framework of the non-parametric production and cost function. Morrison (1986), on the other hand, presents indices within a parametric cost model with dynamic optimization and many others have laboured in this area.

2.5.6 Depreciation of Capital Stock

Depreciation is the decline in value of capital goods with age at a given point in time, so the estimates of depreciation depend on the relative efficiencies of capital goods of different ages. The correct measure of the economic life of capital based on the average age of capital assets has a considerable impact on productivity measures as it affects the degree of embodied new technology. Interestingly, Chen (1997) argues that with net capital, there is a tendency to over-state depreciation because 'obsolescence' rather than physical deterioration is the dominant feature of depreciation. Capital becomes economically obsolete before it has outlived its physical usefulness, but obsolete equipment is still capable of contributing to production. Thus the flow of capital services is said not to decline with age at the rate frequently suggested by depreciation allowances (Kennedy and Thirlwall 1972).

The two most commonly used sets of depreciation rates are shown below. From considerable painstaking empirical work, the depreciation studies of Hulten and Wykoff (1981) conclude that a pattern of geometric decay[16] in the efficiency of real capital stocks is reasonable for measuring real capital input based on vintage price data that depends on age of the capital goods. The arrival of new better vintages of capital (or the embodied technical change) will depress the process of existing old vintages of capital if the new technology cannot be grafted onto older assets. Jorgenson and Yun (1990), on the other hand, incorporate tax rates in their calculation. Both sets of rates are somewhat similar as seen in Table 2.1.

Table 2.1 Depreciation rates (%)

Assets	Hulten and Wykoff (1981)	Jorgenson and Yun (1990)
Furniture and fixtures	12	13.8
Agricultural machinery	12	11.8
Industrial machinery and equipment	12	12.3
Service industry and equipment	18	16.5
Equipment average	13.3	14.1
Office and computing equipment	30	27.3

Source: Jorgenson and Yun (1990) and Hulten and Wykoff (1981).

But these rates are often specific to asset types rather than industries, and they do not change over time. However, the mix of assets in a given industry may well change significantly through time. To accommodate this feature for the manufacturing industries, Norsworthy et al. (1988) use capital flow tables showing expenditure shares by type of equipment asset for all sectors from the input–output tables, and interpolate them to obtain annual weights for expenditure on each asset for each manufacturing industry group. The depreciation rates are then used in a vintage model to obtain annual depreciation rates for the net stock of equipment.

2.6 TO MEASURE OR NOT TO MEASURE TFP GROWTH?

This section hopes to be productively provocative on some aspects of the TFP growth concept and interpretation problems without being definitive on any aspect of the problem. While it is highly possible that some important studies have been missed in this task, the general impression given is a fair one.

To set the stage, let us consider the terminologies related to TFP growth measure which are often used interchangeably with technological change or progress, technical change or progress, embodied technical change and disembodied technical change. Based on this, the definition of TFP is set up as follows before summarizing the discussion in the literature on the divided opinions of the interpretation of TFP:

$$\text{TFP growth} = \text{Technical / technological change} \quad (2.9)$$

$$= \text{Technical / technological progress} \quad (2.10)$$

$$= \text{Embodied technical change} + \text{Disembodied technical change} \quad (2.11)$$

$$= \text{Changes in technical efficiency} + \text{Technological progress} \quad (2.12)$$

While the definitions led by equations (2.9) and (2.10) for TFP growth are identical but used with different terms, equations (2.11) and (2.12) (the latter equation was popularized by Nishimizu and Page 1982) are conceptually similar in that changes in technical efficiency in equation (2.12) essentially refer to embodied technical change, and disembodied technical change in equation (2.11) corresponds to technological progress in equation (2.12). But since the 'birth' of the TFP concept, equation (2.11) (or equation (2.12) for that matter) has remained contentious given the varied views in the literature.

First, let us understand what embodied and disembodied technical change is. Embodied technical change results from the efficient use of new and better types of capital and is considered endogenous. It captures the effects of learning by doing (experience), advances in applied technology, managerial efficiency and industrial organization which transform into better methods and organization that improve the efficiency of both new and old factor inputs. With embodied technical change, more output is obtained with a given quantity of inputs, or the same output can be produced with lesser inputs at the same cost, and this results in movements towards known production boundaries. Disembodied technical change, on the other hand, is not embodied in factor inputs and refers to technology as useful knowledge pertaining to the art of production where concern is with the knowledge-creating activities of research, invention and development (Kennedy and Thirlwall 1972), thereby resulting in the expansion of production boundaries themselves due to increases in knowledge.

While early works such as Tinbergen (1942) and Solow (1957) interpreted TFP growth as disembodied technical change represented as shifts in an aggregate production function, Solow (1960) developed a vintage-capital model to incorporate explicitly the changes in the age distribution of capital stocks, and interpreted TFP growth as technical change embodied in new capital goods. He, however, distinguished disembodied technical change as that which raises the productivity of both old and new investment goods without requiring gross investment, and examples provided include managerial and organizational changes.[17] Brown (1968), on the other hand, modelled disembodied technical change as a trend term and embodied technical change with capital vintage effects, and explained that embodied technical change can be neutral or non-neutral depending on the elasticity of substitution between labour and capital.[18] But Denison (1962) showed that embodied technical change was so unimportant and insignificant that TFP growth is best interpreted as disembodied technical change.[19] This prompted Abramovitz (1962) to call for an urgent examination of the factual gap between these two views. In response to this call, Jorgenson (1966) provided evidence that both embodied and disembodied technical change have precisely the same factual implications. Jorgenson also tried to convince readers that there is a one-to-one correspondence between the two types of technical change and, in view of this, he concludes that one can never distinguish a given rate of growth in embodied technical change from the corresponding rate of growth in disembodied technical change. Although there is some truth in his conclusion, it was based on the rather simplistic and easily refutable assumption that the price of investment good is an index of the quality of investment good.

Essentially, some of the confusion in the early literature on the embodied and disembodied technical change resulted from the inclusion or omission of the quality of inputs and this is reviewed below.

2.6.1 Quality Changes in Inputs

As a complete survey of the large literature on quality change lies outside the scope of this book, this section only reviews some selected issues.[20] One is the issue of eliminating aggregation errors. Jorgenson and Griliches (1967) explain the need to eliminate such errors arising from limitations on the number of separate inputs that may be distinguished empirically. The choice of commodity groups to serve as distinct 'inputs' and 'outputs' involves aggregation within each group by simply adding together quantities of all commodities within the group, and aggregation among groups by computation of the Divisia index. But the resulting price and quantity indices are Divisia price and quantity indexes of the individual commodities only if the rates of growth of either the prices or the quantities within each group are identical. Jorgenson argues that these errors are often mislabelled as 'quality change'. Quality change in this sense occurs whenever the rates of growth of quantities within each separate group are not identical. For example, if high-quality items grow faster than items of low quality, the rate of growth is biased downwards relative to an index treating high-quality and low-quality items as separate commodities. Thus, to eliminate this bias, it was argued that there was a need to construct a Divisia index of individual items within the group, by using disaggregated or more detailed data essentially capturing the changes in the composition of the use of various capital assets in aggregate capital and various types of labour in aggregate labour inputs. In this way, all factor inputs are ensured that they are of constant quality.

While Jorgenson and Griliches (1967, 1972a) detail how quality change considering various types of disaggregation in both capital and labour is measured, to illustrate the concept further here, Fraumeni and Jorgenson's (1981) decomposition of capital input is used:

$$K_t = Q_{k,t} \ X \ A_{t-1} \tag{2.13}$$

where K_t is aggregate capital input;
$Q_{k,t}$ is the quality of capital stock; and
A_{t-1} is aggregate capital stock at the beginning of the period.

It must be noted that $Q_{k,t}$ is an index that transforms aggregate capital stock into aggregate capital input. The growth of aggregate capital input can then decomposed into the sum of components associated with growth in capital stock and growth in capital quality.

Labour quality, on the other hand, has been measured using the ratio of number of workers measured to total hours as was done by Jorgenson et al. (1987), while Gapinski and Western (1999) used average years of schooling, and Jorgenson and Fraumeni (1989) went to great lengths to construct constant quality indices of labour inputs by deriving lifetime labour incomes by applying asset pricing equations (equivalent to those used for tangible assets) to wage rates.

Star (1974) notes that the numerical results of the TFP residual depended on the particular order in which data on inputs were disaggregated, and thus cautions against labelling any of these factors as the cause or explanation for TFP growth. For example, when he disaggregated labour by sex first and then education, all the improvement in the residual appeared to have been caused by the differences between the sexes while education contributed nothing to the reduction in the residual. When the order of disaggregation was reversed, the opposite result was obtained.

Star (1974), however, asserts that the great advantage of using disaggregated data is that quality changes in inputs are transformed into quantity changes in inputs and these are attributed to input growth and not TFP growth. But quality changes affect embodied technical change in the long run. For instance, the age and educational level of workers can be expected to affect their efficiency and their willingness to work with more advanced technology or capital. With capital, more use of computers and less of other office equipment would clearly change the dynamics of productivity in the workplace. Thus when quality changes in inputs are translated to quantity changes in output, they constitute embodied technical change and are attributed to TFP growth. This means that the gains from quality changes in inputs are somewhat suppressed in the contribution of inputs in the short run, but they get measured when they emerge in the output growth component in the long run. Hence, with significant changes in the composition of inputs, one must be careful to interpret the often understated potential for growth as given by the estimated TFP growth measure. Or alternatively, in the short run, measures of input quality changes can be indicative of potential embodied technical change in the long run.

This formed the premise for one of the many disagreements in one of history's classic heated debate and exchange on productivity between Jorgenson and Griliches (1967, 1972a, 1972b) and Denison (1972a, 1972b). Jorgenson and Griliches (1972a, 1972b) point out that quality changes estimated from differences in marginal product or related to different vintages should be counted as inputs, which essentially means that all embodied technical change is to be transferred to inputs and thus the residual TFP measures only disembodied technical change. Denison (1972a), on the other hand, claims that the contribution of such 'unmeasured quality changes' to growth is embodied technical change as the development of better capital goods leads to advances in knowledge. So, should the quality of factors be necessarily adjusted for? Kennedy and Thirlwall (1972) assure readers that this depends on the purpose of the study. If the purpose is simply to measure the increase in the productivity of factors over time, it makes no sense to adjust factors for quality changes. However, if interest is in advances in knowledge or to understand the conditions for growth, the effects of factor quality changes need to be isolated.

Chen (1997), on the other hand, believes that if labour and capital are correctly measured encompassing the quality changes, then the residual TFP, strictly speaking, is confined to being disembodied technical change. Chen's (1997) interpretation of TFP stems from technical change being defined as a function of time and being a trend parameter; it is thus exogenous.

Recent studies have, however, renewed the interest in quantifying and reassessing embodied technical change. This is led by Gordon (1990) who derived new price indices for capital to show the understated effect of capital, and Hulten's (1992) findings indicate that 20 per cent or more of the TFP growth could be attributed to embodied technological change.[21] While models of the disembodied technical change are based on the concept of capital vintages, Hulten (1992) revitalizes the view on capital that successive vintages of investment also embody differences in technical design.[22] For instance, a computer of vintage 1990 will tend to be more efficient at producing output, *ceteris paribus*, than a machine of vintage 1980 even if there is no physical loss of capacity. Thus 'better' is equivalent to 'more' investment and this can be measured by technical-efficiency units discussed by Fisher (1965).

To date, measuring improvements in capital goods are discussed and debated upon as constituting embodied technical change, while improvements in labour that are specific to the firm or industry have remain neglected. Why are training costs or on-the-job training expenditure not explicitly considered as embodied technical change? Is it due to the lack of data? Partly so, and partly because it is likely that since such labour skills are meant to affect organizational and industrial organization, they defy direct quantification and hence have not attracted the attention of research. Thus, Hulten's (1992) study has understated embodied technical change as only attempts to measure capital-embodied technical change have been considered.

In a similar vein, the concept of disembodied technical change has not escaped criticism. Creamer (1972) argues that this form of technical change in the form of knowledge-creating innovations is in fact embodied in the minds of individuals engaged in management. Thus, a comprehensive measure of labour input would embody these so-called disembodied innovations. Robinson (1970) also doubts the reality of the disembodied concept with a parenthetical remark: 'the value of equipment-absorbing disembodied progress (if there is such a thing) ...'

Lucas (1988), on the other hand, tried to offer a theoretical explanation to distinguish between embodied and disembodied technical change by distinguishing between the internal and external effects of human capital accumulation. He explains that learning-by-doing or on-the-job-training provide internal effects since it affects an individual's own productivity and is hence internalized. It can then be thought that schooling is more general and creates external effects where it contributes to the productivity of all factors of production and hence benefits are externalized. Although Lucas explicitly recognized the difficulty in distinguishing between internal and external benefits and how best to measure them, he nevertheless conceded that if it were easy to perform such a classification of internal and external effects, then productivity effects can incorporate internal human capital effects (which one can say is embodied) and exogenous technical effects (which can be called disembodied).

But the term 'learning-by-doing' (Arrow 1962) can be another source of confusion although many studies use it to mean embodied technical change. Learning-by-doing or the acquisition of knowledge is the product of experience, and experience is a function of time. If that is so, it can be considered somewhat exogenous and hence taken to be disembodied technical change. For instance, Arrow (1962) reports that the Horndal ironworks in Sweden had no new investment (and therefore presumably no embodied technical change) for a period of 15 years, yet productivity (output per man hour) rose on the average close to 2 per cent per annum. This steadily increasing performance was imputed to learning from experience. Although the productivity measure used was that of a partial measure, it does drive the point home.

In short, it is no surprise that the distinction between embodied and disembodied technical change is a real one from a theoretical and policy point of view, but making that distinction from the econometric viewpoint remains unreal. The problem is confounded by the causality relationships between the types of technical change as well as input growth, and this is reviewed in the next section.

2.6.2 Causality Relationships

With the parametric approach of econometrically estimating production functions, Kaldor (1957) and more recently Scott (1989) argued that it is pointless and artificial to try and distinguish between shifts in the production function (technical change) and movements along it (input growth) because in the real world, we do not observe the production function but only actual combinations of factors and output in a dynamic process. Nelson (1981) and Shaw (1992) have raised similar concerns on the decomposition concept (of segregating output growth into input growth and TFP growth) given that the inputs as well as the other efficiency measures exhibit complementarity and are interdependent.

Causality between embodied and disembodied technical change

Embodied technical change such as the construction of new and better capital requires advances in technical knowledge (disembodied technical change) that can be transmitted through improvements in capital goods (embodied technical change) or via research and development or experience (both of which are disembodied). Hence there is a very high possibility of bi-directional causality between the two types of technical change which, empirically speaking, defies accurate measurement as it is analogous to the problem of which comes first – the chicken or the egg.

While the above discussion seems to establish that the relationship or correlation between the two types of technical change is positive, this is not necessarily the case, as shown by the empirical evidence provided by Nishimizu and Page (1982) and Mahadevan and Kalirajan (2000). There may well be a high rate of adoption of new technology (disembodied technical change) without technological mastery (embodied technical change) or vice versa.

Causality between technical change and factor input growth

As established earlier on, quality changes and hence factor input growth leads to embodied technical change in the long run. While Rodrik (1997) argues that labour-saving technical change and capital accumulation are not independent, especially in the case of the East Asian economies, Fry (1990) asserts that high rates of return to capital stock due to TFP growth certainly encourage capital accumulation. But capital-embodied technical change would also require skilled labour to manage the advanced capital or machinery. This is the situation of capital-deepening and labour-deepening occurring simultaneously.

By way of the bi-directional causality between the two types of technical change established above, a three-way causality can be said to exist between factor input growth embodied, and disembodied technical change.

2.6.3 The Accounting Identity and the Notion of TFP Growth

Many have argued that the theoretical problems underlying the notion of TFP growth are so significant that the whole concept should be seriously questioned. Here, a brief review of what has been said to this effect and why this may or may not be true is discussed.

One fundamental view is based on the premise that aggregate production functions do not exist in the first place as they are derived from an income accounting identity (Shaikh 1980) and thus the estimation of TFP growth does not make sense. Extending this argument and using the Equifinality theorem, Felipe and McCombie (2003) dispute the estimation of the production function on two grounds. First, they show that the (putative) production function precludes any testing and is far from estimating TFP growth as it only yields a weighted average of the growth rates of wage and profit rates. The accounting identity in growth rates (assuming factor shares are constant) is given by:

$$Y_t = (1\text{-}a)\, w_t + a r_t + (1\text{-}a)\, L_t + a\, K_t \ = \phi_t + (1\text{-}a)\, L_t + a\, K_t \qquad (2.14)$$

where Y_t is real value added;
w_t is the real wage rate;
r_t is the real average profit rate;
$\phi_t = (1\text{-a})\, w_t + a r_t$;
$(1\text{-a}) = (w_t L_t)/Y_t$ is labour's share; and
$a = (r_t K_t)/Y_t$ is capital's share.

Felipe and McCombie (2003) show that the above expression can be mathematically formulated to resemble any production function and, as such, the 'estimated' production function being an identity provides no information on TFP growth. In addition, they also prove that if factor shares are constant, and wage and profit rates grow at constant rates, then the Cobb-Douglas production function will always give a good fit.

Interestingly, Jorgenson and Griliches (1967) explain that the accounting identity is important in defining an appropriate method of measuring TFP and it provides a useful check on the consistency of any proposed definitions of total output and total input. The fundamental identity for each accounting period is that the value of output is equal to the value of input:

$$q_i Y_i = p_j X_j \qquad (2.15)$$

where q_i is the price of the ith output;

Y_i is the quantity of the *i*th output;
p_j is the price of the *j*th input; and
X_j is the quantity of the *j*th input.

Dension (1972b), however, claims that no such accounting identity exists except in one special case, that of a current-dollar series (not in constant prices) for gross or net national product valued at factor cost. The identity is said to hold in this series because the value placed upon each unit of output is, by definition, the amounts earned by the factors providing it. But most productivity studies use GDP valued at (constant) market prices and according to the above argument, this is not based on the identity. This questions Felipe and McCombie's (2003) assertion that TFP measurements are not valid as they are derived from 'identities'. Ironically, Denison had not only accused Jorgenson and Griliches (1967) of making their estimates satisfy the accounting identity, but he further concluded that productivity change is precisely a measure of the degree to which the identity does not hold.

On a different note, Felipe and McCombie (2003) maintain that one cannot move on to estimating the aggregate production function from the theoretical notion of firm-level production function by merely summing up the latter as this requires heroic assumptions which do not hold. Nataf (1948) has also pointed out that aggregation over sectors was possible if and only if micro production functions were additively separable in their inputs. For instance, the equilibrium conditions underlying the micro variables may not hold at the macro level and/or the separability conditions of inputs in a aggregate production function related to their marginal rate of substitution among the various inputs may not be satisfied. Star (1974) explains that in order to add together different units of items in the heterogeneous component of inputs, each item must be a perfect substitute for any other unit, that is, the marginal rate of substitution is constant and the unit measurement are chosen so that the marginal products of every unit are equal.

Nevertheless, Felipe and McCombie (2003) are willing to accept the notion of a production function if the output and input variables are measured in physical quantities as this defies the use of the income accounting identity. But this would not necessarily give a better measure of TFP growth as the problems of capacity utilization, accounting for changing physical characteristics of mix of output, and the elusive measure of capital stock would still not vanish. Thus some studies advocate a different type of analysis, that of a microeconomic nature where productivity growth, organization and management, and government policies are explicitly studied. Perhaps more should be drawn from other lines of research such as the views of the evolutionary theory which recognizes technical progress as an uncertain and costly business.

2.6.4 TFP – A Truly Fruitful Possibility or Totally False Proposition?

While Felipe (1999) claims that by definition, we cannot explain what we do not know, namely the residual, Hulten (2001) feels that static residual measure only correctly measures the shift in the production possibilities but does not capture the induced effects of technology on growth. Griliches (1988) sums up the sentiments of the many critics of TFP growth measures by stating that, 'despite all this work, there is still no general agreement on what the computed productivity measures actually measure, how they are to be interpreted and what are the major sources of their fluctuations and growth'. Of late, attempts to explain or solve the productivity puzzle have been directed at understanding the effect of computers and information technology on the economy. This leads one to wonder if TFP growth explanations are getting murky because of the strong temptation to link the explanations to factors that are themselves rather blurred conceptually and hence difficult to measure. Perhaps, this is due to a rush to develop exciting new fields of research and by 'doing more' in this sense may leave us wiser but with much of the original productivity puzzle still intact.

Generally speaking, the contention is that past productivity work based on production functions is not completely futile as today we do know more about the nature of productivity and output growth than we did five years ago. And that is what learning and academic progress is meant to bring forth. One has to start somewhere and the first steps, however shaky or inaccurate, still need to be taken in order to lead us closer to the truth. Griliches and Mairesse (1997) agree that in most cases, the production function is estimated as a tool for answering questions which are too interesting to give up even though the framework used may be problematic. Thus instead of wallowing in the discussion of the possible abuse and misuse of TFP growth measures, we should appreciate the wealth of insight and analysis into production economics and technical change that has been acquired over time. And then take the relevant criticisms that have been hurled in the right stride and continue working towards better measures of productivity growth and more accurate interpretation of it.

However, just how important TFP has been, will always be a matter of ongoing controversy. Krugman (1990a) puts it succinctly: 'Productivity isn't everything, but in the long run it is almost everything'. The continued strong interest in the measurement and explanation of productivity and efficiency changes is due to the development of new and better theoretical models, the availability of new and better data and estimation techniques, and the advent of large-scale computers (with ready to use specialized econometric packages). These have made possible the testing of refined hypotheses which have widened the scope and scale of applications in the framework of productivity analysis. Despite the controversies and criticisms underlying the TFP growth measure, the utility and significance of the idea of TFP is considerable and very appealing. This is demonstrated in the case studies presented in Part III.

Here, it is conceded that the TFP growth measure is necessary but not sufficient to draw strong conclusions and make policy prescriptions about growth, much less to predict its future. The quantitative empirical investigation needs to be complemented with extensive and more comprehensive qualitative discussion provided by surveys and interviews at the disaggregated or firm level. There is clearly a need to work at the micro level to better understand the dynamics of productivity growth at the macro level.

NOTES

1. Tinbergen's paper was first written in German and was not published in English until 1959.
2. While Fare et al. (1994) have used DEA and Koop et al. (1999, 2000) have used the Bayesian approach to frontier modelling in a multi-country context using data on the aggregate economy, there is always the looming doubt on results obtained from macro-level data with the use of a technique that was designed with micro-level analysis in mind. For instance, with the decomposition of productivity growth itself, Koop admitted that this was difficult to do as the model was highly parametrized and required a good deal of data. Thus restrictions had to be placed for appropriate estimation and this questions the basis of the choice of restrictions.
3. Interested readers may refer to Diewert and Nakamura (1993) for more details on the theoretical and applied literature on the index number approach.
4. This is provided free of charge by Tim Coelli and can be downloaded from http://www.uq.edu.au/economics/staff/coelli.htm.
5. Other examples of flexible functional forms include the normalized quadratic, the generalized Leontief and the generalized Mcfadden but the derivation of production functions from these forms are intractable and hence hardly used.
6. Marschak and Andrew (1944) were the first to recognize this.
7. See for example, Olley and Parkes (1992), Griliches and Mairesse (1997) and Sakellaris and Wilson (2002).
8. See Kumbhakar and Lovell (2000) for the decomposition of the profit and revenue functions.
9. Elsewhere in the literature, Timmer (1971), Richmond (1974) and Schmidt (1976) have defined the frontier using a single error component.
10. See Kumbhakar (1990) and Greene (1990).
11. A copy of the software is available on request from Professor Kali Kalirajan of the Graduate Research Institution of Policy Studies in Tokyo via the following e-mail address: kalirajan@grips.ac.jp.

12. The rule of thumb is to ensure that the sample size is at least three times that of the total sum of inputs and outputs in the model.
13. Norsworthy and Malmquist (1983) provide comprehensive empirical testing of this condition.
14. For a more through discussion, see Baily and Gordon (1988) and Griliches (1992).
15. Note that if labour is hoarded, this will tend to underestimate unutilized capital.
16. Although there is some controversy surrounding the use of this approach (Dension, 1972b provides an excellent critique), it has been argued in the literature that the geometric decay is more plausible than the constant efficiency and straight-line depreciation pattern.
17. Solow (1960) goes further to show that in the long run, the embodied and disembodied models yield the same rate of TFP growth when the elasticity of substitution between labour and capital is unity. But when the elasticity of substitution differed, differential rates of growth may result.
18. It was explained that if the elasticity is less than unity, a rise in the stock of capital (for any given capital labour ratio) lowers the income share of capital, and embodied technical change is capital-saving.
19. As this view was supported by other studies such as Wickens (1970), You (1976), Gregory and James (1973) and Baily and Gordon (1988), the formulation of vintage models proved quite popular only for a while.
20. For instance, the use of hedonic pricing method is omitted here. Interested readers are referred to Chapters 2 and 3 of Gordon (1990) for a more complete discussion on quality change.
21. Sakellaris and Wilson (2002) find that embodied technical change accounted for about two-thirds of total technical change between 1972 and 1996 in their sample of US manufacturing plants, and assert that the role of investment is even larger than previously estimated.
22. This was, however, first noted by Denison (1972b) who questioned the measurement of capital input on the grounds that newer vintages incorporate design improvements.

3 The measurement of technical efficiency in production frontier models

3.1 INTRODUCTION

A rigorous analytical approach to the measurement of efficiency in production originated with the work of Koopmans (1951) and Debreu (1951). Koopmans (1951) provided a definition of what we refer to as technical efficiency: an input–output vector is technically efficient if, and only if, increasing any output or decreasing any input is possible only by decreasing some other output. While the definition and concept of technical efficiency is straightforward and easily understood, the measurement of technical efficiency has proved difficult and complex.[1] This chapter, although not exhaustive, is devoted to the main measurement techniques from the production function to obtain technical efficiency measures. Here, technical efficiency is measured from the production function as the use of the cost function would require price data which is often inaccurate and difficult to obtain.

There are basically three arguments favouring the measure of technical efficiency. The first and most compelling reason lies in the gap that exists between the theoretical assumption of full technical efficiency and empirical reality. Leibenstein (1966) drew attention to this in the 1960s. Second, there are discrepancies between the theoretical notion of a production function and the modelling and estimation of production functions using conventional statistical procedures. Third, the measure of technical efficiency can be used to rank a firm's efficiency performance. This allows the study of the most efficient firm's characteristics so as to draw up policy lessons for the less efficient firms.

This chapter is set out as follows. While the next section explains the concept of technical efficiency, the following section attempts to provide a unified framework of the various methods of measuring technical efficiency under the frontier and non-frontier approaches using a flowchart. The rest of the discussion deals with the theoretical framework and estimation methods underlying the main models and highlights the similarities and differences between them.

3.2 THE CONCEPT OF TECHNICAL EFFICIENCY

Technical efficiency is the capacity and willingness of an economic unit to produce maximum possible output from a given technology and a mix of inputs. While the concept of technical efficiency is old, the measurement of technical efficiency is relatively new and this is possibly due to the fact that neoclassical production theory presupposes full technical efficiency. In the neoclassical production function, technology is often taken to be disembodied and exogenous and is either allowed to vary with time or with respect to some input. There is no separate adjustment for technological improvement embodied (also known as gains in technical efficiency) in labour or the capital stock where the new inputs are more efficient than the old inputs. However, more recent studies have tried to control for embodied improvements in the capital stock by use of vintage models or otherwise. Embodied improvements in labour have been made by making qualitative adjustments in the age–sex–education composition of the labour force. But there is yet to be a consensus on the most suitable way of capturing this embodied technology component.

The concept of embodied technology forms the very essence of Romer's (1986) endogenous growth models which argue for sustainable growth in the long run. Hulten's (1992) findings indicate that 20 per cent or more of the residual TFP could be attributed to embodied technological change. Endogenous technological change can be due to the accumulation of knowledge in the learning-by-doing process, improvement in the instructions for mixing together raw materials, diffusion of new technology, improved managerial practice, research and development undertaken by government or profit-maximizing agents, or can be affected by the overall market structure of industry because it affects the methods used for acquiring, developing or modifying technology.

Another theory underlying the importance of embodied technological change is Vernon's (1966) product cycle theory which Krugman (1979, 1990b) and Dollar (1986) had drawn upon to explain trade that takes place between North and South countries. There are two kinds of goods, new and old, and these are determined over time by two processes of technological change. New goods are recently developed products through the process of innovation and this superior ability to exploit new technology can be found in the developed countries in the North. Once the production of a good becomes standardized, it is possible to produce it far from the main market. Thus, due to lower costs of production in the South, production in the form of foreign direct investment takes place in the South or the South could also 'borrow' this technology (often embodied in capital) in the form of patents and start producing these goods. The product cycle arises because what is a new good in one period eventually becomes an old good. The technology lag which takes the form of technical efficiency change, allows the South to produce and export old products. The 'flying geese' pattern is a development along this concept.[2] The existence of technical efficiency is thus not just a theoretical concept and there is a need to address and quantify this measure.

Consider the production frontier of the ith firm, producing a single output with multiple inputs following the best practice techniques which can be defined as:

$$Y_i^* = f(x_{i1}, x_{i2}, .,.., x_{im}) \mid A \qquad (3.1)$$

where x_{ik}'s and Y_i^* are the kth input and frontier output of the ith firm respectively, and A is the given technology that is common to all firms in the sample.

Consider the situation where the firm is not producing its maximum possible output owing to some slackness in production induced by various non-price and socio-economic organizational factors. The production function of the firm can be written as

$$Y_i = f(x_{i1}, x_{i2}, .,.., x_{im})\, exp(u_i) \qquad (3.2)$$

where u_i represents the combined effects of various non-price and socio-economic organizational factors which constrain the firm from obtaining its maximum possible output. In other words, u_i which is firm-specific, reflects the firm's ability to produce at its present level, which is otherwise called the firm's technical efficiency. When the firm is fully technically efficient, then u takes the value of 0 and when the firm faces constraints, u takes a value less than 0. The value of u reflects the extent to which the firm is affected by the constraints. A measure of technical efficiency of the firm can be defined as

$$\exp(u_i) = Y_i \,/\, Y_i^* = \text{Actual output / Maximum possible output} \qquad (3.3)$$

where the actual or realized output is observed output for a given set of inputs and the potential output is the technologically feasible maximum output for the same set of inputs under the production environment faced by firms.

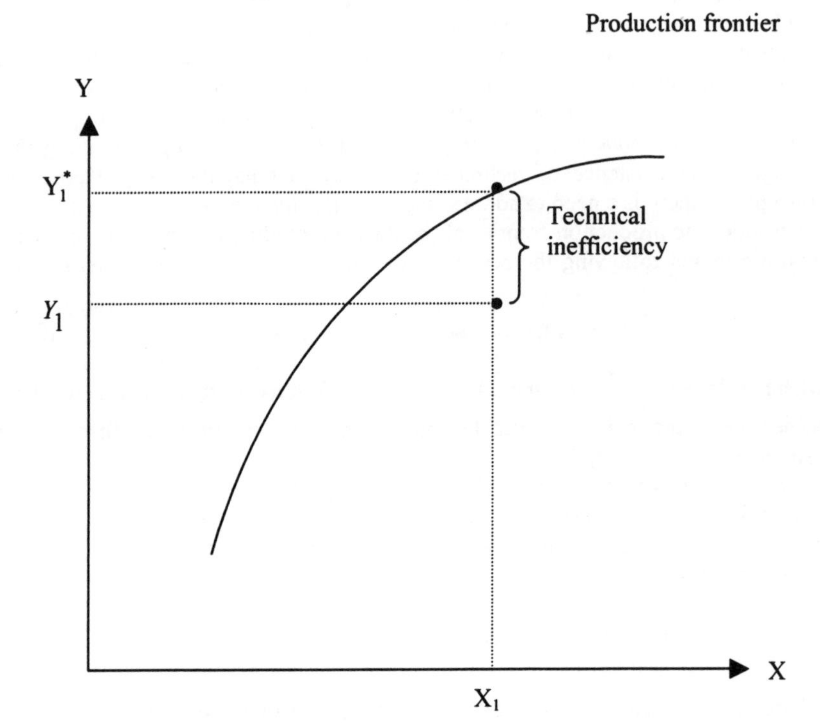

Figure 3.1 Technical inefficiency

Diagrammatically, Y^* is the frontier output and Y_1 is the observed output if firm uses X_1 input combination. Thus, technical inefficiency is represented by the gap between Y^* and Y_1. Equation (3.3) is the basic model used for measuring technical efficiency. In this model, the numerator is observable but the denominator is not and hence needs to be determined. The next section discusses the various methods based on different assumptions that have been used in the literature to estimate the denominator and thereby $\exp(u_i)$.

3.3 APPROACHES TO MEASURING TECHNICAL EFFICIENCY

The measurement of technical efficiency is linked with the estimation of production frontier because one needs a standard against which to measure efficiency. Thus it is not surprising that the literature on efficiency measurement and estimation of production frontier both began with the same article, namely Farrell (1957). The flowchart in Figure 3.2 provides an overview of technical efficiency measuring methods that are conveniently grouped under one-error and two-error structures.

The one-error structure assumes that there are no random errors and that all of the noise in the error structure is technical inefficiency arising from firm-specific factors. The two-error structure on the other hand allows for both technical inefficiency as well as random errors (due to weather, strike, luck, and measurement errors). There are various models available for estimation under these structures but the discussion here is selective and based only on core models used specifically for measuring technical efficiency and the changes and improvements in the measure of technical efficiency are traced using the models that have evolved over time.

3.3.1 The One-Error Structure

a) Deterministic approach

This was conceived by Aigner and Chu (1968) who specified the following Cobb-Douglas production function:

$$\ln Y = \ln f(X) - u$$

$$= \alpha_0 + \sum_{j=1}^{m} \alpha_i \ln X_{ij} - u, \quad u \geq 0 \qquad i = 1,2, \ldots, n \text{ and } j = 1, 2, \ldots, m \qquad (3.4)$$

where the error term forces $f(x) \geq y$ as the frontier output is defined as the maximal output attainable by firm given its inputs and technology. The elements of the parameter vector $\alpha = (\alpha_0, \alpha_1, \ldots, \alpha_N)'$ can be estimated either by linear programming (minimizing the sum of the absolute values of the residuals subject to the constraint that each residual be non-positive), or by quadratic programming (minimizing the sum of squared residuals subject to the same constraint). Although Aigner and Chu did not do so, the technical efficiency of each observation can be computed directly from the vector of residuals since u represents technical efficiency.

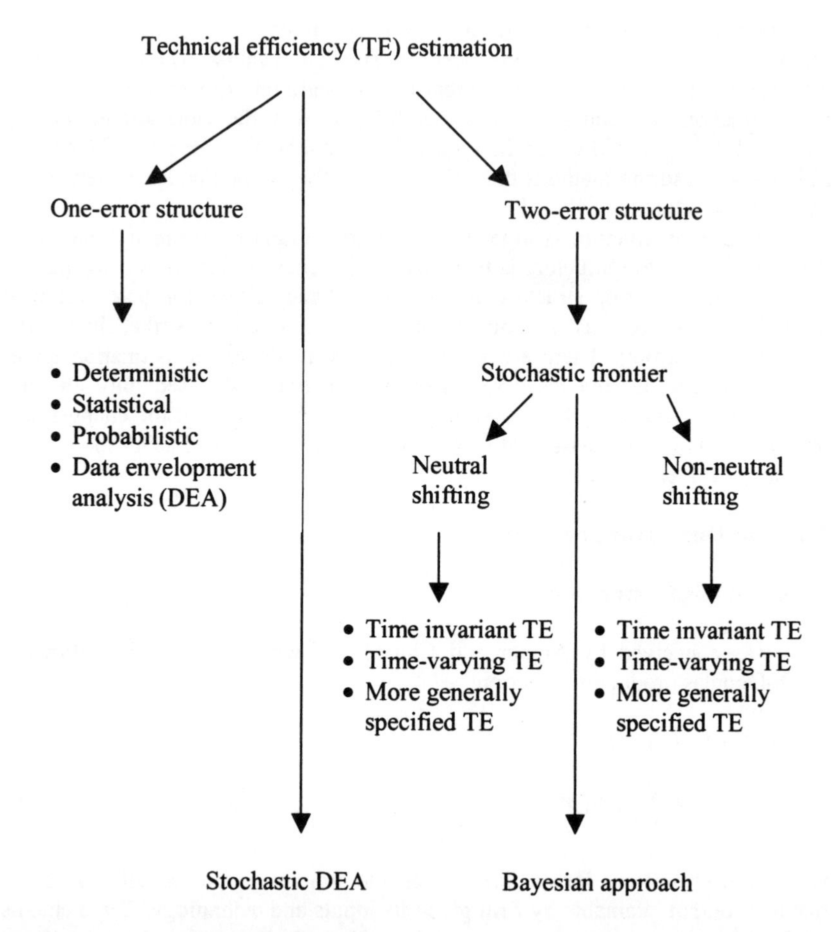

Figure 3.2 Measuring technical efficiency

By tightly enveloping data with linear segments, the programming approach lends itself naturally to the construction of frontier technology and provides a simple means of computing the distance to that frontier. This means of measuring the distance to the frontier yields an interpretation of efficiency as maximal/minimal proportionate changes in an activity, given technology.

However, there are four problems with this method. The first problem is the assumption of constant returns to scale and the underlying technology being linear homogenous. An extension of the method to incorporate non-constant returns to scale is rather cumbersome as shown by Seitz (1970). The second problem is that the shape of the frontier is supported by a subset of the data and thus the technical efficiency measures are extremely sensitive to outliers. One way around this problem is to discard a few observations until a certain percentage of the observations lie outside the input set or until the parameter estimates stabilize. This was pointed out by Timmer (1971) who suggests estimating a probabilistic frontier by deleting 3 per cent of the observations assuming they were affected by statistical errors. This approach was, however, not widely followed as the selection of the 3 per cent was purely arbitrary and lacked economic and statistical justification.

The third problem is that the estimates have no statistical properties because there are no assumptions made about the regressors or the error term. Hence without standard errors, inferential results cannot be obtained. However, resampling techniques such as bootstrapping and jackknifing can be used to derive empirical distributions as a basis for statistical inference. The fourth drawback is that the above approach is unable to deal with multiple output but this is easily dealt using DEA.

b) Statistical approach

Consider the following production function:

$$\ln Y_i = \alpha_0 + \sum_{j=1}^{m} \alpha_i \ln X_{ij} - u \tag{3.5}$$

where α_0 is the intercept term;
α' is the vector of parameters; and
u is the residual.

It has been shown that estimating equation (3.5) by OLS provides a best linear unbiased estimate of α' but α_0 which is not consistently estimated enters into the measure of technical efficiency since potential output is given by ($\hat{\alpha}_0 + \hat{\alpha}' \ln X_i$). Thus, for the measure of technical efficiency, it is important that the above model is corrected by Richmond's (1974) method of corrected ordinary least squares (COLS). Thus, we can write equation (3.5) as:

$$\ln Y_i = (\alpha_0 - \mu) + \sum_{j=1}^{m} \alpha_i \ln X_{ij} - (u_i - \mu) \qquad (3.6)$$

where μ is the mean of u and the new error term (u-μ) satisfies all the standard OLS conditions of zero mean and constant variance but not the normality condition. Now, u can assume any distributional specification and we can estimate the parameters from the higher-order (second, third, and so on) moments of the distribution of the OLS residuals. Since μ is a function of these parameters, μ can then be estimated consistently and used to 'correct' the OLS constant term. However, Olson et al. (1980) warn that the computation from the second and third moments of the OLS residuals often causes large variance in the COLS estimators which then affect the efficiency of the estimators. Also, since the standard errors of both the error components of the disturbance must be non-negative, the second and third moments of the regression residuals have restrictions on their feasible sets.

Unfortunately, the COLS only corrects the intercept term and this implies that the structure of 'best practice' production technology is the same as the structure of the 'central tendency' production technology. This is undesirable since the structure of best practice production technology ought to be permitted to differ from that of production technology down in the middle of the data where producers are less efficient than best practice producers (Kumbhakar and Lovell 2000). In other words, the COLS function does not necessarily bound the data from above as closely as possible, since it is required to be parallel to the OLS regression.

Another difficulty with the COLS technique is that the correction to the constant term is not independent of the distribution assumed for u. Thus, one can expect different estimates of technical efficiency for different assumed distributions. Furthermore, with the COLS, even after correcting the constant term, some of the residuals (u-μ) may be non-negative and thus have the 'wrong' sign. Such observations end up above the estimated production frontier. One response to the above problems has been to first estimate equation (3.1) by OLS and then to correct the constant term by shifting it up until no residual is positive and one residual takes on the value of zero. Another response is to use the stochastic frontier model which is discussed next.

3.3.2 The Two-Error Structure

The two-error structure was developed to take explicit account of statistical errors as efficiency scores may be contaminated by noise or measurement error. This relaxes the strong assumption of the single error structure that all observations in the data set are accurate. The stochastic frontier with the two-error structure is given by:

$$\ln Y_i = \beta_0 + \sum_{j=1}^{m} \alpha_i \ln X_{ij} + u_i + v_i \tag{3.7}$$

where u is the difference between the individual firm's practice and the best practice technique; and v represents statistical errors and other random factors. The two-error structure allows us to find out whether the deviation of firm's actual output from its potential output (that is, technical inefficiency) is mainly because the firm did not use the best practice technique or because of external random factors.

Many empirical applications have already been undertaken using various distributional assumptions on u to obtain average technical efficiency estimates. However, for a long time, the advantage of the single-error structure was that technical efficiency could be measured for each observation while the disadvantage with the two-error structure was that this was not possible as the separation of the error term into two components for each firm was a considerable task. This was soon resolved when Jondrow et al. (1982) and Kalirajan and Flinn (1983) independently predicted the random variable u under the assumption that $u+v$ is known. That is, considering the expected value of u, conditional on $u+v$, given by the minimum mean-square-error prediction. But Waldman (1984) showed that such prediction led to inconsistent estimators as the estimates did not converge to the true value.

Panel data estimation

The estimation of technical efficiency for a single cross-section of firms however depended heavily on the explicit distributional specification of u, thereby providing different technical efficiency estimates for different distributions. Schmidt and Sickles (1984), however, argue that such strong assumptions are not required for the consistency of estimates when panel data are available. This is because panel data allows the noise to be averaged in the overall residual and this is possible as the inefficiency terms are observed a few times rather than only once as in the case of the cross-section data. In addition, Sheehan (1997) and Griliches and Mairesse (1997) explain that using within or differencing transformation (that is, the fixed effects model) in panel data reduces the sensitivity of the results to capital stock measures which are often fraught with problems. Furthermore, the assumption that inefficiency effects and input levels are independent can be also be relaxed in the fixed effects model. This relaxation of the assumption is realistic, as it is unreasonable for a firm not to change its input mix if it knows it is technically inefficient.

However, Griliches and Mairesse (1997) raise the issue of sample selectivity problem in panel data using firm-level or plant-level data. They explain that if observations (and data) are not missing at random, estimates that are based on 'clean' and 'balanced' sub-samples could be badly biased. For example, Griliches and Regev (1995) found that there was a negative correlation between estimated technical efficiency and future probabilities of exit among the Israeli firms in their sample. If the impact of technical efficiency on exit is stronger for smaller firms (the larger ones having more resources to survive them), then this will induce a negative correlation between technical efficiency and, say, the stock of capital among the surviving firms, and bias the estimated capital coefficient downward in such samples.

a) Fixed effects model

There are various types of models that can be used to estimate technical efficiency with panel data. Let the stochastic frontier model in a panel data framework, consisting of n firms, each observed over a time period of T be written as:

$$Y_{it} = \beta_0 + \beta X'_{it} + v_{it} + u_{it} \quad i = 1, 2, \ldots, n \text{ and } t = 1, 2, \ldots, T \tag{3.8}$$

The above model can be estimated assuming that the technical efficiency effects are time-invariant or time-variant. For time-invariant models, only the intercept is allowed to vary over firms while the level of efficiency for each firm is assumed not to change over time. This can be estimated by the fixed-effects model using two ways in the panel data literature.

One way is to suppress the constant term and add a dummy variable for each of the n firms or, equivalently, by keeping the constant term and adding (n-1) dummies. But as n becomes large, this estimation becomes highly parameterized leading to a large loss of degrees of freedom and the estimation is often not feasible as too many dummies bring upon the problem of multicollinearity. Thus, the popular way is to express all data in terms of deviations from the firms' means. This is done by rewriting equation (3.8) as:

$$Y_{it} = \beta_{0i} + \beta X'_{it} + v_{it} \tag{3.9}$$

where $\beta_{0i} = \beta_0 - u_{it}$ and the n intercepts are recovered as the means of the residuals by firm. Here, the parameters are estimated conditionally on fixed values of the u_i's and hence, the 'within' estimators of β's can be obtained by the OLS estimation of:

$$Y_{it} - \overline{Y}_i = \beta'(X_{it} - \overline{X}_i) + v'_{it} \tag{3.10}$$

where $\overline{Y}_i$ and $\overline{X}_i$ are the means of the (Y, X) set for the ith firm over T.

One advantage of the fixed effects models is that it allows the inefficiency effects to be correlated with the regressors as the within transformation eliminates the time-invariant regressors and thus u_{it} would include the influence of all variables that are time-invariant at the firm level within the sample. The disadvantage is that this would make technical efficiency comparisons difficult unless the excluded variables influence all firms in the sample equally. Also, this rules out the realistic possibility that firm-specific effects and responses are important to obtain accurate technical efficiency estimates. Kalirajan and Shand (1994) further explain that, since the intercept term in equation (3.10) cannot be identified. This implies that different values of β's and u_i may lead to the same conditional mean $E(Y_i|X_i)$, making the estimation of the intercept and thus, technical efficiency measures somewhat arbitrary to some extent.

However, another advantage of the fixed effects model is that it does not rely on any distributional assumptions on efficiency since in treating u_i as fixed, the within estimator simply proceeds conditionally from whatever their realizations may be (Schmidt and Sickles 1984). While Simar (1992) showed that the fixed effects model provided a poor estimation of the parameters, and consequently, unreasonable technical efficiency estimates, Kumbhakar (1987) found the technical efficiency estimates from the fixed effects model to be greater than those from the random effects model, which is another type of panel data model, discussed below.

b) Random effects model

Time-invariant models can also be estimated using the random effects model in the panel data literature. Unlike the fixed effects model, this model allows for firm-specific attributes and thus includes time-invariant regressors, but in doing so it has to rely on the assumption that the inefficiency effects and input levels are independent. This assumption stems from Zellner et al. (1966) who argue that firms often maximize expected profit and this implies that input quantities are exogenous. The random effects model is often said to be preferred (resulting from gains in efficiency) to the fixed effects model since it utilizes the 'between' estimator in addition to the 'within' estimator of the fixed effects model. It should, however, be noted that the heterogeneity in both slopes and intercepts reflecting variation within and across firms lends itself to the high parameterization of the random effects model which can be a disadvantage.

Which model and estimation technique to use?

Mundlak (1978) argues that the decision on the nature of the effects, whether it is random or fixed, is both arbitrary and unnecessary. He says that it is up to the user to decide whether he wants inference with respect to the population of all effects (random effects) or only with respect to the effects that are in the sample (fixed effects).

Statistically speaking, the choice between the fixed effects and random effects model can be made by testing if the regressors, X_{it}, are correlated with the technical efficiency effects using the procedure of Hausman and Taylor (1981). If the null hypothesis of correlation could not be rejected, then the instrumental variable estimation can be used to estimate the random effects model with the assumption that all or some of the X_{it} are correlated with u_{it}.[3] If indeed, there is no correlation between X_{it} and u_{it}, then the random effects model can be estimated using either maximum likelihood estimation (MLE) or generalized least squares (GLS) method. Also, one criticism that can be levelled at the traditional panel data approaches is that both the inefficient and efficient firms have equivalent influence upon the shape of the estimated frontier, whereas the most efficient firms have a greater influence upon the shape of the estimated frontier when MLE is used (Coelli et al. 1998). The advantage of the GLS technique is that, unlike the MLE, the GLS does not require a distributional specification for u_{it} since it operates on the premise that the components of the variance of the residuals are unknown. But if the distributional specification underlying u_{it} is accurate, then the ML estimators are generally more efficient (asymptotically) than the GLS estimators since they exploit distributional information unlike the GLS estimators.

Schmidt and Sickles (1984) further explain that the choice of panel data estimation is also dependent on the size of n and T. When n is large and T is small, GLS estimation is strongly advised. If T is large but n is small, one is restricted to using the within estimator of the fixed effects model. If both n and T are large, any estimation technique would do, based on what one is willing to assume regarding the distributional assumptions of u and the correlatedness between the regressors and u. With different distributional assumptions on u, there is little doubt that values of technical efficiencies would vary, but there is some evidence provided by Greene (1990) that a ranking of the individual technical efficiency scores or the composition of the top and bottom efficiency scores deciles is not particularly sensitive to the assigned distribution of u. If this is true, then it may be best to use relatively simple distributions such as the half-normal or exponential rather than a more flexible distribution such as the gamma distribution.

Time varying technical efficiency

As the sample size becomes larger, the assumption that technical inefficiency effects are time-invariant is more difficult to justify since one would expect firms to learn from their previous experience in the production process, so that their technical inefficiency would change over time. Thus, in the last decade or so, along with the most common assumption that u_{it} follows a half-normal or general truncated-normal distribution, many empirical studies have relied on MLE using panel data estimation by adopting various time-varying specifications for the technical inefficiency effects.

For instance, Kumbhakar (1990) modelled technical efficiency effects as a product of an exponential function of time involving two parameters, γ and δ, as well as a time-invariant non-negative random variable, u_i:

$$Y_{it} = \beta_0 + \sum_{j=1}^{m} \beta_i X_{ijt} \; u_{it} + v_{it} \tag{3.11}$$

where $u_{it} = g(t)\, u_i$; and

$$g(t) = [1 + \exp(\gamma + \delta t^2)]^{-1}$$

Although this allows the level of technical inefficiency to be non-constant, its temporal pattern is the same for all firms since it is determined by the form $g(t)$. This model which uses MLE is yet to be supported by any empirical application. However, there are many empirical applications or at least variations of it based on Battese and Coelli's (1992) model:[4]

$$Y_{it} = \beta_0 + \sum_{j=1}^{m} \beta_j X_{ijt} - u_{it} + v_{it} \tag{3.12}$$

where $u_{it} = \{\exp[-\eta(t-T)]\} u_i$; and
η is an unknown scalar to be estimated.

Here, the technical inefficiency effect for the *i*th firm in the last period is u_i and for all earlier periods in the panel, technical inefficiency effects are the product of the technical inefficiency effect for the *i*th firm in the last period and the value of the exponential function exp $[-\eta(t-T)]$, whose value depends on η and the number of periods before the last period of the panel, $(T-t)$. Similar to Kumbhakar's (1990) model, the disadvantage in this model is its rigid parameterization. In particular, the technical efficiency must either increase or decrease at a decreasing rate ($\eta > 0$) or an increasing rate ($\eta < 0$) or simply remain constant ($\eta = 0$). Thus, the model does not account for situations in which some firms may be relatively inefficient initially but become relatively more efficient in subsequent periods.

The specification of Cornwell et al. (1990), however, improved on the above rigid parameterization by assuming that the intercept in parameters for different firms at different time periods was a quadratic function of time (t) with the coefficients varying over firms according to a multivariate distribution. The advantage of this model over Kumbhakar's (1990) and Battese and Coelli's (1992) model is that it uses GLS and hence there is no need to specify any special density function of u_{it} and firm-specific technical efficiency can now be calculated as:

$$\hat{u}_{it} = \hat{\beta}_{ot} - \hat{\beta}_{oit} \tag{3.13}$$

where $\hat{\beta}_{ot} = \max\{\hat{\beta}_{oi}\}$;
$\hat{\beta}_{oit} = \delta_{i0} + \delta_{i1}t + \delta_{i2}t^2$; and
δ_{ij} are parameters to be estimated.

Although the temporal pattern of technical inefficiency is unrestricted as the magnitude of the technical change varies over time, this is assumed to be the same for all firms. Also, the above specification is empirically useful only for relatively small time periods, and for large time periods, the estimation has to be done for too many parameters. The other criticism levelled against these time-varying models is the way in which the inefficiency effects have been modelled. Ahn et al. (2000) argue that such models define inefficiency effects as a fixed function of time and thus only provide reasonable approximations for the dynamics of short-run technical inefficiency and are inappropriate for analysing the long-run dynamics of technical inefficiency. The specifications of the inefficiency effects are only arbitrary functional approximations with little theoretical or intuitive justifications.

More generally specified technical inefficiency models

In the family of stochastic frontier models, a model that has gained popularity is one that assumes that firm-specific factors affecting technical efficiency must be included in the model. As an illustration, first consider the models of Kumbhakar et al. (1991) and Battese and Coelli (1995), both of which specify the distribution of technical inefficiency effects u as $N(m'\gamma, \sigma_u^2)$ where γ is a vector of parameters to be estimated. In other words, technical inefficiency is modelled as a deterministic component explained by a vector of exogenous variables (m) and a random component (θ):

$$u = m'\gamma + \theta \tag{3.14}$$

These authors argue that this type of model firstly avoids the problem of the possibility of correlation between technical inefficiency effects and the inputs. Secondly, this single-step procedure allows the explanation of part of the variation in technical inefficiency in terms of firm-specific factors. If so, it must be cautioned that omitted variable bias might be a problem if all the important firm-specific factors have not been considered. Recently, Koop et al. (2000) used a Bayesian approach to model a similar structure whereby the mean of technical inefficiency was modelled to depend on some explanatory variables that were only allowed to be dummy variables to reduce the computational burden in the Bayesian framework.

Previous studies such as Pitt and Lee (1981) and Kalirajan and Shand (1985) used a two-step procedure where technical efficiency was first obtained and then regressed against the firm-specific factors by OLS. But this procedure was deemed inappropriate as the non-positive nature of technical inefficiency was not accommodated for in the model. One way around this is to use a logit function for estimation and another way is to transform the technical efficiency indices appropriately to comply with the standard OLS assumptions.[5]

In this two-stage formulation, it is assumed that the firm-specific factors influence frontier output indirectly through their effect on estimated efficiency. While these factors do not influence the structure of the production frontier, they help explain the variation in estimated efficiency. However, Coelli et al. (1998) highlight some serious problems with the two-step method. First, the above procedure is based on the assumption that the firm-specific factors are uncorrelated with the inputs. If they are correlated, then the ML estimates are biased and so would be the technical efficiencies, and hence the second stage analysis. Second, in the first stage, the inefficiency effects are assumed to be independently and identically distributed in order to obtain technical inefficiency measures. But in the second stage, the predicted inefficiency effects are assumed to be a function of a number of firm-specific factors, which implies that the inefficiency effects are not identically distributed, unless all the coefficients of the factors are simultaneously zero.

Lee and Schmidt (1993) raise an important issue regarding firm-specific factors affecting frontier output and/or technical efficiency. Consider their model:

$$\begin{aligned} Y_{it} &= \alpha t + X'_{it}\,\beta - u_{it} + v_{it} \\ &= \alpha_{it} + X'_{it}\,\beta + v_{it} \end{aligned} \tag{3.15}$$

where $\alpha_{it} = \alpha_t - u_{it}$; and
$\alpha_{it} = \theta_t\,\delta_i$

The intercept for the ith firm at time t is given by $\alpha_{it,}$ and α_t is the frontier intercept, that is, it is the maximum possible value of $\alpha_{it.}$ Firm-specific factors that do not vary over time are given by δ_i and θ_t are parameters to be estimated. In their model, the firm-specific factors are assumed to affect frontier output and these are controlled for before efficiency is calculated. Alternatively, if some firm-specific variables affect output only because they affect the level of technical inefficiency, then it is appropriate to consider these variables (Z_{it}) as part of the intercept in equation (3.15). That is:

$$\alpha_{it} = Z_{it}\gamma + \theta_t\,\delta_i \tag{3.16}$$

and γ is the set of parameters to be estimated. Here, the exogenous or firm-specific factors influence the structure of the production frontier and thus, this formulation is a more accurate characterization of production possibilities and consequently more accurate estimates of efficiency. However, variation in efficiency is not explained by the above formulation. In fact, whether a particular firm-specific variable affects frontier output, or the level of technical efficiency only, or both, is not a question we can expect to answer easily from the data.

Non-neutral shifting frontier models

All of the stochastic production frontier models discussed so far (regardless of whether their estimation is based on cross-sectional, time-invariant or time-varying panel data) are neutral shifts from the realized production function. This form of shifting frontier suffers the serious drawback of constant marginal rate of technical substitution (MRTS) at any input combination. Consider the following conventional stochastic frontier model:[6]

$$Y = f(X) + v + u \tag{3.17}$$

where $E\,(Y|\,X,\,u) = f\,(X) + u\ <\ f\,(X)$. That is, the efficiency index shifts average observed output is below the frontier output due to the presence of technical inefficiency, u, which is non-positive. And the unit isoquant moves upwards in such a way that the MRTS at any input combination remains unchanged.

Let us now define the following for input i:

$$\text{Let } E_i\,(Y|\,X,\,u) = \frac{\delta\ E(Y\,|\,X,u)}{\delta\ X_i} \quad \text{and} \quad F_i(X) = \frac{\delta\ f(X)}{\delta\ X_i} \tag{3.18}$$

$$\text{Then MRTS} = \frac{E_i(Y\,|\,X,u)}{E_j(Y\,|\,X,u)} = \frac{F_i(X)}{F_j(X)} \tag{3.19}$$

That is, the MRTS is independent of u. The technically inefficient firms (those with $u < 0$) suffer a uniform reduction in input productivity without altering optimal input mixes but this is hard to justify. Such neutral (or otherwise called parallel) shifting frontier is unrealistic and can only be considered as a special case of the non-neutral shifting frontier.

While the studies of Huang and Liu (1994) and Kalirajan and Shand (1994) consider non-neutral shifting frontier models, there are significant differences in the formulation of their models (based on the source of the non-neutrality as well as the type of efficiency measures obtainable from the two models) and these are discussed in the next section.

Time varying and input-specific technical efficiency model

This model, also known as the stochastic varying coefficients frontier, was developed by Kalirajan and Shand (1994) who argue that there is no logic behind the parallel-shifting frontier which essentially remains constant with the exception of the intercept term. Thus, there is a need to include observation-specific production behaviour that varies across observations and therefore results in different input response coefficients across observations. They further explain that technical efficiency is determined by the method of application of inputs regardless of the levels of the input use. This implies that different methods of applying inputs will influence output differently, that is, both the intercept and slope coefficients will vary from firm to firm and this forms the basis for the concept of non-neutrality in the analysis. Also, depending on which firm uses which best practice technique with which input, the frontier production coefficients would not necessary all come from the same firm.

The stochastic varying coefficients frontier model is as follows:

$$Y_{it} = \sum_{j=1}^{m} \beta_{ijt} X_{ijt} + \varepsilon_{it} \tag{3.20}$$

The intercept of the ith firm in the tth period is given by β_{i1t}, when $j = 1$ and when $j \neq 1$, the slope coefficient of the jth input is given by β_{ijt}. Equation (3.20) implies that the production response coefficients are specific to each firm in each time period but unfortunately, the model cannot be estimated as the number of parameters exceeds the number of observations. This necessitates the reduction in the number of parameter estimation by imposing the following restrictions:

$$\beta_{ijt} = \overline{\beta}_j + u_{ij} + v_{jt} \tag{3.21}$$

$$\sum_{i}^{n} u_{ij} = 0 \text{ and } \sum_{t}^{T} v_{jt} = 0 \tag{3.22}$$

where u_{ij} and v_{jt} respectively denote cross-sectional and temporal variation of the production coefficients β_{ijt}. The model is estimated using GLS, thus non-specific distributional assumptions on u are necessary. The highest magnitude of each response coefficient and the intercept, form the production coefficients of stochastic production function. That is:

$$\beta^*_{jt} = \max_i \{\beta_{ijt}\} \tag{3.23}$$

where β^*_{jt} is the frontier coefficient of the jth input in the tth period.

An important observation is that the frontier coefficients need not necessarily coincide with the response coefficients for any single individual observation as they may represent the best combination of response coefficients derived from different individual observations. This implicitly assumes that not all firms use all the inputs efficiently. In addition to firm-specific technical efficiency measures, this model also provides input-specific technical efficiency measures. The technical efficiency (TE) of using the jth input by the ith firm can be calculated as:

$$\text{TE}_{ij} = \frac{\hat{\beta}_{ij}}{\beta^*_j} \tag{3.24}$$

The above information allows one to distinguish between firms which are more or less efficient in the use of each of the inputs and this would indicate the most appropriate direction for policy-making.

The hybrid time-varying technical efficiency model

Such a model was developed by Huang and Liu (1994) who believed that the technical inefficiency effects on productivity may be greater on some inputs than on others since it is likely that firms would have acquired more information, knowledge and experience with respect to one input productivity than to another. Or that the effect of some government policy or regulation on the use of input and productivity processes may either constrain or benefit some inputs but not all inputs and in the same way. Thus, they specify the following:

$$\text{The unobserved stochastic frontier output, } Y^* = f(X) + v \tag{3.25}$$

$$\text{Technical efficiency, } u = Y - Y^* = f(Z) + w \tag{3.26}$$

where Y is the observed output;

Z are the variables identifying the sources of technical efficiency; and

W is the random error representing residual efficiency.

Since u is non-positive, w must be truncated from above and the truncation point depends on $f(Z)$, that is:

$$W \leq -f(Z) \tag{3.27}$$

Thus, the above model which is a hybrid of a stochastic frontier regression (3.25) and a truncated regression (3.21) is said to have a composite error, $v+w$. The estimation of such a model is then accomplished by having varying truncation points for w.

In their empirical application, Huang and Liu (1994) first obtain estimates of the frontier model:

$$Y = \beta_0 + \Sigma\, \beta_i X_i + v \tag{3.28}$$

and then obtain Y^*, the frontier output as $\hat{\beta}_0 + \hat{\beta}_i X_i$

Next, the following non-neutral efficiency regression is estimated:

$$Y - Y^* = \sum_i \alpha_i Z_i + \sum_i \sum_j \alpha_{ij} Z_i X_j + w \tag{3.29}$$

where technical efficiency is given by the left-hand side of the above equation by substituting the estimated parameters, $\hat{\alpha}_i$ and $\hat{\alpha}_{ij}$. The specification of the efficiency regression in (3.29) allows for the non-neutral shift of the observed output from the frontier. This results from the interaction between a firm's characteristics and input usage.

3.3.3 Some Recently Developed Lines of Research

This section is not meant to be exhaustive but is intended to briefly introduce the three relatively new methods, and these include the stochastic DEA, the Bayesian approach and the dynamic frontier approach to frontier modelling. These methods are in their infancy stages for empirical purposes as they are still being explored and improved. One reason for the lack of serious empirical pursuit using these models is that the sort of additional information required for these approaches is not easily available. Second, these methods are computationally very demanding which makes then difficult for applied empirical work unless one has the necessary software skills or enlists the help of computer programmers to help with the number-crunching.

One fairly recent approach in frontier modelling is the use of the Bayesian approach[7] which takes parameter uncertainty (a characteristic bound to be important in small sample size) into account in deriving posterior densities for the efficiencies. Here, interest lies in providing confidence intervals for the point estimates of the efficiency levels. Bayesian inference is carried by formulating a prior probability density function and combining it with the likelihood function of the sample data to form a posterior probability density function. Often, the uncertainty concerning which sample model to use can be treated by mixing them over with posterior model probabilities as weights. Otherwise, a particular distribution for use can be chosen using Bayes factors or posterior odds as a criteria for model selection. By incorporating new information obtained either deductively or inductively, the Bayesian approach overcomes the limitation of imposing *a priori* sampling distribution on technical inefficiency effects.

However, Broeck et al. (1994), who used the Bayesian approach in frontier modelling, explain that this approach has its own share of problems. First, the estimates obtained are sensitive to the choice of prior and there is no rule as to what and how this is done. Second, the Bayesian empirical application is computationally not a trivial exercise as it relies on Monte Carlo integration taking into account all prior and sample information. Third, it has been noted that the verification of the suitability of a Bayesian model including prediction and diagnostic testing of the assumptions still require the satisfactory development of additional statistical computational methods. Although Kim and Schmidt (2000) do not find much difference between Bayesian and classical results, studies by Koop et al. (1999, 2000) and Koop (2001) at the very least provide a reasonably useful alternative for flagging interesting analyses.

The stochastic DEA models are a significant contribution to frontier modelling as they attempt to marry the strengths of the stochastic frontier approach and DEA models. The model by Sengupta (1998), for instance, applies a filtering method to the stochastic data set so that only the systematic components are utilized to obtain a non-stochastic data set for DEA programming models. Then, the efficiency measures are checked for robustness by deriving the probability distribution of the optimal output vector and inefficiency output vector. If the statistical distance between these two frontiers is small, the efficiency measure is robust in the sense that the outlier effect is small. But if the skewness and variance associated with the distribution of the efficiency or optimal output vector is still very large, then there may be outlier sensitivity. The drawback in filtering data, however, arises when the errors are non-Gaussian. Here, Sengupta arbitrarily resorts to using common Gaussian distributions (such as the exponential or half-normal distribution) to approximate the required conditional density function of the input vector.

An alternative approach to allowing DEA to capture the effects of random noise without the deterministic frontiers themselves becoming stochastic, is to use the 'chance-constrained efficiency analysis' introduced by Land et al. (1993). Here, DEA is extended to consider the stochastic inputs and outputs such that constraints are violated but not too frequently. This allows a 'soft' frontier where output observations are permitted to cross over as it is acknowledged that the enveloping efficiency frontier is not necessarily an absolute barrier. The main drawback of the mathematical programming technique for this type of analysis is the heavy data requirements in terms of availability and quality that is necessary to derive the joint probability distribution of all random variables. Land et al. (1993) explain that the probability distribution typically relates to hypothetical repeat situations that, by the nature of things, cannot really be investigated experimentally and often numerical experimentation is resorted to, and this does not necessarily represent the actual situation. Furthermore, information on the nature and type of uncertainty responsible for the stochastic data is also necessary to formulate the appropriate chance-constraints. Another type of chance-constrained DEA developed by Olesen and Petersen (1995) uses a piecewise linear envelopment of confidence regions for observed stochastic inputs and outputs. Li (1998) provides numerous references of alternatives to the stochastic DEA but she acknowledges that these methods require a large number of parameters to be estimated. And although this can be facilitated by assumptions which reduce the computational task, nevertheless it appears that such assumptions on the relationship of the inputs and output components are often not necessarily flexible and are made simple to keep the estimation tractable.

An interesting extension to frontier modelling has been proposed by Ahn et al. (2000) who identify the need for a dynamic frontier model to consider the long-run dynamics of the inefficiency effects. They use a model which assumes that technical inefficiency evolves autoregressively over time due to firms' inability to adjust their productivity in a timely manner. Their model reduces to the usual dynamic panel model if the speed of adjusting inefficiency is assumed to be the same for all firms. They also considered various estimation procedures and specification tests depending on whether the frontier is deterministic or stochastic.

NOTES

1. On the other hand, the measurement of allocative and scale efficiency is less controversial and if there is a problem, it lies with the availability and reliability of price data rather than the analytical and empirical technique used for measurement.
2. The 'flying geese' model was first used to describe the life cycle of industries in the course of economic development (Akamatsu 1962). The model has now been extended to study the shift of industries from a country.

3. However, one problem with the instrumental variable method is that if lagged dependent variables are used as instruments, then the estimation would lose degrees of freedom and thus only a large enough time series can enable such an estimation. Otherwise, as an alternative, Mundlak (1978) and Chamberlain (1980) offer some possibilities of modelling the correlation between the regressors and u.
4. One likely reason for this is that Coelli's (1996a) FRONTIER software is free of charge and can easily be downloaded from the web. See note 4 in Chapter 2.
5. Such a transformation is used in the case study in Chapter 8.
6. This is drawn from Huang and Liu (1994).
7. See Zellner (1971) for an introduction to Bayesian inference.

PART II

Applications

4 The non-frontier approach: a case study of Hong Kong's manufacturing sector

4.1 INTRODUCTION

This chapter focuses on the non-frontier approach which formed the basis of productivity growth measurement since the very notion of TFP growth was conjured up in the early 1950s. Here, the theoretical underpinning of both the parametric and non-parametric methods are explained and used with Hong Kong's manufacturing sector as a case study.

4.2 THEORETICAL FRAMEWORK

4.2.1 The Translog-Divisia Index

Consider the production function of

$$Q_t = F\,[K_t, L_t, t] \tag{4.1}$$

Equation (4.1) expresses value added Q as a function of the stock of capital K, employment L, and a shift factor t which proxies the effects of TFP growth. Assuming that the argument 't' is separable from K and L,

$$Q_t = A_t\,F\,[K_t, L_t,] \tag{4.2}$$

$$\Rightarrow \; A_t = \frac{Q_t}{F[K_t, L_t]} \tag{4.3}$$

Differentiating (4.3) and expressing in growth rates (denoted by, $\dot{A}$, q, l and k):

$$\frac{\dot{A}_t}{A_t} = q_t - \frac{L_t}{Q_t}\frac{\partial Q_t}{\partial L_t} l_t - \frac{K_t}{Q_t}\frac{\partial Q_t}{\partial K_t} k_t \tag{4.4}$$

The expressions in front of l_t and k_t are the respective output elasticities. By assuming perfect competition and profit maximization, the price elasticity of demand for all the factors is infinite, and the factor elasticities equal the factor shares in output, and thus (4.4) becomes:

$$\frac{\dot{A}_t}{A_t} = (q_t - k_t) - a_t(l_t - k_t)$$

$$= q_t - k_t(1 - a_t) - l_t a_t \tag{4.5}$$

where a_t and $(1\text{-}a_t)$ are the respective labour and capital shares.

For TFP studies, the most commonly used index is the Theil-Tornqvist index or the Translog-Divisia index approach that was developed by Jorgenson et al. (1987). The latter index using the gross output approach is defined over two time periods t and t-1as:

$$\bar{V}_t = LnQ_t - LnQ_{t-1}$$

$$- \bar{V}_M(LnM_t - LnM_{t-1}) - \bar{V}_K(LnK_t - LnK_{t-1}) - \bar{V}_L(LnL_t - LnL_{t-1}) \tag{4.6}$$

where $\bar{V}_M = 1/2\ (V_{M,t} + V_{M,t-1})$

$\bar{V}_K = 1/2\ (V_{K,t} + V_{K,t-1})$

$\bar{V}_L = 1/2\ (V_{L,t} + V_{L,t-1})$

with $\bar{V}_M$, $\bar{V}_K$, and $\bar{V}_L$ denoting the shares of intermediate M, capital K, and labour L inputs, Q and t being gross output and time respectively, and a bar indicating a simple average over two successive time periods, t and t-1. The average productivity growth is given by $\bar{V}_t$ and this is defined to be Hicks neutral (exogenous) in that it is not associated with any particular input and may vary with the growth of any input or all inputs and time, and hence is often described as being disembodied.

Under assumptions of competitive factor markets and constant returns to scale, the Vs are equal to income shares of the respective factors and the $\bar{V}_S$ are interpreted as output elasticities with respect to the various inputs, that is:

$$V_K = \frac{\sum_K P_{Kk} K_k}{qQ}, \quad V_M = \frac{\sum_m P_{Mm} M_m}{qQ}, \text{ and } \quad V_L = \frac{\sum_l P_{Ll} L_l}{qQ} \tag{4.7}$$

where q denotes price of output;
Q denotes quantity of output;
P_{Kk} is price of capital asset type k;
P_{Mm} is price of intermediate input m;
P_{Ll} is price of labour type l;
K_k is quantity of capital asset type k;
M_m is quantity of intermediate input m; and
L_l is quantity of labour type l

As Jorgenson et al. (1987) provide full details on the construction of the above variables, further elaboration on this is omitted.

4.2.2 Average Production Function

Consider the following Cobb-Douglas production function as an example:

$Y = A K^{\alpha_k} L^{\alpha_L}$ or taking logarithms and introducing an error term,

$$Ln\, Y = A' + \alpha_K\, Ln\, K + \alpha_L\, Ln\, L + \varepsilon \tag{4.8}$$

where Y = value added output;
K = capital expenditure;
L = labour;
α_K and α_L are the capital and labour shares; and
$\varepsilon \sim N(0,\sigma^2)$

The estimates of α_K and α_L are interpreted as output elasticities with respect to inputs and usual assumption is that constant returns to scale prevail, that is, $\alpha_K + \alpha_L = 1$. This also means that the production function is homogenous of degree 1, that is, proportional changes in capital and labour result in proportional changes in value added output. The above model is then estimated using OLS with the assumption that the error term ε is identically and independently distributed with mean zero and a constant variance.

Using the parameter estimates of $\hat{\alpha}_k$ and $\hat{\alpha}_L$, TFP levels can be calculated as $(Y - \hat{Y})$ and TFP growth is given by the difference in TFP levels. Alternatively, TFP growth can be calculated as:

$$\left(\dot{Y} - \hat{\alpha}_k \dot{K} - \hat{\alpha}_L \dot{L}\right) \tag{4.9}$$

where a dot represents observed growth rates of the variables. Sometimes, TFP growth is defined as a function of time, and being a trend parameter it is thus exogenous. At other times, a trend effect is included and the residual is measured as TFP growth. But often, adjustments by statistical agencies in constructing time series data from surveys involve allocations and interpolations that are more or less smooth with respect to time. Consequently, in such series there is a built-in correlation with time, and the use of trend variables may therefore capture and 'explain' more variation in the data than inherent in original data record.

Consider the following two versions of the flexible Translog production function:

$$\begin{aligned} Ln\ Y = \alpha + \alpha_K Ln\ \mathrm{K} + \alpha_L Ln\ \mathrm{L} + \alpha_{KK}(Ln\ \mathrm{K})(Ln\ \mathrm{K}) + \alpha_{LL}(Ln\ \mathrm{L})(Ln\ \mathrm{L}) \\ + \alpha_{KL}(0.5)(Ln\ \mathrm{K})(Ln\ \mathrm{L}) \end{aligned} \tag{4.10}$$

$$\begin{aligned} Ln\ Y = \alpha + \alpha_K Ln\ K + \alpha_L Ln\ L + \alpha_{KK}(0.5)(Ln\ K)(Ln\ K) \\ + \alpha_{LL}(0.5)(Ln\ L)(Ln\ L) \\ + \alpha_{KL}(Ln\ K)(Ln\ L) + \alpha_T(T) + \alpha_{TT}(0.5)T^2 \\ + \alpha_{KT}(Ln\ K)(T) + \alpha_{LT}(Ln\ L)(T) \end{aligned} \tag{4.11}$$

where *T* is a time tend.

There are other similar variations of the Translog model and the choice for use depends on econometric considerations as well as what is being investigated. For example, for information on technical biases in inputs, one needs the model which has interaction terms of time and inputs given by equation (4.11). If the nature of productivity growth increase over time is of interest, then the α_{TT} term in equation (4.11) would be necessary. A positive α_{TT} means that the acceleration of productivity growth is positive or that the rate of productivity growth increases over time. Also, the share elasticity term of α_{KL} in equation (4.11) can be used to obtain implications on the pattern of substitution on the distribution of the value of output between capital and labour. However if sample size is limited and one has strong reasons to believe that the production function is Hicks-neutral, then to make econometrically valid inferences on the estimates based on sufficient degrees of freedom, the model given by (4.10) would suffice.

The Translog model given by equation (4.11) allows testing for various hypotheses. For example, to test for the existence of Hicks neutral technology (that is, the biases of productivity growth with respect to any one input is equal to zero):

$$\text{Test if } \alpha_{KT} = \alpha_{LT} = 0 \tag{4.12}$$

If the above hypothesis is accepted, then the productivity growth bias is neutral and the shifts of the production function are parallel whereby the marginal rate of substitution of labour and capital is constant. If the above hypothesis is rejected, then input biased can be checked for. That is, if $\alpha_{LT} > 0$, then the positive bias means that productivity growth is labour-using and that the estimates bias can be interpreted as the change in the share of labour with respect to time, holding all other inputs constant. On the other hand, if $\alpha_{KT} < 0$, then negative bias means that productivity growth is capital-saving and that rate of productivity growth decreases with respect to quantity of capital.

The above Translog model can also used to check if the Cobb-Douglas or indeed the Translog model is more appropriate for the data. The test involves investigating if the second order conditions are significantly different from zero:

$$\text{Test if } \alpha_{KK} = \alpha_{LL} = \alpha_{KL} = 0 \tag{4.13}$$

If the above null hypothesis is rejected, then the second-order conditions cannot be ignored and thus the Translog function is to be used for estimation. If that is the case, one may be interested to check if the conditions for concavity (that is, the estimated elasticities of the share of each of the input with respect to the quantity of the input itself must be non-positive) which are necessary for the Translog model are satisfied:

$$\text{Test if } \alpha_{KK}, \alpha_{LL}, \alpha_{KL} < 0 \tag{4.14}$$

If the above hypothesis is accepted, then the share of each of the input is non-increasing in the quantity of the input itself.

4.3 CASE STUDY: HONG KONG'S MANUFACTURING SECTOR

4.3.1 Introduction

The manufacturing sector of Hong Kong is chosen as a case study since most TFP studies on Hong Kong have been on the aggregate economy. These include Chen (1977), Young (1992, 1995), the World Bank (1993), Kim and Lau (1994), Takenaka (1995), Drysdale and Huang (1997), Hsieh (1997) and Tang (2000). The conclusions from the non-frontier approach used by all these studies are quite varied. Young (1992) estimated TFP growth to be about 2 per cent from the late 1960s to the late 1980s, Färe and Grosskopf (1997) found a similar result for 1975–90, Koop et al. (2000) found TFP growth to be 4.72 per cent over 1965–90, and Kim and Lau (1994) found TFP growth not to be significantly different from zero. Recently, Tang (2000) showed that the Hong Kong economy experienced an average TFP growth of 3.4 per cent for 1989–93 and 3.2 per cent for 1994–97.

For sector-based studies, while Kwong (2000) is the first study on Hong Kong's service sector (and he concludes that except for a few isolated service industries, all others experienced no TFP growth over 1984–96), to date, Kwong et al. (2000) and Mahadevan (2002) are the only studies on Hong Kong's manufacturing sector. The latter study used the stochastic production frontier approach to analyse TFP growth of 17 manufacturing industries over 1991–96 and the findings were that TFP growth was positive and increasing at an average of 4.8 per cent per annum. Kwong et al. (2000), on the other hand, calculated the Translog-Divisia index of the non-frontier approach using the gross output measure for 29, three-digit manufacturing industries over 1984–93. They found that TFP growth was mostly negative and declined over time and this arose from an increase in the use of capital goods and a rapid rise in material inputs use, the latter being the result of the massive inflow of half-finished goods from the relocation of Hong Kong manufacturing operations in China.

In this exercise, an attempt is made to estimate the Translog-Divisa index and the Cobb-Douglas production function using value added, capital and workers employed in the manufacturing sector from 1983 to 1999. Besides comparing the results from these two non-frontier methods, the issues of interest are as follows. First, what is the contribution of each of the inputs to manufacturing output growth? Second, is output growth in the manufacturing sector input-driven or TFP growth-driven? Third, what are the implications for future growth? The rest of the chapter is organized in the following way. The next section provides a brief overview of the Hong Kong economy and its manufacturing sector. The following section sets out the method of TFP growth estimation and explains the data sources. Then the empirical results are presented and analysed. Lastly, the conclusion summarizes the key findings.

4.3.2 Overview of the Hong Kong Economy

For more than three decades, Hong Kong has been experiencing some of the highest growth rates in the world. In 1996, its per capita income was US$24 490, which was 85.1 per cent that of the USA. Today, with a population of about 6 million, Hong Kong is the second-richest economy in Asia after Singapore. It is often said that industrialization occurred almost by accident in Hong Kong. The key factors were the mass migration of industrialists from mainland China in the 1950s, and the wave of immigrants, many of whom were illegal, who fled from the Cultural revolution in the mainland in the 1960s. The first wave brought capital and technology to Hong Kong while the second wave brought cheap labour. Cost advantages coupled with available physical and social infrastructure posed attractions to foreign manufacturers and buyers. The manufacturing sector then developed on its own without any direction from the government by taking subcontracts from overseas.

Table 4.1 shows some macroeconomic data on Hong Kong. It can be seen that Hong Kong's real GDP growth rate was much stronger before the 1990s, after which it experienced slower growth. Dosdworth and Mihaljek (1997) explain that this is caused by the slow recovery from the 1989 recession; the uncertainties about the future course of economic reform in China following the 1989 events; the consolidation of the asset market from mid-1994 to mid-1996; and the recovery from the 1997 Asian financial crisis. However, Hong Kong has clearly been a service economy since the 1970s and its services have grown at an annual rate of 17 per cent since 1983, faster than any other economy in the world (Enright et al. 1997). The manufacturing sector's value added share, on the other hand, shrunk considerably, reflecting the significant movement of Hong Kong's manufacturing operations to South China since the 1980s following China's 'open door' policy.

Table 4.1 Some macroeconomic indicators (%)

	Real GDP growth rate	Sectoral contribution to GDP	
		Manufacturing	Services
1983	6.3	21.74	69.24
1987	12.9	20.99	71.64
1990	3.4	16.88	75.49
1993	6.1	10.32	82.72
1996	5.0	6.71	85.48
1999	2.9	5.78	85.83

Source: Asian Development Bank, *Key Indicators* (various issues).

Concurrently, the services sector expanded its share and according to Wong (1996), the share of consumption services in GDP declined from 29.5 per cent to 28.7 per cent over 1983–93 while the share of intermediate or producer services in GDP rose from 27.2% to 42.8% during that time. This rapid increase in services was brought on by the expanding manufacturing operations of Hong Kong in China. The composition of Hong Kong's manufacturing sector (not considering its activities in China) is shown in Table 4.2. It can be seen that the food, beverage and tobacco industry has increased its value added share over the years, stemming from an increase in domestic demand. The textile and wearing apparel industry remains a dominant industry representing about 25 per cent of value added manufacturing output. Its decline in contribution over time is explained by the movement of firms to China due to cost pressures and the restrictions caused by the import quotas for the garments under the Multifibre Agreement. Nevertheless, Hong Kong is still the world's largest leading textiles exporter and the world's second-largest clothing exporter after the Chinese mainland. Although insignificant, industries such as the non-metallic mineral products, basic metal industries and industrial machinery have increased their contribution slightly due to increased demand from the industrializing China. Compared to Singapore, Hong Kong's manufacturing operations are not at the high end of the chain and although the electronics industry has increased its importance and is the largest merchandise export earner for Hong Kong, it is primarily producing consumer electronics for original equipment manufacture customers.

Table 4.2 Industry share in value added of the manufacturing sector

Industries	1985	1990	1995	1999
Food, beverage and tobacco	4.77	6.62	6.04	9.91
Textiles	14.94	15.23	15.06	11.06
Wearing apparel	24.20	20.52	12.05	11.01
Footwear, leather and leather products	1.82	0.86	0.29	0.09
Printing and publishing	5.40	7.42	12.34	16.34
Paper and paper products	1.40	2.33	2.24	1.28
Chemicals and chemical products	1.65	1.84	2.34	3.34
Petroleum and coal	-	0.11	0.15	0.16
Rubber and plastic products	9.54	6.56	3.02	2.04
Non-Metallic mineral products	0.82	1.02	2.42	4.24
Basic metal industries	0.57	0.71	1.25	0.98
Fabricated metal products	7.13	6.05	5.42	3.07
Industrial machinery	3.81	6.54	7.19	7.37
Electrical machinery	2.29	1.74	1.10	0.42
Electronic products	8.10	10.58	11.75	12.17
Transport equipment	2.44	2.82	4.29	4.61

Source: Various Issues of *Annual Survey of Industrial Production*, Census and Statistics Department of Hong Kong.

4.3.3 Data and Methodology

Data sources

Annual data for 1983–99 on value added, net book value of fixed capital assets, number of workers and gross fixed capital formation deflator for manufacturing were obtained from the *Annual Survey of Industrial Production*. The GDP deflator for the manufacturing sector was obtained from Ramstetter (1999). Data on average monthly salaries to workers in the manufacturing sector is obtained from the *Monthly Digest of Statistics*. As this is only available from 1994 to 1999, the data for 1983 to 1993 was linearly extrapolated by the average growth in the salaries over 1994–99.

With capital, as there was no data on gross investment related to capital expenditure on maintenance and repair, capital stock services was proxied by deflating fixed capital assets.

Models used

In spite of the intuitive appeal of the gross output measure (including intermediate consumption comprising energy and materials inputs), the value added measure was used for three reasons. First, Hong Kong's manufacturing activities were relocated to China, which were then imported by Hong Kong as semi-finished goods, it was considered more appropriate that the value added instead of gross output would be more accurate as an output measure. Second, the parametric estimation of the Cobb-Douglas production function provided an implausible negative intermediate consumption share coefficient. Third, there was no appropriate deflator for intermediate consumption and perhaps the choice of the Index of Industrial Production as a proxy deflator could have resulted in the implausible coefficient.[3] Hence, the value added measure was used. However, as the estimation of the translog production function would not leave many degrees of freedom (given the sample period) to obtain reliable estimates, the following Cobb-Douglas production function was estimated for Hong Kong's manufacturing sector:

$$Ln\ Y_t = A + \alpha Ln\ K_t + \beta Ln\ L_t \tag{4.15}$$

where Y = value added manufacturing output at 1990 prices;
K = capital stock measured in 1990 prices;
L = number of workers employed;
t = 1983 to 1999; and
α and β are the respective capital and labour shares.

In addition, the Translog-Divisia index with periodic variations in the factor shares that allow for changes in the weights associated with the inputs growth over time was also calculated. Here, the value added measure was obtained from the sum of remuneration and operating surplus. The share of labour is approximated by the ratio of total salaries paid out (by multiplying average monthly salaries by 12 and the number of workers employed in the manufacturing sector) to that of value added output. Under perfect competition and constant returns to scale (in line with the parametric estimation of the Cobb-Douglas function), the capital share is simply one minus the share of labour.

4.3.4 Empirical Results and Analysis

Table 4.3 below shows the input shares from the Translog-Divisia index calculation. The shares obtained below not only varied greatly over time but they

Table 4.3 The non-parametric estimation of input shares

	Capital share	Labour share
1984–89	0.32	0.68
1990–94	0.49	0.51
1995–99	0.59	0.41
1984–99	0.46	0.54

Note: The above shares are annual averages.

were also very different from previous studies. For example, Young (1992) estimated a labour share of 0.609 for the Hong Kong economy over 1986–91 while this study reported a share of 0.624 for the manufacturing sector alone. But one would expect the labour share for the manufacturing sector to be lower than that for the aggregate economy. For the manufacturing sector, Kwong et al. (2000), on the other hand, found the labour share to be stable around 0.2 while the capital share which was stable around 0.32 over 1984–89 declined to 0.15 in 1993. Although these results are not directly comparable with those reported above based on different output measures, it is clear that the above reported share calculations suffer from the extremely crude estimation method used.[4] Hence, it was deemed undesirable to use these highly implausible input shares to obtain the Translog Divisia TFP growth index.

For the parametric method, using the OLS estimation, equation (4.15) was obtained as:

$$\underset{}{Ln\ Y = \underset{(0.184)}{1.13^*} + \underset{(0.036)}{0.62^*}\, Ln\ K + \underset{(0.017)}{0.38^*}\, Ln\ L} \tag{4.16}$$

where standard errors are given in parentheses and * indicates significance of the estimated coefficients at the 5 per cent level of significance.

At the outset, it should be noted that the diagnostic tests showed that the above estimation did not suffer from functional misspecification or heteroscedasticity but was corrected for autocorrelation using the exact maximum likelihood method. The higher capital input share reflects the capital-intensive nature of the manufacturing activities. Using the above paramcter estimates, the sources of output growth were then calculated using equation (4.9). The results are tabulated in Table 4.4.

Table 4.4 The parametric estimation on the sources of output growth (%)

	Output growth	Capital input growth	Labour input growth	TFP growth
1984–89	3.11	1.10	-0.07	2.08
1990–94	0.71	-0.92	-0.21	1.84
1995–99	-0.03	0.35	-0.67	0.29
1984–99	1.31	0.22	-0.33	1.42

Note: The above rates are annual averages.

Output growth fell in the early 1990s reflecting the relocation of manufacturing activities to China due to low costs there. In 1989, trade flows related to such outward processing activities accounted for 55 per cent of the total value of visible trade between Hong Kong and China and this share rose to 67 per cent in 1998. On the other hand, the fall in output in the late 1990s was mainly caused by the effects of the Asian financial crisis. In general, similar to Mahadevan's (2002b) findings for the 1990s, TFP growth as seen above was positive but declined over time. This worsening effect is in line with the results of Kwong et al. (2000) except that the latter report negative TFP growth. This is hardly surprising as Kwong found that material input growth was the most significant contributor to manufacturing output growth and using the gross output measure, this is expected to lead lower TFP growth results compared to the use of value added measure here.[5] Overall, TFP growth was the driving force of manufacturing output growth and this is similar to the results for Hong Kong's aggregate economy obtained by Gapinsky and Western (1999) and Tang (2000).

Over time, labour input growth has declined consistently and this reflects the falling share of employment in the manufacturing sector from 35.7 per cent in 1985 to 8.3 per cent in 1998. Sung and Wong (2000) speculate that the shrinking manufacturing sector in Hong Kong would only reduce human capital formation and the effects of immigration from China can be expected to further reduce Hong Kong's average human capital capability. While Gapinski and Western (1999) document a consistent fall in the labour quality accounting for output growth in the economy for the decade of the 1980s,[6] this may not necessarily be the case for the 1990s as there is evidence to suggest that there is an increase in the skill level of manufacturing workers. For instance, the share of employed population with tertiary education in manufacturing rose from 20.5 per cent in 1993 to 28.9 per cent in 1998.

Capital input growth, on the other hand, has remained positive and this conforms to the findings of Kwong et al. (2000) who explain that this is due to manufacturers trying to substitute capital for labour which was in high demand due to the rapidly expanding service sector. Also, drawing from Deardorff's (1994) analysis, the significant outward FDI from Hong Kong would have prevented the marginal product of capital in Hong Kong from declining too much, and this would raise or maintain a positive rate of return such that investment in capital is sufficiently attractive. It can also be anticipated that capital input growth is likely to pick up since Hong Kong is not high on the technological ladder and thus there is room for gains from the use of better and more advanced technology in its production inputs. This is borne out by the frontier approach of Mahadevan (2002b) who provides empirical evidence of positive and increasing embodied technological progress over 1991–96. On the other hand, Kwong et al. (2000) remain sceptical about this possibility and maintain that upgrading required a radically different set of skills and knowledge which the manufacturers lacked. Thus manufacturers were unwilling to bear the risks of upgrading given the profits they enjoy from lower production costs in China, and being engaged in mainly original equipment manufacturing they only needed to transfer their old knowledge to their new location with little innovation. In addition to that, Berger and Lester (1997) point to the practices of Hong Kong's financial sector which are heavily predisposed towards short-term trade credit and working capital while long-term loans for research and development, and capital investment have been relatively scarce even for larger firms. Perhaps government intervention in the financial system could create efficiencies in the allocation of funds.

Hong Kong is also said to violate the industrial structure characteristics that are often argued to be essential for technology adoption as Hong Kong companies are not large and operate in a fairly competitive market. However, it is still possible that external competitive pressures might induce firms to seriously consider upgrading and moving into higher value added operations to stay viable in the export market. Also, while Enright et al. (1997) explains that Hong Kong's small and medium-sized enterprises respond well to changes in the global market, Berger and Lester (1997) document evidence of great flexibility in Hong Kong's production techniques from their extensive survey of firms. Thus, Hong Kong is a fine example of having avoided the bureaucracy of large firm operations and has thrived on the philosophy of 'small is beautiful'. The one-stop shopping at Hong Kong where production networks can be rapidly activated from the centres there is another attractive feature highlighted by the survey.

The sustainability of these features in the future somehow remains questionable. As the role played by multinational companies and FDI in Hong Kong manufacturing is small, the channels for new technology and automation may be slow to come. In addition, the tight labour market conditions in Hong Kong, the thriving services sector, and the attitude of shunning blue-collar work by the local people, would make it difficult to attract skilled workers into manufacturing. This would make the adoption of capital-using innovation costly.

Nevertheless, a slow pace of technology adoption may well be advantageous as it lowers adjustments costs for adapting new technology and gives workers time to absorb and better understand how to work the technology efficiently. As noted by Young (1992), Hong Kong's output growth was due to the significant learning-by-doing gains by slowly progressing up the technology ladder in its manufacturing operations, allowing workers to build upon their acquired knowledge over time. Kwong (2000), however, disagrees with this view and provides evidence that Hong Kong's output growth was not driven by technological progress but rather by an increase in the service price relative to manufacturing price.

Although small, the Hong Kong government has also had a role to play in providing a conducive environment for the manufacturing sector. Tang (2000) reports on the huge infrastructure development undertaken in the 1990s which facilitated the conduct of higher value added activities at greater efficiency. Although in the past, the Hong Kong government relied more on market forces to obtain efficiency, the Hong Kong Special Administrative Region (SAR) government has, however, taken on a more active role lately. This is partly because, unlike the colonial era where the governor was appointed by a foreign polity, and was immune to local political pressure, the Chief Executive of the Hong Kong SAR government was elected by a committee of local people and is thus pressured or obliged to do more. For instance, the government-established Industrial Support Fund and the Applied Research Fund are evidenced to have funded a significant number of projects in the last five years. In August 1998, while a Special Finance Scheme was launched to provide financial support to the small and medium-sized enterprises, a Small and Medium Enterprise Office was also set up to coordinate services and assistance for smaller businesses. Technology training, on the other hand, is more focused through the expansion of degree places and the increase in subsidy from 50 per cent to 70 per cent of the total training costs via the New Technology Training Scheme in February 1997. Sung and Wong (2000) also explain that there are influential people in China who favour a more active technology policy in Hong Kong. For example, in July 1999, China's State Council designated Shenzen as a development area and Beijing has already approved the setting up of about 50 high-tech development institutions there to cooperate jointly with Hong Kong businesses. Upgrading Hong Kong is perceived to be in the interest of other Chinese provinces such as Guangdong and such proposals can be expected to lead to increased migration of Chinese skills to Hong Kong and the impact of this in terms of human capital formation has implication for productivity growth.

4.4 CONCLUSION

Although the output growth of the manufacturing sector of Hong Kong is largely TFP growth-driven, TFP growth has, however, been found to be low and declining. But the TFP growth values obtained in this exercise need to be interpreted with the following caveats in mind. First, the use of the value added measure creates an upward bias in the TFP residual. Second, inputs have not been appropriately disaggregated to take into account changes in input quality thereby inflating the TFP values. Nevertheless, some implications can still be drawn based on the results obtained.

There seems to be pressure on Hong Kong from both internal and external forces, to progress up the technology ladder. Although this has benefits, it is important that a balance between the speed of technology adoption and the spread of diffusion of new knowledge is struck. If technology adoption is too rapid, this would slow down the technology diffusion process considerably and lower TFP growth.

In general, the non-interventionist approach of the Hong Kong government did not affect TFP growth adversely, but what can be said of the future? For a start, Hong Kong has weathered the 1997 Asian financial crisis well and can be expected to enjoy higher TFP growth in the manufacturing sector if its regional trading partners' economies stay buoyant. Of late, the government has increased its role to help the manufacturing sector but it is too early to judge the effects of this involvement. Chan (1996) documents the active role that the Hong Kong Productivity Council has taken to help extend the value added chain in manufacturing activities. But how well the manufacturing firms in Hong Kong adjust to their new political and economic environment so heavily influenced by China also has a bearing on its productivity performance.[7]

At this stage, the appropriate level of government and other institutional support needed for the viability of Hong Kong's manufacturing sector is unclear.

NOTES

1. This example could also be used with gross output (for *Y*) and intermediate inputs in addition to capital and labour as explanatory variables.
2. *Y* is observed output level and $\hat{Y}$ is the estimated output level using the OLS parameters for α and β.
3. Kwong et al. (2000) admit that their use of proxies from trade statistics to deflate material inputs was not satisfactory as the commodity categories from the trade statistics could not be matched with the industry survey.
4. No attempt was made to compute the price and quantity indices separately.
5. This is due to the upward bias in TFP growth created by the omission of intermediate goods and services when value added output measure is used.
6. First, Gapinski and Western (1999) used a simplistic measure of average years of schooling to measure labour quality. Second, by 1980, Hong Kong's average schooling years was already high by international standards, and it is difficult to expect increasing returns over time. Third, their results are not directly relevant as they are not specific to the manufacturing sector.
7. Gapinski and Western (1999) and Bumgarner and Prime (2000) discuss the future of 'One China' and its implications for the Hong Kong economy.

5 The stochastic production frontier approach: a case study of Singapore's services sector

5.1 INTRODUCTION

While the previous chapter used OLS and index number methods of the non-frontier approach which ignore the possibility of technical inefficiency in production, this chapter explicitly considers the inefficiency issue. In particular, here, both the parallel and non-parallel shifting stochastic production frontiers are parametrically estimated and since price data is not used, one can only obtain information on technical efficiency and not allocative efficiency. The next section sets out the theoretical framework underlying the models. By way of illustration, the simple Cobb-Douglas production frontier is estimated for Singapore's services sector and the empirical results on the TFP growth and the two components of TFP growth, technological progress and technical efficiency, are compared and analysed.

5.2 THEORETICAL FRAMEWORK

This section deals exclusively with panel data estimation given the nature of the case study that follows.

5.2.1 The Parallel Shifting Stochastic Production Frontier

As discussed in Chapter 3, this parametric model can be estimated by assuming various distributions for technical efficiency effects, u_{it}. While u_{it} can take the more general truncated normal distribution where $u_{it} \sim N(\mu, \sigma_u^2)$, here, we consider the case where u_i takes on the half-normal distribution where $u_{it} \sim N(0, \sigma_u^2)$. Other related assumptions are:

$$v_{it} \sim N(0, \sigma_v^2)$$

$$E(u_{it}\ u_{i't'}) = 0 \qquad \text{for all } i \neq i' \text{ and } t \neq t'$$

$$E(u_{it}\ u_{i't'}) = \sigma_u^2 \qquad \text{for } i = i' \text{ and } t = t'$$

$$E(v_{it}\ v_{i't'}) = 0 \qquad \text{for all } i \neq i' \text{ and } t \neq t'$$

$$E(v_{it} v_{i't'}) = \sigma_v^2 \qquad \text{for } i = i' \text{ and } t = t'$$

$$E(u_{it}\ v_{i't'}) = 0 \qquad \text{for all } i \text{ and } t$$

The above equations imply that the variance of the inefficiency effects is a constant but the variance between any two inefficiency effects is zero as the inefficiency effects across firms over time are assumed to be uncorrelated. The estimation is then carried out as follows:

The density function of ε_{it} (where $\varepsilon = u + v$) is given by:

$$f(\varepsilon_{it}) = \frac{1}{\sigma(2\pi)^{1/2}} \quad [1 - F(\varepsilon_{it} / \sigma_v^2)] \ \exp(-1/2)\,[(\varepsilon_{it}^2 / \sigma_u)^2 - (\varepsilon_{it}/\sigma_v^2)^2] \tag{5.1}$$

where $\sigma^2 = \sigma_u^2 + \sigma_v^2$ and $F(\cdot)$ is the cumulative distribution function of the standard normal random variable.

The density function of Y can be obtained by substituting $(Y_{it} - X_{it}\beta)$ for ε_{it} in equation (5.1). The log-likelihood function can then be written as:

$$\begin{aligned} L^*(\theta\,;Y_{it}) = {} & \frac{1}{2}(N_t T_i \ln\sigma^2 + \ln 2\pi) \\ & -\frac{1}{2}[\Sigma(Y_{it} - X_{it}\beta)'(Y_{it} - X_{it}\beta)]/(1-\gamma)\sigma^2 \\ & +\sum_{i}^{N}\sum_{t}^{T}\ln[1 - F(-Z_{it})] + \frac{1}{2}\sum_{i}^{N}\sum_{t}^{T}(Z_{it}^2) \end{aligned} \tag{5.2}$$

where $\theta = (\beta, \sigma^2, \gamma)$;

$\gamma = \sigma_u^2 / \sigma^2$; and

$z_{it} = -\gamma (Y_{it} - X_{it}\beta) / [\gamma(1-\gamma)\sigma^2]^{1/2}$

Given that u_{it} and v_{it} are independent of X_{it}, Aigner et al. (1977) showed that a system of equations can be formed by taking the partial derivatives of $L^*(\theta; Y_{it})$ with respect to θ. The estimates of β, σ^2 and γ are obtained when these partial derivatives are set to 0.

The explanatory power of the model is given by γ, which is the ratio of the variance of the inefficiency effects of the half-normal distribution to that of the variance of the residual term in the model. A zero value for γ means that all deviations from the frontier are due to noise, since the variance of inefficiency effects is zero. In other words, all the u_{it}'s are zero, implying that all firms are fully efficient and this means that the OLS estimation of the average production function instead of the stochastic frontier model should be undertaken. However, one also needs to check on the statistical significance of the γ value. The test statistic is that of the one-sided likelihood ratio test with a chi-square distribution and the critical values can be found from Table 1 in Kodde and Palm (1986). For interpretation, while a statistically significant γ means that the stochastic frontier production model would fit the data appropriately, a γ value close to one means that the stochastic frontier model has high explanatory power.

5.2.2 Econometric Packages

There are a few ready-to-use stochastic frontier estimation routines by the maximum likelihood method in the LIMDEP software, the FRONTIER program of Coelli (1996a), and TEALEC,[1] a Fortran program developed at the Australian National University. All these packages first estimate the OLS parameters and use them to evaluate the likelihood function for various values of γ. These are then used as starting values in an iterative maximization procedure to provide estimates that maximize the likelihood function. Both FRONTIER and TEALEC use the Davidson-Fletcher-Powell iterative program. Alternatively, one could use the numerical optimization routine in statistical software such as SAS or GAUSS, or try coding the methods directly using a computing language such as C or Fortran.

5.2.3 The Non-Parallel Shifting Stochastic Production Frontier

Here, we adopt Kalirajan and Shand's (1994) stochastic varying coefficients model. Assuming a Cobb-Douglas technology:

$$\ln Y_i = \beta_{1i} + \sum_{k=1}^{K} \beta_{ki} \ln X_{ki} \qquad i = 1, 2, ..., N \text{ (no. of firms)} \tag{5.3}$$

where Y_i is the output level of the ith firm; X_{ki} is the level of the kth input used by the ith firm; β_{1i} is the intercept for the ith firm; and β_{ki} is the actual response of the output to the method of application of the kth input by the ith firm. It is further assumed that the individual response coefficient of output with respect to an input fluctuates around its mean value, that is:

$$\beta_{ki} = \bar{\beta}_k + u_{ki} \quad \text{for } k = 1, 2, \ldots, K \text{ and } i = 1, 2, \ldots, N \tag{5.4}$$

where $E(\beta_{ki}) = \bar{\beta}_k$;

$E(u_{ki}) = 0$; and

$\text{Var}(u_{ki}) = \sigma_{ukk}$ for $j = k$ and 0 otherwise.

Also, the intercept term $\beta_{1i} = \bar{\beta}_1 + u_{1i}$ and equation (5.3) can be written as

$$\ln Y_i = \bar{\beta}_1 + \sum_{k=1}^{K} \bar{\beta}_k \ln X_{ki} + w_i \tag{5.5}$$

where $w_i = \sum_{k=2}^{K} u_{ki} \ln X_{ki} + u_{1i}$;

$E(w_i) = 0$ for all i;

$\text{Cov}(w_i, w_j) = 0$ for $i \neq j$; and

$\text{Var}(w_i) = \sigma_{u11} + \sum_{k=2}^{K} \sigma_{ukk} (\ln X_{ki})^2$

Following Aitken's generalized least squares method suggested by Hildreth and Houck (1968), the mean response coefficients ($\bar{\beta}$'s) and the variances (σ_{ukk}) can be estimated and the individual response coefficients (β_{ki}'s) can be obtained as described in Griffiths (1972). The highest magnitude of each response coefficient and intercept form the frontier coefficient of the potential production function. If β_k^* are the parameter estimates of the frontier production, then, β_k^* $= \max_i \{ \beta_{ki} \}$ where $k = 1, 2, ..., K$ and $i = 1, 2, ..., N$. The potential output of the individual firm can be realized when the 'best practice' techniques are used and this is given by

$$\ln Y_i^* = \beta_1^* + \sum_{k=2}^{K} \beta_k^* \ln X_{ki} \quad (5.6)$$

There are two important points about β_k^*'s. First, the 'best practice' method varies from input to input since not every firm would be applying all the inputs efficiently. Consequently, the frontier coefficients β_k^*'s need not come from any single observation. For example, β_1^* may come from the eight firm, β_2^* may come from the twelfth firm and so on. But the possibility that all the β_k^*'s may be selected from a single observation cannot be completely ruled out.

The validity of the application of the random coefficient specification to the data can be examined by following the method of Breusch and Pagan (1979). They have noted that the random coefficient specification as described above fits the class of heteroscedastic error models and have proposed a Lagrangian multiplier (LM) test which has the same asymptotic properties as the likelihood ratio test in standard situations but is computationally simpler.

5.2.4 Econometric Package

The user-friendly TERAN program developed by Kalirajan is available on request to estimate the non-neutral frontier model. It comes with a manual and is designed in much the same way as the FRONTIER. The parameters such as sample size and number of time periods as well as the number of regressors can be easily changed in the source code and a FORTRAN compiler can then be used to compile and produce an executable program.

5.2.5 Decomposition of Output Growth and TFP Growth

Using the frontier coefficients from the models, output growth can be decomposed into not just input growth and TFP growth but TFP growth can be further decomposed into technological progress and gains in technical efficiency using the framework in Figure 5.1.

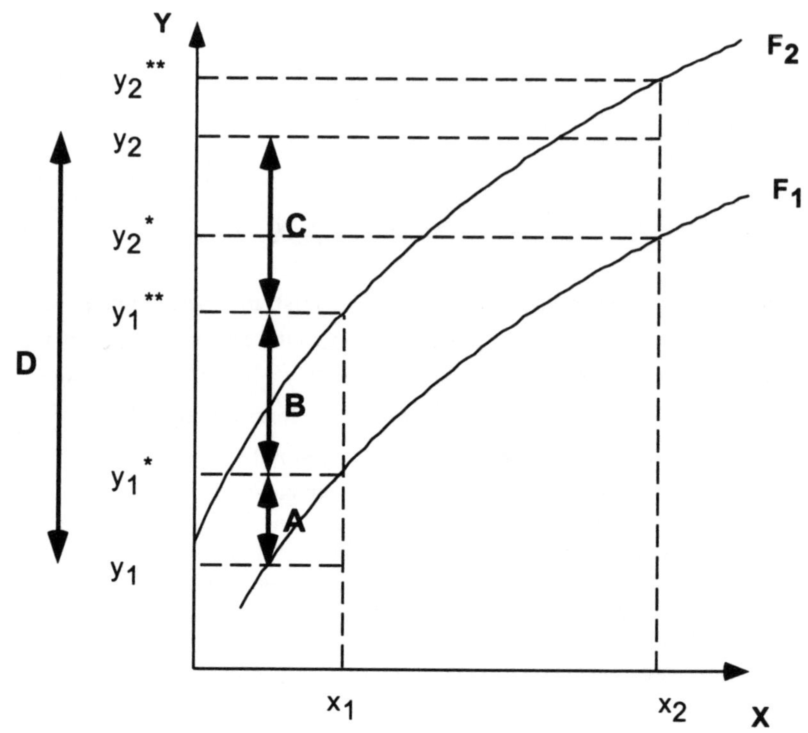

Source: Mahadevan and Kalirajan (1999).

Figure 5.1 A frontier approach to the decompositional framework

Assume that the industry faces production frontiers F_1 and F_2 in period 1 and period 2 respectively. If the industry experiences technically efficiency (TE), output would be on the frontier, that is, the industry would be able to produce output y_1* in period 1, using x_1 input level and output y_2** in period 2, using x_2 input level. However, in periods 1 and 2, industry may be producing output y_1 and y_2 respectively, due to technical inefficiency in production. Technical inefficiency in terms of output forgone is represented by the distance between the frontier output and actual output of a given industry in the figure. The industry in period 1 is said to experience TE1 in period 1 if it is able to increase production from y_1 to y_1* and TE2 in period 2 if it is able to increase production from y_2 to

y_2**. Thus, change in technical efficiency over time is the difference between TE1 and TE2 and technological progress is measured by the distance between frontier 2 and frontier 1 given by, $y_1^{**} - y_1^{*}$, evaluated at x_1 input level. The input growth between the two periods denoted by Δy_x causes output growth of $y_2^{**} - y_1^{**}$. This output growth can be decomposed into three components, that is, input growth, technological progress and improvements in technical efficiency, the sum of the latter two constitutes total factor productivity growth. The decomposition can be mathematically expressed as follows:

$$
\begin{aligned}
D &= y_2 - y_1 \\
&= A + B + C \\
&= [y_1^* - y_1] + [y_1^{**} - y_1^*] + [y_2 - y_1^{**}] \\
&= [y_1^* - y_1] + [y_1^{**} - y_1^*] + [y_2 - y_1^{**}] + [y_2^{**} - y_2^{**}] \\
&= [y_1^* - y_1] + [y_1^{**} - y_1^*] - [y_2^{**} - y_2] + [y_2^{**} - y_1^{**}] \\
&= \{(y_1^* - y_1) - (y_2^{**} - y_2)\} + (y_1^{**} - y_1^*) + (y_2^{**} - y_1^{**}) \\
&= T\dot{E} + T\dot{P} + \dot{y}_X^* \\
&= T\dot{F}P + \dot{y}_X^*
\end{aligned}
$$

where $y_2 - y_1$ = output growth between two periods

$\dot{TE}$ = change in technical efficiency

$\dot{TP}$ = technological progress

$\dot{y}_x^*$ = change in output due to input growth

$\dot{TFP}$ = total factor productivity growth.

5.3 CASE STUDY: SINGAPORE'S SERVICES SECTOR

5.3.1 Introduction

The East Asian miraculous growth according to Krugman (1994) is a myth as it was found that output growth in the newly industrializing Southeast Asian economies was input-driven and TFP growth was insignificant. Although much investigation has been done on the aggregate economy and the manufacturing sector of these economies, there is a dearth of such studies on the services sector.[2] Thus, this chapter focuses on the services sector and Singapore is an appropriate case study as services have been identified as an important engine of growth for this high-performing Asian economy after the 1984/85 recession. Unlike many economies, the agricultural sector is virtually non-existent in Singapore, and thus the services sector has thrived alongside that of the manufacturing sector since the early 1970s.

The following are the issues of interest. How true or relevant is Krugman's claim of the mythical growth for Singapore's services? To answer this question, first, the sources of services' output growth and TFP growth are empirically investigated. Is output growth of services input-driven as was found for Singapore's aggregate economy and manufacturing sector? If so, does that necessarily mean that Krugman is right?

To date, only two studies, Rao and Lee (1995) and Tan and Virabhak (1998), have attempted to estimate the TFP growth in Singapore's services sector. Both these studies found that output growth was input-driven using the non-frontier approach to estimate TFP growth without acknowledging the fact that TFP growth is made up of two components, technological progress (TP) and changes in technical efficiency (TE). Hence, the frontier approach is used in this case study to analyse Singapore's services sector productivity growth performance using 17 service industries over 1974–94. In addition, two models, the parallel and non-parallel shifting production frontier models are parametrically estimated for robustness and their results are compared and analysed.

5.3.2 Model Specification

The following Cobb-Douglas functional form with industry and time-specific dummies was used for the estimation of the parallel-shifting stochastic frontier model:

$$\text{Ln } Y_{it} = \phi + \beta \text{ Ln } L_{it} + \alpha \text{ Ln } K_{it} + \sum_{t=1}^{19} \delta_t + \sum_{j=1}^{s} \lambda_j - u_{it} + v_{it} \tag{5.7}$$

where i = 1, 2, ...,17 (no. of industries);
t = 1,2, ..., 20 (no. of years);
j = 1, 2, 3 (no. of dummies representing single digit service industry codes);
Y = value added output measured in 1985 prices;
L = number of workers employed;

K = capital used measured in 1985 prices;
δ = time dummies representing time periods;
λ = grouped service industry dummies;
u_{it} = the combined effects of non-price and organizational factors that constrain firms from achieving their maximum possible output from the given set of inputs and technology at time t and $u_{it} \sim N(0, \sigma_u^2)$; and
v_{it} = statistical random disturbance terms.

The non-parallel shifting frontier model is slightly modified from the above model. As it estimates separate input shares for each industry, no industry-specific dummies were needed. The model is as follows:

$$ln\ Y_{it} = \beta_{1i} + \sum_{j=1}^{2} \beta_{ij}\ ln\ X_{ijt} + w_i \qquad (5.8)$$

where $i = 1, 2, ..., 17$ (no. of service industries);
$j = K$ and L (no. of inputs used);
$t = 1, 2, ..., 20$ (no. of years);
Y = value added output in 1985 constant prices;
X_K = capital expenditure measured in 1985 prices;
X_L = number of workers employed;
β_{1i} = intercept term of the ith industry; and
β_{ij} = actual response of output to the method of application of the jth input used by the ith industry.

5.3.3 Data Sources

The value added output,[3] capital expenditure and net value of fixed assets in each service industry can be obtained from the *Report on Survey of Services* for various years, *The Service Sector 1990–93*, *Census of Services 1994*, as well as separate *Economics Survey Series* published on Wholesale and Retail, Transport and Communication, Financial and Business Services. Appendix 5.2 provides the list of industries in the services sector.

Data on workers employed were obtained from the *Singapore Yearbook of Labour Statistics* and the *Report on the Labour Force Survey of Singapore*, various issues. The GDP deflators for services and the gross domestic fixed capital formation price deflators for the various categories of capital assets as well as the property price indices are obtained from the *Singapore Yearbook of Statistics*.

5.3.4 Construction of Variables

Capital assets were considered separately according to the following categories: (1) land and building, (2) transport equipment, (3) machinery and equipment. Jorgenson's (1990) depreciation rates were first used to depreciate capital and then the figures were deflated appropriately by various price indices. For various types of land and building, appropriate property price indices were used.[4] The capital stock series was then calculated using the following perpetual inventory method with the net value of fixed assets for 1974 as the initial capital stock.

$$K_{it} = (1\text{-}d_i)\, K_{i,\,t\text{-}1} + I_{t\text{-}1} \qquad (5.10)$$

where K_{it} = capital stock of asset category i at time t;
d_i = depreciation rate by asset category i; and
I_{t-1} = gross investment at time t-1.

Labour was measured by the number of workers employed in each sector and adjusted according to average weekly hours worked using 1974 as a base index and the following three occupational groups: (1) professional, administration, management and related workers, (2) production, transport and other related workers, (3) clerical, sales, service and related workers. Appendix 5.5 provides details on this.

5.3.5 Empirical Results

The parallel shifting frontier (model 1) was estimated using TEALEC and the results are reported in Table 5.1. The value of γ is significant at the 1 per cent level given by the one-sided likelihood ratio test statistic of 76, which tests the null hypothesis that $\gamma = 0$. The result suggests that the residuals are dominated by u_{it} and hence, the frontier production function is significantly different from the traditional Cobb-Douglas function which does not involve non-negative industry effects, u_{it}. The input shares of 0.3 for capital and 0.69 for labour are statistically significant and the significance of the time and industry dummies show the importance of including them to obtain accurate estimates.

Table 5.1 Estimates from model 1

Variable	Model estimates
ϕ	5.48 * (0.529)
α	0.30 * (0.017)
β	0.69 * (0.031)
γ	0.7
Time dummies	18 of the 19 dummies were significant
Industry dummies	All 3 dummies were significant

Notes: Figures in parenthesis are the asymptotic standard errors.
*means that the coefficient is significant at the 5 per cent level of significance.

The non-parallel shifting frontier (Model 2) was estimated using TERAN and the results are reported in Table 5.2. The assumption of random coefficients was tested using the Breusch-Pagan LM test. The test statistic produced a chi-square value of 6.39 with 2 degrees of freedom, which is significant at the 5 per cent level. This lends support to the varying coefficient model where the response coefficients were allowed to vary across industries. The maximum values of the actual response coefficient for each input form the frontier coefficients. As expected, there is some difference in the magnitudes of the estimates obtained from the two models. One observation is that the capital (labour) share frontier estimates of model 2 are generally higher (lower) than model 1. However, there is no discernible pattern in the variation of the input share estimates of model 2 over time. Using these estimates, first the sources of output growth and TFP growth for each industry were obtained for the two models following the decomposition framework explained in Figure 5.1.

Then the decomposition results for the services sector as a whole are tabulated by a weighted average approach using the share of each service industry's value added to the total value added of all the industries in the services sector. Previous studies' results are also reported for comparison in Table 5.3. It can be seen that technological progress was consistently decreasing for almost all service industries over time because services are especially prone to limits in technology use and often the provision of services requires a personal touch.

At the disaggregated level (see Tables 5.4 and 5.5), technological progress is the dominant source of TFP growth for 47 per cent of the 17 service industries

Table 5.2 Estimates from model 2

Year	Variable	Frontier coefficients
1978	β_1	2.23
	β_K	0.45
	β_L	0.53
1983	β_1	2.92
	β_K	0.51
	β_L	0.46
1987	β_1	2.65
	β_K	0.48
	β_L	0.53
1990	β_1	3.14
	β_K	0.39
	β_L	0.63
1994	β_1	2.82
	β_K	0.43
	β_L	0.55

during 1976-84, for 82 per cent of the industries during 1986–90, and 53 per cent of the service industries in the early 1990s.

With changes in technical efficiency, for 1976–84 and the early 1990s it is positive for four service industries, and for 1986–90, it is positive for the communications and wholesale trade industries only. Thus, at the disaggregated industry level, the deterioration in technical efficiency was very clear and this could result from poor diffusion process of new technology and little accumulation of knowledge from learning-by-doing amongst other factors.

With real estate, during 1976–84, there was increasing demand for condominiums and five-room apartments and new housing estates with shopping centres were cropping up. In the early 1990s, competition was high as the property market was intense with rising demand for private housing and even bigger apartments as well as office space. Thus, those involved in the property market and legal business had the incentive to improve and provide the best service possible to satisfy the needs of an increasingly sophisticated society. The rise in property prices over the last five years also contributed to the expansion of the financial and business services.

Table 5.3 Decomposition of output growth in the services sector

Period	Output growth	Input growth	Input growth	Total factor productivity growth				Change in technical efficiency		Technological progress	
		Model 1	Model 2	Rao and Lee (1995)	Tan and Virabhak (1998)	Model 1	Model 2	Model 1	Model 2	Model 1	Model 2
1976-84	2.70	1.93	3.71	0.6	-3.76	0.77	-1.01	-0.39	-3.28	1.16	2.27
1986-90	1.25	0.54	1.98			0.71	-0.73	-0.17	-1.86	0.88	1.13
1990-94	0.97	0.7	1.89			0.27	-0.92	-0.27	-1.86	0.54	0.94
1987-92	1.11	0.57	1.92		6.5	0.54	-0.81	-0.21	-3.16	0.75	2.35
1987-94	1.03	0.53	1.65	2.6		0.50	-0.62	-0.29	-3.49	0.79	2.87

Note: Since 1985 is a recession year, it was excluded from the above estimate.

Table 5.4 Decomposition of output growth in service industries, 1976-84 and 1986-90

	1976-84					1986-90				
Industries	Output growth	Input growth	TFP growth	Change in technical efficiency	Technological progress	Output growth	Input growth	TFP growth	Change in technical efficiency	Technological progress
61	1.373	1.475	-0.102	-0.618	0.516	1.987	0.559	1.428	0.763	0.665
62	1.028	1.689	-0.662	-1.726	1.065	1.778	0.796	0.981	-0.302	1.283
63	2.555	5.863	-3.308	-5.238	1.930	1.813	1.045	0.767	-0.973	1.740
711	1.610	2.576	-0.966	-2.565	1.599	0.844	0.801	0.043	-1.019	1.062
712	1.053	0.719	0.334	-0.979	1.313	0.926	0.249	0.677	-0.134	0.811
713	1.846	2.117	-0.271	-0.924	0.652	0.778	0.432	0.346	-0.163	0.509
714	2.928	5.888	-2.960	-3.885	0.926	1.329	1.450	-0.120	-3.057	2.937
715	3.021	3.485	-0.465	-1.149	0.684	0.889	0.562	0.327	-0.487	0.815
72	2.529	2.328	0.201	-0.679	0.879	1.015	-0.143	1.157	0.483	0.675
81	6.780	2.994	3.786	2.779	1.007	1.051	0.417	0.634	-0.392	1.026
82	2.027	1.715	0.312	-0.713	1.025	0.999	0.427	0.572	-1.124	1.697
831	8.989	5.136	3.853	1.301	2.553	0.698	0.786	-0.088	-0.661	0.573
832	4.700	3.829	0.871	0.017	0.854	0.856	0.135	0.721	-0.009	0.730
833	2.908	1.784	1.124	0.045	1.079	0.943	0.603	0.340	-0.286	0.626
834	11.488	13.172	-1.684	-3.501	1.818	2.451	4.011	-1.560	-2.526	0.966
835	3.919	2.909	1.010	-0.060	1.069	1.120	0.981	0.139	-0.805	0.944
836/9	5.158	8.06	-2.902	-4.25	1.348	1.348	0.618	0.730	-0.748	1.478

Note: See Appendix 5.1 for information on the service industry codes.

Table 5.5 Decomposition of output growth in service industries, 1990-1994

Industries	Output growth	Input growth	TFP growth	Change in technical efficiency	Technological progress
61	0.731	0.646	0.085	-0.233	0.317
62	2.017	0.771	1.246	0.631	0.615
63	0.398	0.432	-0.034	-0.852	0.818
711	0.666	1.056	-0.390	-1.189	0.799
712	0.555	0.753	-0.198	-0.702	0.504
713	0.397	0.554	-0.157	-0.566	0.409
714	1.003	1.325	-0.321	-1.930	1.609
715	1.481	2.122	-0.641	-1.228	0.587
72	0.728	0.350	0.378	0.052	0.326
81	1.423	1.018	0.405	-0.214	0.620
82	1.330	0.566	0.763	-0.232	0.995
831	1.268	0.447	0.821	0.264	0.558
832	1.528	0.844	0.684	0.234	0.450
833	0.782	0.399	0.383	-0.093	0.476
834	2.350	2.491	-0.141	-0.937	0.797
835	1.731	1.584	0.147	-0.525	0.672
836/9	2.034	2.381	-0.347	-1.130	0.783

5.4 CONCLUSION

The empirical evidence from both frontier models showed that service output growth is input-driven and TFP growth is insignificant. Thus Krugman's (1994) 'perspiration theory' based on Young's (1992) aggregate economy data also holds true for the services sector. This is not to say that the services sector or Singapore's growth is mythical and that the services sector would not be able to contribute to growth in the long run. A simple point to this is that, instead of a static view, a more dynamic view on growth potential should be undertaken. That is, being an economy which has been input-driven does not preclude the possibility that this will change as the economy (in particular, the services economy in this context) matures.

Another important consideration is that service output is extremely difficult to measure accurately and the failure to do so might have resulted in the worrying magnitudes and trends in TFP growth estimates in the empirical investigation. However, this leads us to the next question of the choice between two evils – not to attempt to measure service productivity using the service output measures, or to make the most of the existing service output measures and do some analysis. Here, the latter choice was considered the less of the two evils as having some idea on service productivity was better than having none at all.

The above finding allows for the following important implications. First, it highlights the difference in conclusion from the frontier estimation of the exercise above and that of the non-frontier estimation of the previous studies. Earlier studies methodology assumed that industries were technically efficient and hence when TFP growth was found to be insignificant, it was concluded that technological progress was also insignificant. This was shown to be inaccurate from the estimated frontier models. Although there was declining technological progress (it was positive), it was the lack of technical efficiency that caused the low and insignificant TFP growth. Thus, unlike Krugman (1994) and many others, we claim that technological progress alone may no longer be able to sustain long-term growth (especially as the services sector becomes increasingly mature) and improvements in technical efficiency hold the key to such growth.

Second, the empirical evidence clearly identified a source of potential for growth (as Krugman does) that exists in improving technical efficiency. If technical efficiency can be improved, then input growth should not be dismissed lightly as it is possible that more output can be obtained by using resources and given technology efficiently.

Lastly, the prospects for Singapore's services sector are not as grim as the empirical evidence suggests. As the relocation of manufacturing activities abroad is in line with the government's policy of building an external wing, more resources, especially labour, will be available for the expansion of the services sector. This is crucial given the labour shortage situation in Singapore. Hence, some growth in service output in the future can be expected from input growth. This can, however, be constrained by the limits of substitution of capital and labour use between the manufacturing and services sectors but the possibility of retraining labour in particular could lead to TFP growth via improvements in technical efficiency in the services sector.

Strong international demand in the absence of negative shocks in the region for Singapore's services clearly augurs well for the potential of growth in the services sector. Singapore's geographical location and its excellent infrastructural and communications facilities have been a great advantage for the export of services. Given that neighbouring countries like the second-tier newly-industrializing economies are wooing foreign direct investment in manufacturing activities, the demand for support services are bound to be significant and Singapore is well placed to cash in on the situation. The government's attempt to get its multinational companies to set up operational headquarters in Singapore to service and oversee its manufacturing operations in the region has also met with great success.

NOTES

1. See note 11 in Chapter 2.
2. Appendix 5.1 provides a summary of the main TFP studies done on Singapore.
3. Appendix 5.3 details how output in various service industries is measured in Singapore.
4. Appendix 5.4 shows the use of property price indices for the various service industries.
5. One can expect that an increase in the volume of real estate services resulting in sale of property is likely to result in an increase in the volume of legal services.

APPENDIX 5.1 TFP GROWTH ESTIMATES FOR SINGAPORE (%)

Source	Time period	Overall economy	Manufacturing	Services
Bloch and Tang (1999)			Less than 0.05	
Bosworth, Collins and Chen (1995)	1960–92	0.60		
Chen (1977)	1955–70 1960–70	3.62	 3.34	
Collins and Bosworth (1996)	1960–73 1973–84 1984–94	0.90 1.0 3.10		
Department of Statistics (1997)	1973–80 1980–85 1985–90 1990–96	-0.5 -0.6 3.8 1.8		
Drysdale and Huang (1997)	1960–90	0.80		
Kawai (1994)	1970–80 1980–90	0.70 1.60		
Kim and Lau (1994)	1964–90	1.90		
Leung (1997) Leung (1998)	1983–93 1983–93		2 to 3 4.6	
Mahadevan and Kalirajan (2000)	1976–84 1987–94		0.92 -0.52	
Nehru and Dhareshwar (1994)	1960–87 1960–73 1973–87	-0.80 4.70 1.50		

APPENDIX 5.1 (continued)

Source	Time Period	Overall economy	Manufacturing	Services
Owyong (2001)	1960–69	2.87		
	1970–79	0.95		
	1980–89	1.65		
	1990–96	2.87		
Rao and Lee (1995)	1966–73	1.30		
	1976–84	0.60	0.40	0.90
	1987–94	2.60	3.20	2.20
Sarel (1995)	1975–90	0.02		
Sarel (1997)	1978–96	2.23		
	1991–96	2.46		
Takenaka (1995)	1970–92	-2.40		
Tan, Lall and Tan (2000)	1980–85		-0.70	
	1986–91		2.27	
Tan and Virabhak (1998)	1976-92			-0.40
	1976-84			-3.78
	1987-92			-6.00
Tsao (1982)	1966–72	0.60	0.06	
	1972–80	-0.90	2.16	
Tsao (1985)	1970–79		0.08	
Van Eklan (1995)	1961–91	1.80		
World Bank (1993)[a]	1960–90	1.19		
		-3.01		
Wong and Gan (1994)	1981–85		-0.80	
	1986–90		4.01	
Young (1992)	1966–85	-0.50		
Young (1994)	1970–85	0.10		
Young (1995)	1966–90	0.20		
	1970–90		-1.00	

Note: [a] The lower value was obtained using a sample of high-income and low-income countries while the higher value was obtained using a sample of high-income countries only.

APPENDIX 5.2 LIST OF INDUSTRIES IN THE SERVICES SECTOR

Industry codes	Service industry
61	Wholesale trade
62	Retail trade
63	Hotels and catering
711	Land transport
712	Water transport
713	Air transport
714	Services allied to transport
715	Storage and warehousing
72	Communications
81	Finance services
82	Insurance services
831	Real estate
832	Legal services
833	Accounting, auditing and book-keeping services
834	Information technology services
835	Engineering, architectural and technical services
836/839	Other business services

APPENDIX 5.3 MEASURING SERVICE OUTPUT IN SINGAPORE[1]

Service output is measured using the 'single deflation' method which involves deflating current estimates of value added or net output by appropriate price indices. The underlying assumption in this method is that prices of output and inputs change by the same proportion and in the same direction. This is not true in many cases and hence actual physical quantities of output or relevant indicators of real output are used whenever they are available.

Output of the components of commerce are valued in different ways. For entrepot trade, the value added at current prices is obtained by taking the difference between the estimated gross margin on re-exports less intermediate costs such as transport and rental costs. The gross margin on re-exports is the difference between the value of re-exports at f.o.b. (free on board) and the corresponding imports at c.i.f. (cost, insurance and freight). Then the current-price series is deflated by the relevant subgroup indices of the import price index. For domestic trade, it is similar but the gross mark-ups on retained imports and production are used. Deflation is then undertaken using appropriate price indices. For hotels and restaurants, value added is operating surplus, deflated using suitable subgroup indices of the CPI (consumer price index) and hotel-room days occupied.

For transport and communications, volume indicators like seaborne cargo handled, passenger-kilometres and tonnage-kilometres of airborne cargo, volume of postal articles handled, number of international telex and telephone calls transmitted, number of bus tickets sold, number of registered taxis and number of boats licensed are used to estimate the value added at constant prices.

For financial services, value added is the sum of actual and imputed bank service charges (the latter is an estimate of net interest income which is the excess of interest income received from loans and advances over interest paid) less purchases of goods and services for intermediate consumption and the overall GDP deflator is used for converting current prices to constant prices.

For insurance companies, value added is the excess of premium income over claims paid and less any intermediate expenses for general insurance and for life insurance, net additions to actuarial reserves are also included. Where appropriate, volume indicators or premium rates are used for deflation.

For business services, value added is obtained from detailed income and expenditure accounts and constant price estimates are obtained by the extrapolation method using employment data.

For real estate activities, value added is the value of properties transacted and deflated by an index of property prices. For real estate developers, value added is estimated on the volume of work done on residential buildings. With ownership of dwellings, value added is obtained from actual rentals and imputed owner-occupied dwellings, less the estimated cost of maintenance and repairs.

NOTE

1. This section draws heavily on *Singapore National Accounts 1987*.

APPENDIX 5.4 USE OF PROPERTY PRICE INDEX TO DEFLATE LAND AND BUILDINGS

The following are various types of land and building: i) offices, ii) shops, iii) industrial.

The list below shows how the various service industries were classified and where some services do not fit exclusively into any particular category, a simple average was applied.

Industrial	715
Offices/industrial	711 to 714
Offices	81 to 836
Shops	61, 62
Offices/shops	63, 72

APPENDIX 5.5 ASSIGNING WEIGHTS TO OCCUPATIONAL GROUPS TO CALCULATE THE HOURS WORKED BY OCCUPATIONAL GROUPS

Select the occupational group which has the largest number employed within the chosen industry. Assign weights to the other occupational groups according to the formula below. If category (iii) has the highest number, then:

Weight for (i) = Number employed in (i)/ Number employed in (iii)
Weight for (ii) = Number employed in (ii)/ Number employed in (iii)

The weights obtained using 1987 values are assumed to remain the same for all the years from 1988 to 94. Thus for any given year, number of weekly hours worked by those in (iii) can be found from the equation below:

Number of weekly hours for industry (overall weekly hours is available)
= [share (iii) + weight for (i) * share (i) + weight for (ii) * share(ii)] * Number of weekly hours by those in (iii)

where share (j) = ratio of number employed in the *j* th occupation to total employment for the service sector in the given year.
* represents the multiplication operator.

Using the above information, weekly hours for those in (i) and (ii) can then be calculated using appropriate weights and shares.

6 The data envelopment analysis (DEA) approach: a case study of Korea's banking sector

6.1 INTRODUCTION

In this chapter, only the Malmquist DEA technique of the non-parametric frontier approach is chosen for discussion and application since there is a lot more to DEA and many books have already covered much of the material.[1] Hence, there is little to gain from replication without depth and at the outset it must be stressed that the chief purpose of this chapter is at the very least to recommend DEA as the best approach to study bank performance and to provide some insight to DEA application that would be particularly appreciated by the uninitiated.

The DEA technique is widely used to develop productivity and efficiency measures for the service industries such as public sector services, hospitals, schools, insurance firms, and transport services such as port services and airlines and so on. This is partly because services often produce multiple outputs that can then be assigned appropriate optimal weights by DEA to provide single performance measures for the firm or industry. But if there is a concern that variables would be under-represented or over-represented in weights assigned by DEA, then weight restrictions on inputs and outputs can be imposed based on prior information to better reflect the situation under study.[2]

The next section sets out the theoretical framework underlying the Malmquist model and the decomposition of the Malmquist TFP growth index to technical change, technical efficiency change and scale efficiency change. Various issues such as sensitivity analysis, available software programs and advantages and disadvantages underlying DEA are also discussed. The rest of the chapter is devoted to investigating the effectiveness of Korean financial deregulation efforts since the 1980s prior to 1997.

6.2 THEORETICAL FRAMEWORK OF THE MALMQUIST PRODUCTIVITY INDEX

DEA is a non-parametric technique that converts multiple input and output measures into a single comprehensive measure of productivity. This is done by linear programming which constructs the frontier technology from data and calculates the distance to that frontier for individual observations (firms) or what are known as decision-making units (DMUs). The frontier technology is formed as linear combinations of observed extremal activities, yielding a frontier consisting of facets, and the performance of each DMU is evaluated by comparing against a composite DMU that is constructed by floating a piecewise flexible linear surface on the observations. Thus only part of the entire frontier is relevant in when evaluating a DMU's performance and this relevant portion is called a facet. In Figure 6.1, only the facet from F_1 to F_3 is considered for evaluating firm F_2. Similarly, only the facet from F_3 to F_5 is used to evaluate the firm F_4.

It should be noted that DMUs identified as efficient are only efficient in relation to other DMUs in the same sample. It is conceivable for a DMU outside the sample to attain a higher efficiency score than the best practice DMU in the sample. Thus DEA labels a DMU as efficient or inefficient compared to its reference set which consists of efficient DMUs most similar to that DMU in their levels of inputs and outputs. Reference contributions or peer weights would enable the identification of the efficient DMU that has contributed the most to determining the efficiency score of the inefficient DMU. The DMU that appears the most number of times in reference sets is the global leader.

To define the Malmquist output-based productivity index,[3] we assume that for each time period t = 1, 2, ..., T, the production technology S_t models the transformation of inputs into output in the following way:

$$S_t = \{(x_t, y_t): x_t \text{ can produce } y_t \tag{6.1}$$

That is, the technology consists of the set of all feasible input/output factors.

Following Shephard (1970) or Färe (1988), the output (hence denoted with the subscript 'o') distance function[4] is defined at t as:

$$D_o^t(x_t, y_t) = \inf\{\theta : (x_t, y_t/\theta) \in S_t\} \tag{6.2}$$

$$= \sup\{\theta : (x_t, \theta\, y_t) \in S_t\}^{-1} \tag{6.3}$$

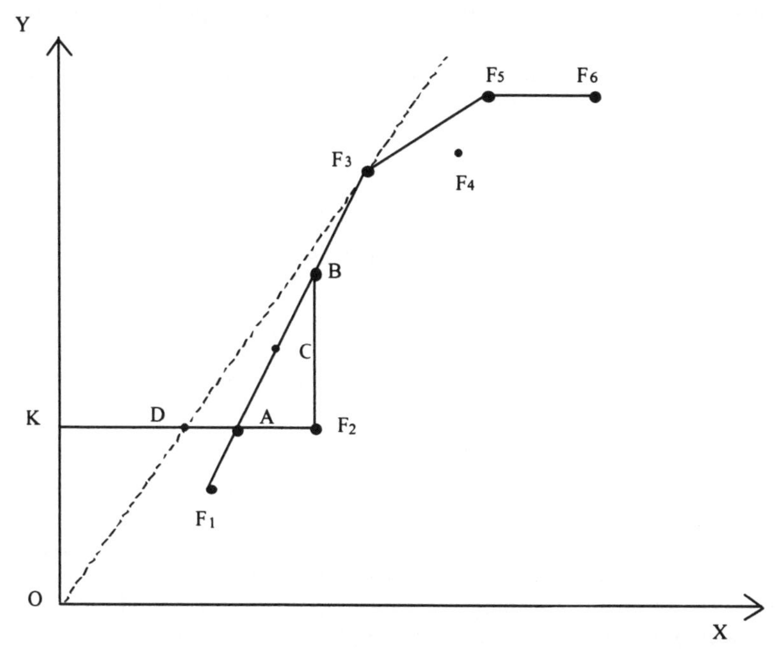

Figure 6.1 Production frontier and efficiency subset

$D_o^t(x_t, y_t)$ represents the distance from period s observation to the period t technology and (6.2) which is homogenous of degree +1 in outputs is defined as the reciprocal of the maximum proportional expansion of the output vector y_t given x_t. The expression (6.3) with the inverse sign is the input distance function (which characterizes the production technology by looking at a minimal proportional contraction of the input vector, given an output vector) and under constant returns to scale, the above relationship between the input and output distance functions is true. Also, distance functions are independent of the units of measurement because the technique radially contracts the inputs of inefficient DMUs (under input orientation) or expands the outputs (under output orientation) towards the efficient frontier by the same proportion.

Note that $D_o^t(x_t, y_t) \leq 1$ if and only if $(x_t, y_t) \in S_t$ and $D_o^t(x_t, y_t) = 1$ if and only if (x_t, y_t) is on the frontier technology. That is, when production is technically efficient and this follows from Farrell's (1957) output-oriented technical efficiency measure whose reciprocal is equivalent to the Malmquist output-oriented index.

Similarly, we define the output distance function to relate an input-output vector's (x_{t+1}, y_{t+1}) distance at time period $t+1$ to the frontier technology (S) at time period $t+1$:

$$D_o^{t+1}(x_{t+1}, y_{t+1}) = \inf \{\theta : (x_{t+1}, y_{t+1}/\theta) \in S_{t+1}\} \tag{6.4}$$

We also have mixed-period distance functions defined as:

$$D_o^{t}(x_{t+1}, y_{t+1}) = \inf \{\theta : (x_{t+1}, y_{t+1}/\theta) \in S_{t}\} \tag{6.5}$$

$$D_o^{t+1}(x_{t}, y_{t}) = \inf \{\theta : (x_{t}, y_{t}/\theta) \in S_{t+1}\} \tag{6.6}$$

For instance, the distance function $D_o^t(x_{t+1}, y_{t+1})$ measures the maximum proportional change in outputs required to make (x_{t+1}, y_{t+1}) feasible in relation to the technology at the previous period t. In both the mixed-period cases, the value of the distance function may exceed unity and this can occur if the observation being evaluated is not feasible in the other period. This is most likely in (6.5) as we would expect technical progress to have occurred from period t to $t+1$ but it could also occur in (6.6) if technical regress has taken place but this is less likely. Using the above four distance functions, Färe et al. (1994) defines the Malmquist output-based productivity index as a geometric mean of two of the indices as:

$$m_0(x_{t+1}, y_{t+1}, x_t, y_t) = \left[\frac{D_o^t(x_{t+1}, y_{t+1})}{D_o^t(x_t, y_t)} \times \frac{D_o^{t+1}(x_{t+1}, y_{t+1})}{D_o^{t+1}(x_t, y_t)} \right]^{1/2} \tag{6.7}$$

An equivalent way of writing this productivity index is

$$m_0(x_{t+1}, y_{t+1}, x_t, y_t) = \frac{D_o^{t+1}(x_{t+1}, y_{t+1})}{D_o^t(x_t, y_t)} \left[\frac{D_o^t(x_{t+1}, y_{t+1})}{D_o^{t+1}(x_{t+1}, y_{t+1})} \text{ x } \frac{D_o^t(x_t, y_t)}{D_o^{t+1}(x_t, y_t)} \right]^{1/2} \tag{6.8}$$

$$\text{where technical efficiency change} = \frac{D_o^{t+1}(x_{t+1}, y_{t+1})}{D_o^t(x_t, y_t)} \tag{6.9}$$

$$\text{and technical change} = \left[\frac{D_o^t(x_{t+1}, y_{t+1})}{D_o^{t+1}(x_{t+1}, y_{t+1})} \times \frac{D_o^t(x_t, y_t)}{D_o^{t+1}(x_t, y_t)} \right]^{1/2} \tag{6.10}$$

That is,

$$\underset{}{\text{TFP growth}} = \underset{\text{(Catching up effect)}}{\text{Technical efficiency change}} \times \underset{\text{(Frontier effect)}}{\text{Technical change}} \tag{6.11}$$

A value of m_o greater than one signals positive TFP growth from period t to period t+1 while a value less than one signals a TFP growth decline. While the product of the technical efficiency change and technical change by definition equals the Malmquist index, the components themselves may move in opposite directions. For instance, a Malmquist index of 1.25 (which indicates a productivity gain) could result from a catching up effect of less than 1 (say, 0.5 which indicates a deterioration in technical efficiency performance) and a frontier effect of greater than 1 (say, 2.5).

The catching up effect measures how much closer to the frontier the DMU is by capturing the extent of diffusion of technology or knowledge of technology use while the frontier effect measures the movement of the frontier between the two periods with regards to the rate of technology adoption.

The ratio outside the square brackets in (6.8) measures the change in the output-oriented measure of Farrell technical efficiency[5] between period t (given by OF/OE) and t+1 (given by OB/OA). The remaining part of the index in (5.8) is a measure of technical change or the shift in technology between the two periods, evaluated at time period t (given by OC/OE) and at time period t+1 (given by OA/OD). The decomposition of TFP growth is illustrated in Figure 6.2 for the case of the constant returns to scale.

While there are a few ways of calculating the Malmquist index, here we follow Färe (1989) to obtain the solution to the distance function using linear programming techniques under the following assumptions.

There are k = 1, 2, …, K observations of n = 1, 2, …, N inputs $x_n^{k,t}$ in each period t = 1, 2, …, T, which are employed to produce k = 1, 2, … K observations of m = 1, 2, …, M outputs denoted $y_m^{k,t}$ in each period t = 1, 2, …, T. Also, the number of observations do not change over time, that is, $K^t = K$. Then we can describe the technology in period t as follows:

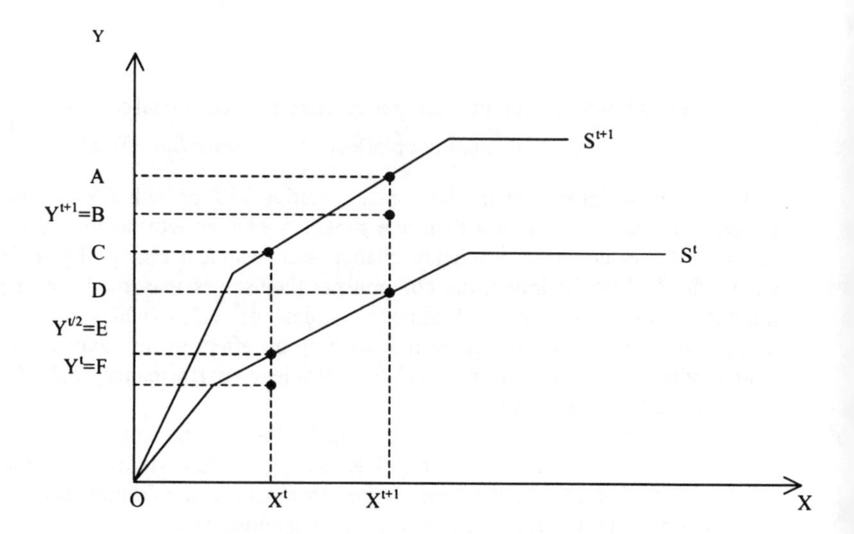

Source: Adapted from Färe et al. (1994).

Figure 6.2 The Malmquist output-based productivity index

$$S^t = (x_t, y_t): \quad \sum_{k=1}^{K} \lambda^{k,t} X_n^{k,t} \le x_n^t, \qquad n = 1,2, \ldots, N$$

$$\sum_{k=1}^{K} \lambda^{k,t} Y_n^{k,t} \le y_m^t, \qquad m = 1,2,\ldots,M$$

$$\sum_{k=1}^{K} \lambda^{k,t} \le 1; \quad \lambda^{k,t} \ge 0, \quad k = 1,2, \ldots, K \tag{6.12}$$

where $\lambda^{k,t}$ is an intensity variable which serves to form the convex combinations of observed inputs and outputs, thus forming the technology or reference set.

To obtain the Malmquist productivity index given by (6.2), we need to calculate the four distance functions, $D_o^t(x_t, y_t)$, $D_o^{t+1}(x_t, y_t)$, $D_o^t(x_{t+1}, y_{t+1})$, and $D_o^{t+1}(x_t, y_t)$ by solving the linear programs for each of them. Let us first consider the linear program to find $D_o^t(x_t, y_t)$ and to minimise notational clutter, omit the number of observations *K*, outputs *M* and inputs *N* in the following expression.

$$D_o^t(x_t, y_t) = \min_{\theta\lambda} \theta, \tag{6.13}$$

subject to (st)

$$y_{kt}/\theta \geq Y_t\lambda,$$
$$\lambda X_t \leq x_{kt}$$
$$\lambda \geq 0,$$

The above problem can be rewritten to reflect the traditional Farrell output-oriented measure as well as the standard DEA models as:

$$[D_o^t(x_t, y_t)]^{-1} = \max_{\phi\lambda} \phi, \tag{6.14}$$

st

$$-\phi y_{kt} + Y_t\lambda \geq 0,$$
$$x_{kt} - X_t\lambda \geq 0,$$
$$\lambda \geq 0,$$

The other three linear programs can be similarly derived as:

$$[D_o^{t+1}(x_{t+1}, y_{t+1})]^{-1} = \max_{\phi\lambda} \phi, \tag{6.15}$$

st

$$-\phi y_{k,t+1} + Y_{k,t+1}\lambda \geq 0,$$
$$x_{k,t+1} - X_{t+1}\lambda \geq 0,$$
$$\lambda \geq 0,$$

$$[D_o^t(x_{t+1}, y_{t+1})]^{-1} = \max_{\phi\lambda} \phi, \tag{6.16}$$

st

$$-\phi y_{kt} + Y_{t+1}\lambda \geq 0,$$
$$x_{kt} - X_{t+1}\lambda \geq 0,$$

$$\lambda \geq 0,$$

and
$$[D_o^{t+1}(x_t, y_t)]^{-1} = \max_{\phi\lambda} \phi, \quad (6.17)$$
st
$$-\phi y_{kt} + Y_{t+1}\lambda \geq 0,$$
$$x_{kt} - X_{t+1}\lambda \geq 0,$$
$$\lambda \geq 0,$$

where y_{kt} is a $MX1$ vector of output quantities for the observation k at time t;
x_{kt} is a $NX1$ vector of input quantities for the observation k at time t;
Y_t is a KXM matrix of output quantities for all K observations at time t;
X_t is a KXN matrix of input quantities for all K observations at time t;
λ is a $KX1$ vector of weights; and
ϕ is a scalar.

In the above formulation, ϕ is the efficiency score and it will take a value between 0 and 1. The linear programs must however be solved K times, once for each observation in the sample.

The above formulation can be varied for various types of technology. For non-increasing returns to scale, the condition that $\sum\lambda_k \leq 1$ is needed. Following Afriat (1972), one may allow for variable returns to scale (increasing, constant or decreasing) by having $\sum\lambda_k = 1$ as a restriction in all of the linear programs. Färe et al. (1994) illustrates the returns to scale phenomena for scalar input and output for one period t as shown in Figure 6.3.

Suppose there are three observations A, B, and C. If we have $\sum \lambda_k \leq 1$, then technology will be bounded by OAB and the horizontal extension from B. If we impose constant returns to scale by allowing non-negative values for λ, the technology will be the area on the right side of the extended ray OA. Finally, in the variable returns to scale case, the technology is bounded by $x_A^t AB$ and the horizontal extension from B. Figure 6.4 is used to illustrate the exposition on the technology boundary.

Consider the F_1F_3 facet in Figure 6.4. Firms located on this facet exhibit increasing returns to scale because a proportionate rise in their input places them inside the production frontier. A proportionate decrease in their input and output is impossible because it would move them outside the frontier. This is illustrated by a ray from the origin that passes through the F_1F_3 facet at F_2. Firms located on the F_3F_5 facet exhibit decreasing returns to scale because a proportionate

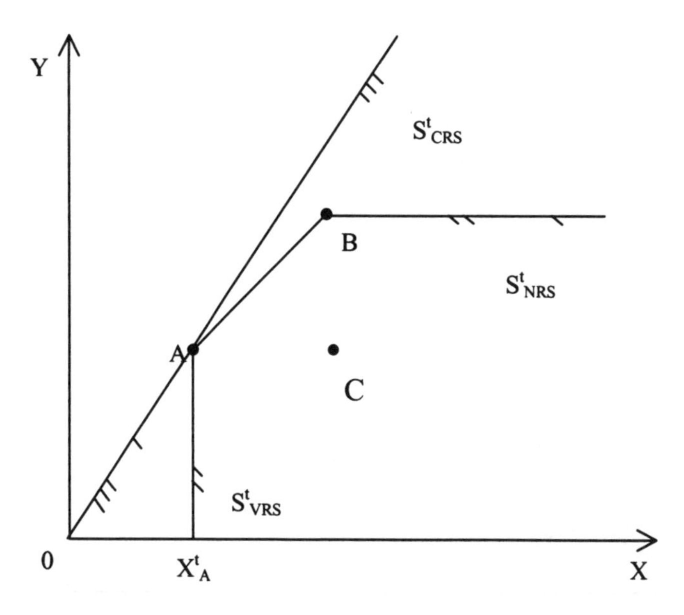

Figure 6.3 Construction of reference technology (S^t)

increase in their input and output places them inside the production frontier and a proportionate increase in their input and output is impossible as it would move them outside the frontier. Constant returns to scale occur if all proportionate increases or decreases in inputs and output move the firm long the ray from the origin and this is given by F_3 in the diagram. The variable returns to scale condition is necessary in order to obtain information on scale efficiency which is a measure of how close the observed decision making unit (DMU) is to the most productive scale size.

A DMU may be scale inefficient if it exceeds the most productive scale size (thus experiencing decreasing returns to scale), or if it is smaller than the most productive size (thus failing to take full advantage of increasing returns to scale). This efficiency component is constructed as the ratio of the distance function satisfying constant returns to scale to the distance function satisfying variable returns to scale. More specifically, it is calculated from the technical efficiency measures obtained from both the constant returns to scale (CRS) and variable returns to scale (VRS) technologies in the following way:

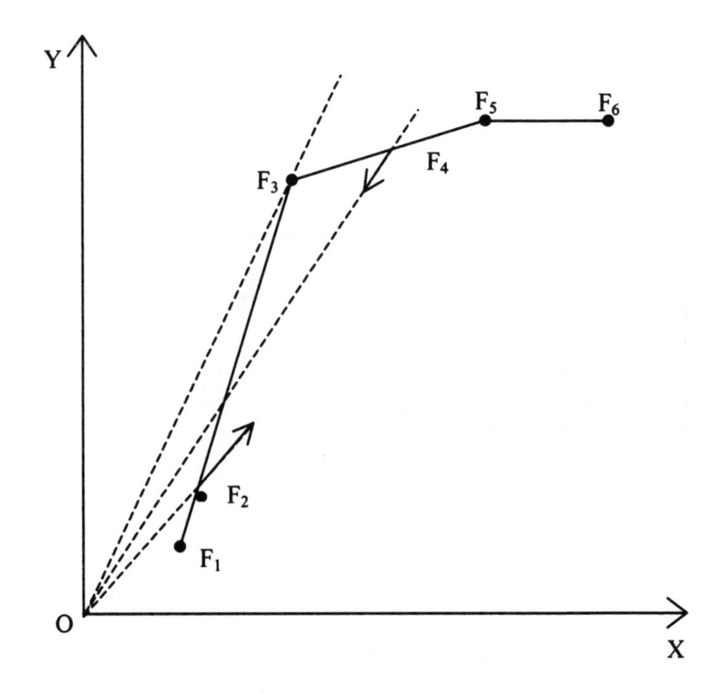

Figure 6.4 An illustration of scale efficiencies

Technical efficiency index$_{CRS}$

$$= \text{Technical efficiency index}_{VRS} \text{ X Scale efficiency index} \qquad (6.18)$$

Thus, Färe et al. (1994) decomposed the catching up effect (given by technical efficiency change under the constant returns to scale technology) into 'pure' technical efficiency change (given by technical efficiency change under the variable returns to scale technology) and scale efficiency change. That is:

$$\begin{matrix}\text{Technical efficiency} \\ \text{change index}\end{matrix} = \begin{matrix}\text{Pure technical} \\ \text{efficiency change index}\end{matrix} \text{ X } \begin{matrix}\text{Scale efficiency} \\ \text{change index}\end{matrix} \qquad (6.19)$$

To obtain the above measures, the constant returns to scale linear programming problem can be modified by adding the convexity constraint $\sum\lambda_k = 1$ and this would form a convex hull of intersecting planes which envelop the data more tightly than the constant returns to scale hull and thus provide technical efficiency scores which are greater than or equal to those obtained under the constant returns to scale model. If there is a difference in the two technical efficiency scores for a particular DMU, then this indicates that the DMU has scale inefficiency and the variable returns to scale model ought to be used as the appropriate model. Otherwise, we can work with the constant returns to scale model without being concerned about scale inefficiency confounding the measure of technical efficiency.

One shortcoming of the scale efficiency measure is that the value itself does not provide any information on the nature of the returns to scale that the DMU is experiencing. This can however be determined by running the linear programming problems by non-increasing returns to scale imposed, that is having $\Sigma\lambda_k \leq 1$. If the technical efficiency score of the variable returns to scale model and that of the non-increasing returns to scale are unequal (equal), then, increasing (decreasing) returns to scale is said to exist for the DMU. By definition, non-increasing returns to scale implies constant returns to scale or decreasing returns to scale. So, if the technical efficiency score of a DMU under variable returns to scale equals the score under the non-increasing returns to scale, then that DMU is operating under decreasing returns to scale. If the score under variable returns to scale is not equal to the score under non-increasing returns to scale, this means that the DMU is operating under increasing returns to scale.

Interestingly, Ray and Desli (1997) raised a problem of internal consistency with Färe et al.'s (1994) decomposition of expressions (6.11) and (6.18). This is because the technical change measure corresponds to shifts over time in the constant returns to scale frontier while pure efficiency change and scale efficiency changes are derived from the variable returns to scale frontiers. Ray and Desli argued that such a decomposition was misleading under the variable returns to scale technology and they proposed a decomposition using a variable returns to scale frontier instead and found remarkably different results. But Färe et al. (1997) explain that decompositions under the constant and variable returns to scale provide alternative benchmarks and they do not require the data to satisfy either the constant or the variable returns to scale technology. However, Färe et al. (1997) warn that the mixed-period distance functions may not have a finite solution under the variable returns to scale frontier and show how the resulting scale efficiency term may incorrectly identify the scale properties of the underlying technology.

It should be noted that the DEA example in this chapter assumes strong input and output disposability. That is, it is assumed that a DMU can reduce its consumption of inputs without incurring additional disposal expenses. Where this is not possible, congestion inefficiency or input slack will emerge and this occurs when a DMU is operating on the sections of the piecewise linear frontier which runs parallel to the axes. For instance, a DMU would be considered inefficient even though it is on the efficient frontier if it could reduce the amount of input and still produce the same amount of output. Likewise, there can be output slack if a DMU can increase its output without using any more inputs.[6] But Coelli and Rao (2001) explain that slacks are not important if there are lots of data as this would enable the DEA frontier to be a collection of many small facets providing a near-smooth surface with minimal slack regions.

6.3 SOME ISSUES IN DEA ESTIMATIONS

As DEA efficiency scores are determined by extreme values in the dimensional space created by the choice of inputs and outputs, it has been said that this extremal process would misclassify 'corner' points (points for which one of the inputs or outputs has a very small or large value) as being efficient because there are not an adequate number of reference points to compare with a 'corner' point to establish its inefficiency. These 'corner' points are also known as 'outliers' as they do not fit the pattern of the remaining data and are not at all typical of the rest of the data (Gunst and Mason 1980). The outliers should be deleted only if they arise from recording or measurement errors but nevertheless they should be explainable so that sources of dispersion result from conditions the researcher desires to be endogenous (Burgess and Wilson 1993). In addition, it is well known that when two or more outliers are present in a sample, one may mask the effect of another, and hence testing whether individual observations are outliers may fail to detect outliers that lie near other outliers. Consequently, Wilson (1995) not only tests whether pairs, triplets and so on of observations might be outliers but also provides significance levels which may be used to rank the observations by the likelihood that they may be outliers.

While the outlier analysis is one way of reducing unwanted effects on efficiency, sensitivity analysis in a more formal sense is crucial to non-parametric estimations such as DEA since it assumes away statistical noise. Thus it is not enough to know whether the Malmquist index estimators indicate increases or decreases in productivity, but whether the indicated changes are significant in a statistical sense or merely due to sampling noise. One way to test this is to use a bootstrap method. Simar and Wilson (1999) develop such a procedure which may be used to estimate confidence intervals for distance functions used to measure efficiency components, and they demonstrate that the key to obtaining statistically consistent estimation of these confidence intervals lies in the replication of the unobserved data-generating process.[7]

Fairly recent is the conceptual issue raised by Xue and Harker (1999). They point out that the efficiency scores generated by DEA models are dependent on each other in the statistical sense as the DEA efficiency score is a relative efficiency index and not an absolute efficiency index. Thus using (Tobit) regression analysis in a two-stage estimation with the DEA scores would yield inaccurate results. To overcome this, they propose a bootstrap procedure to obtain bootstrap replications and standard errors for these replicators by fitting a (Tobit) regression model within each bootstrap sample.

In DEA, the DMUs are benchmarked against actual performance rather than a theoretical benchmark that may not be achievable. However, since DEA provides a relative efficiency measure within the sample rather than an absolute efficiency measure, it can be expected that two different samples cannot be directly compared. The relative efficiency scores are also sensitive to the number of inputs and outputs specified in the model. Thus it may be useful to test the sensitivity of the results to changes in input–output specification. Also, unless we work with a sample size larger than the product of the number of inputs and number of outputs, the analysis loses discriminatory power. The other advantages and disadvantages have been discussed elsewhere in Chapter 2.

As with any empirical technique, there are mixed opinions about DEA. While Schmidt (1985–86) stated, 'I see no virtue whatsoever in a non-statistical approach to data ... very sceptical of non-statistical efficiency measurement exercises, certainly as they are now carried out and perhaps in any way that they could be carried out', Seiford and Thrall (1990) observed that the parametric description of the production technology would be provided by the production function only 'if it were known' and in reality, the production function is not known, thereby supporting DEA. Bauer (1990), on the other hand, is concerned that, 'the calculated frontier may be warped if the data are contaminated by statistical noise'. Stolp (1990), however, maintains that, 'DEA makes it possible for the data to speak for themselves rather than speak in the idiom of some imposed functional form'.

While Seiford and Thrall (1990) claim that the more than 400 articles appearing in the non-parametric literature since the initial study by Charnes et al. (1978) is testimony to its strength and wide applicability, one only needs to look around and notice that this is possibly because compared to the parametric frontier estimation, there seems to be greater access to DEA software packages. Although in reality, the task of obtaining DEA-type solutions is time-consuming and can be rather demanding in terms of computational and programming skills, fortunately there are several specialized software packages such as Coelli's

(1996b) DEAP, Cooper et al.'s (1999) DEA-Solver and Thanassoulis and Emrouznejad (1996) Warwick-DEA among many others such as Ideas, Byu-DEA, Pioneer, Onfront, Frontier Analyst and Efficiency Measurement System.[8] However, Charnes et al. (1994) warn that there may well be problems in the available software programs that prevent the algorithm from converging on an optimal solution as a result of implementation trade-offs in DEA software design, but hopefully there are in-built preventive measures to counteract the occurrence of such difficulties.

6.4 CASE STUDY: THE KOREAN BANKING SECTOR[9]

6.4.1 Introduction

The 1997/98 Asian financial crisis has once again rekindled the debate on the role of government intervention in economic development. As a result of the crisis, the South Korean economy has been compelled to try and 'clean up' its financial system although Korea has undertaken financial deregulation since the early 1980s. In fact, the Korean financial sector is one of the most regulated and protected sectors of the economy, given the Korean government's strong interest in directing scarce capital to strategically chosen manufacturing industries since the 1960s. The mixed evidence of financial deregulation on the productivity performance of banks has prompted this study on the TFP growth of Korean banks from 1985–96 before the 1997 crisis.

Here, an attempt is made to explain the effectiveness of the Koran financial deregulation efforts, but at the outset it must be made clear that this study does not suggest or try to determine if financial deregulation before 1997 was the cause of the 1997 crisis in Korea. Instead, it hopes to add to the existing studies on the mixed effects of financial deregulation on productivity[10] by considering the productivity performance of five nationwide and ten regional Korean banks from 1985 to 1996. This is important to assess the role and effectiveness of government intervention in the banking sector which inevitably bears implications for the ongoing bank restructuring process in Korea after the 1997 crisis.

The first deregulation phase in Korea started in the early 1980s with the General Banking Act being revised near the end of 1982 to give banks more discretion in managing their own affairs while boosting public accountability by imposing limits on the amount of bank stocks which could be held by a single shareholder. In addition, a large number of regulations governing the internal management and operations of banks were abolished, and others were simplified. The second phase of deregulation commenced after 1990 when various restrictions on the formation of new banks were lifted. By 1990, five new nationwide banks had started operations, allowing for a more competitive environment in the banking sector. Commercial banks were also allowed to borrow abroad and since 1993, the government is said to discontinue the practice of appointing top management staff in Korean banks.

To date, Gilbert and Wilson (1998) is the only study which has investigated the productive performance of Korean banks. Similar to their study, here, the intermediation approach is adopted and DEA is the empirical technique chosen for the following reasons. First, numerous studies on bank efficiency have used this method[11] and second, DEA allows the consideration of multidimensional output and inputs that characterize bank production. Third, it does not require the explicit specification of a functional form and so imposes little structure on the shape of the production frontier. Our study differs from Gilbert and Wilson's study in three ways.

First, their study consisted of unbalanced panel data from 1980 to 1994 while ours consists of a balanced panel from 1986 to 1996. The difference in the two data sets lies in our inclusion of the Seoul bank (as it is a nationwide bank in the true sense) and the omission of ten nationwide banks. The reasons for doing so are detailed in Appendix 6.1 as the careful selection of an appropriate sample is very important in DEA to ensure that the bank's performance is evaluated with other banks sharing similar characteristics. Otherwise, DEA which is not discriminative in its choice of peer sample evaluation might produce rather obscure results with its relative efficiency measures. Second, a balanced panel was adopted to allow for the productivity performance of the banks to be monitored consistently over time, thereby making a stronger case than an unbalanced panel. This is especially relevant when using DEA which relies on the relative efficiency of banks.[12] Third, there are differences in the input and output components of the intermediation approach undertaken by both studies and this is detailed in a later section. Thus, these sources of differences can be expected to lead to different conclusions of both studies, but strictly speaking, these studies are incomparable.

6.4.2 Data Sources

Although there exists no clear classification of input and output factors in the banking production process compared to manufacturing firms, the banking literature can generally be divided into the intermediation approach and the production approach. These two approaches differ in the way they treat deposits in the process; deposits are inputs in the intermediation approach but are considered as outputs in the production approach. The production approach characterizes banks as producers of services related with loan and deposit accounts. In this approach, the number of loan and deposit accounts are considered as output along with other earning assets.

Here, following Drake (2001) and Lee and Lee (2001), a modified version of the intermediation approach which recognizes that banks in recent years have increasingly been generating income from 'off-balance sheet business and fee income' is adopted. Clearly, these forms of revenue generating activities would not be captured by focusing only on the value of earning assets on the balance sheet. Hence the banks are defined as financial intermediaries that transfer deposits and borrowed funds into loans and interest-earning assets as well as other income such as service fee or commission income. More specifically:

	Our model	Gilbert and Wilson's (1998) model
Inputs	Labour Capital Borrowed funds Deposits (Interest and non-interest bearing)	Labour Capital Purchased funds (All deposits except demand deposits which are non-interest bearing)
Outputs	Loans Assets Service fee	Loans Demand deposits

where in our model:

- Deposits include time, savings and demand deposits as well as certificates of deposit and offshore deposits denominated in domestic and foreign currency.
- Borrowed funds refer to all bank borrowings in bank and trust accounts denominated in domestic and foreign currency as well as call money, private companies issues of certificates and bank drafts.
- Loans include all short- and long-term commercial, industrial and consumer loans in domestic and foreign currency.
- Assets refer to investments and interest-bearing liquid assets such as equity and real estate.

All financial variables in this study were deflated by the consumer price index with 1995 as the base year, obtained from the *Monthly Bulletin* published by the Bank of Korea. Labour was measured by the number of employees, and capital stock was given by the amount of tangible fixed assets. As reported firms' capital stock figures were already deflated but with varying base year prices, they were made comparable with a common base year of 1995 using the gross domestic fixed capital formation deflator obtained from the *National Accounts* published by the Bank of Korea.

The sample in this study covers banks whose stock is listed on the Korean Stock Exchange and they are required to report their financial status in the *Annual Report of Korean Companies* by Korea Investors Service from which the data for this empirical investigation was compiled. The data from 1986 to 1996 consists of five nationwide banks including Sang-up (SP), Seoul (SL), Che-il (CL), Cho Hung (CH) and Hanil (HL), and ten regional banks including Kwangwon (KW), Kyungki (KK), Kyungnam (KN), Kwangju (KJ), Tae Gu (TG), Pusan (PN), Jeon Buk (JB), Che Ju (CJ), Chung Buk (CB) and Chung Cheong (CC). Table 6.1 provides summary statistics of the mean levels of the banks' input and output variables over 1986 to 1996.

Table 6.1 Summary statistics

	Loans	Assets	Deposits	Fees	Labour	Capital	Borrowings
Nationwide banks							
Mean	12004	11 932	16127	163	8775	583	5128
SD	505	1827	860	9	72	21	187
Min	6064	1014	6187	51	7831	330	2147
Max	21803	56 734	31848	364	10087	1061	9536
Regional banks							
Mean	1413	1229	2180	13	1733	98	356
SD	104	127	155	1	90	7	31
Min	198	42	281	1	433	13	26
Max	5411	6004	8919	65	3727	354	1730

Notes: All financial variables and capital expenditure are in billion Korean Won (1995 prices).
SD stands for standard deviation.
Labour is given by the number of workers employed.

As expected, the nationwide banks are larger than the regional banks in their operations but the banks within these two categories varied significantly in size.

6.4.3 Methodology

Here, the Malmquist TFP index is estimated and decomposed using Coelli's (1996b) DEAP software. The chosen output-oriented model is estimated under the constant, variable, and non-increasing returns to scale technology to provide information on the frontier and catching up effect as well as on pure technical efficiency, and scale efficiency. For this sample, 42 linear programs must be solved for each bank.

6.4.4 Empirical Results

The empirical results are first presented and discussed before being analysed to throw light on the deregulation efforts. As no rigorous analysis is used in the latter process, it is best to consider the arguments put forth as suggestive rather than conclusive. In this regard, the following quotation seems appropriate:

> 'We are coming now rather into the region of guess work,' said Dr. Moritimer. 'Say, rather, into the region where we balance probabilities and choose the most likely. It is the scientific use of the imagination, but we have always some material basis on which to start our speculations.'
>
> Sherlock Holmes
> *The Hound of the Baskervilles*

The empirical evidence in Table 6.2 shows the mean efficiency indices of all the nationwide and regional Korean banks under study. It is clear from the table that nationwide banks performed better than the regional banks and all but two regional banks experienced a decline in productivity growth and one with no change in productivity growth. On average, annual TFP growth for nationwide banks was 3.8 per cent while that of regional banks was –7.2 per cent. Nevertheless, both nationwide and regional banks were driven by technical change (frontier effect) rather than technical efficiency change (catching up effect). This is not surprising as Gilbert and Wilson (1998) note that banks were changing their mix of inputs and outputs. This in turn means that they stand to gain from the use of better technology and equipment given the production of new products and combinations of inputs. On average, the estimated contribution of frontier effect to overall productivity growth was higher for regional banks

Table 6.2 Mean efficiency change indices

	TFP growth	Technical change	Technical efficiency	Pure technical efficiency	Scale efficiency	Returns to scale
Nationwide banks						
CH	1.012	1.484	0.682	0.773	0.882	increasing
SP	1.080	1.541	0.701	0.874	0.802	decreasing
CL	1.025	1.107	0.926	0.926	1.000	constant
HL	1.034	1.359	0.761	0.892	0.853	decreasing
SL	1.041	1.162	0.896	0.977	0.917	increasing
Mean	1.038	1.330	0.793	0.888	0.891	
Regional banks						
DG	1.000	1.621	0.617	0.833	0.741	decreasing
PN	0.886	1.282	0.691	0.832	0.831	decreasing
CC	0.995	1.314	0.757	0.809	0.936	increasing
KJ	0.911	1.102	0.827	0.869	0.952	decreasing
CJ	0.887	1.187	0.747	0.903	0.827	decreasing
KK	0.912	1.047	0.871	0.891	0.978	decreasing
JB	0.900	1.261	0.714	0.880	0.811	increasing
KW	0.756	0.984	0.768	0.768	1.000	constant
KN	1.008	1.151	0.876	0.898	0.976	decreasing
CB	1.020	1.611	0.633	0.798	0.793	decreasing
Mean	0.928	1.256	0.750	0.848	0.884	

(134 per cent) than for nationwide banks (129 per cent). The decomposition of the catching up effect for both types of banks shows that both scale inefficiency and pure technical inefficiency were causing the poor performance. It can be seen that eliminating these two forms of inefficiency would enable nationwide banks to reduce input use by 20.7 per cent and regional banks to cut back on input use by 25 per cent without changing their output levels. This would also release resources for use in other service-related industries.

Table 6.2 further shows that, with scale efficiency, only one nationwide bank and regional bank were found to be operating close to optimum scale given by their sufficiently close to unity indices. With nationwide banks, the Bank of Seoul and Cho Hung Bank should expand operations while Sang-up and Hanil would benefit by scaling down their operations. As more than half of the regional banks experienced decreasing returns to scale, a careful study needs to be conducted to identify the ways in which these banks' operations can be curtailed as cost reductions can be enjoyed by avoiding the overutilization of inputs.

Since the financial crisis of 1997, the Korean government has tried to establish banks big enough to enjoy economies of scale through mergers and closing of small inefficient banks. This may not be appropriate as it hinges on the presumption that Korean banks are inefficient largely because of their small size, but this is only true for the regional banks. Hence, instead of an across-the-board policy, the government could consider reallocating bank services among various banks so as to optimize their scale of output. Current efforts to have larger banks could end up introducing new inefficient large banks in Korea without the much-needed gains in pure technical efficiency.

Figures 6.5 and 6.6 show the trends over time in the mean efficiency indices of TFP growth, technical change and technical efficiency change for nationwide banks and regional banks. It can be seen that in general, the TFP growth trend for both types of banks is similar given by the decline over time. Could this trend reflect the ineffectiveness of the deregulation efforts? Gilbert and Wilson (1998), on the other hand, conclude that deregulation efforts have been successful in improving productivity growth especially among nationwide banks while results were mixed for regional banks. But it must be cautioned that their results were not annual averages but relative to the 1980 frontier.

One possible explanation for the declining productivity growth trend obtained in this exercise is the growth of non-bank financial institutions (NBFI) fuelled by the relatively relaxed conditions of operation since the 1980s. While Park (1996) explains that the NBFI created a lot of competition between banks and non-banks, Lee et al. (2000) claim that the NBFI were aggressively used by the chaebols who then became influential in the agenda of the early 1990s financial deregulation measures, thus preventing the operation of the competitive market envisioned by the advocates of financial liberalization. Hamilton (1989) draws attention to similar institutional arrangements surrounding the Korean government-business relationship that diminished deregulation efforts.

Another possible reason for the continued decline in productivity growth is that the liberalization efforts were possibly more external than internal.[13] Park (1996) reports that financial opening or external liberalization proceeded faster than domestic financial deregulation in the latter half of the 1980s because the current account ran surpluses during 1986–89 after chronic deficits in the previous years. Park (1996) and Lee et al. (2000) document Korea's significant step towards external liberalization in the 1990s. Blejer and Sagari (1988), however, warn against inappropriate implementation and sequencing of internal and external

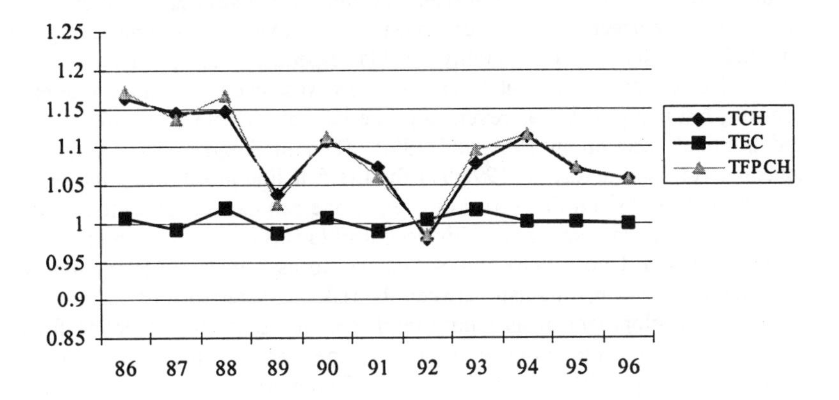

Figure 6.5 Trends of efficiency change indices for nationwide banks from model 2

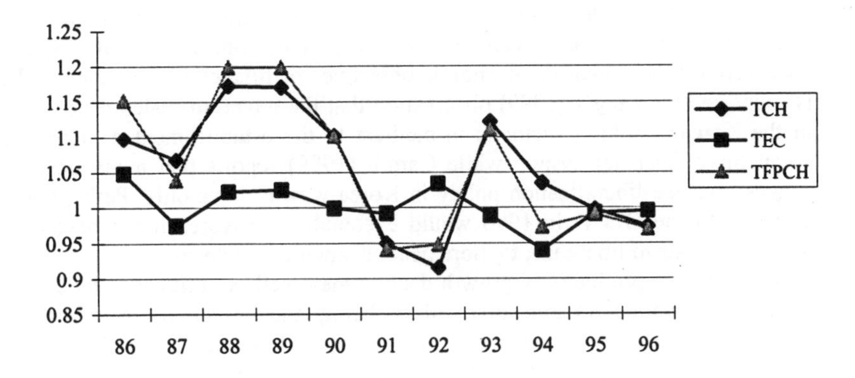

Figure 6.6 Trends of efficiency change indices for regional banks from model 2

Notes: TFPCH: TFP growth index
TCH: Technical change index
TEC: Technical efficiency change index

financial liberalization as both of these different processes may interact to render deregulation ineffective.This, then, questions the extent of internal deregulation undertaken in the Korean economy. In this respect, it must be noted that it was not until December 1988 that a serious effort was made to remove interest rate controls, but this policy was reversed in the face of adverse economic conditions and political reaction in 1989 and 1990. Then in August 1991, a four-phase schedule (to span across to 1996/97) for the full liberalization of interest rates was announced. Given this series of events, one can expect substantial delays in any positive lagged responses to this decontrol to surface. Even with interest rates fully liberalized, Cho (1986) argues that due to asymmetric information, banks are often unable to distinguish between the risk characteristics of customers, and hence the development of an equity market is necessary for complete financial liberalization. But the absence of a developed equity market in Korea was reported by Yang (1999), while Cargill (1999) remarked that the development of the money and capital market in Korea has received little attention.

Cho (1986) also goes on to state that in the absence of a well-functioning equity market, the government may feel justified in intervening in the credit market and this was the case in Korea, as An et al. (2001) notes that despite the privatization of commercial banks, the government continues to exercise its influence in the appointment and dismissal of the bank presidents.

It appears that a decrease in public sector participation was never quite the intention of the Korean government whose political objectives and desire for control ride higher than the economic objectives of financial liberalization. This is supported by Yang's (1999) observation that the government-led restructuring in the Korean banking sector is in contrast to the establishment of a free and competitive financial system while Cargill (1999) reports that many observers suggest that the liberalization policy in Korea was in name only. Perhaps being admitted to the OECD in 1996 would eventually see Korea move beyond the mere intentions to liberalize, to more genuine attempts to do so.

However, the productivity growth decline may well be influenced by external or macroeconomic factors other than being the direct result of internal deregulation efforts. For instance, the empirical evidence can be explained by the strengthening of the Japanese yen after 1985 which boosted Korea's manufactured exports. This expansion of manufacturing output is likely to have been financed by heavy bank borrowing, thereby increasing banking operations. In addition, in the late 1980s huge construction projects supporting the 1988 Seoul Olympics as well as other aspects of infrastructure in the economy were undertaken, thus stimulating bank output. As for the years of 1991 and 1992, the dip in productivity growth of the banks correlates with the exceptionally high inflation rates at that time due to wage increases demanded by the strong labour unions. One also cannot rule out bank characteristics or bank management practices (unrelated to deregulation efforts) which may have affected the efficiency performance of the banks. For example, Park (1996) notes that even though financial deregulation is expected to encourage banks to manage their assets and liabilities more carefully, evidence is to the contrary as variations in sectoral compositions of banks' portfolio followed that of macroeconomic conditions and financial policies.

6.4.5 Sensitivity Analysis

The condition that the number of observations is greater than the sum of inputs and outputs is not sufficient to guarantee efficiency discrimination among DMUs (Seiford and Thrall 1990). Thus, some form of sensitivity analysis is necessary to ensure that the results are reliable and since the software program DEAP does not provide for non-parametric testing such as bootstrapping, an alternative test for sensitivity using the window analysis was undertaken. Window analysis as explained by Charnes et al. (1994) allows for an assessment of the stability of relative efficiency scores over time by using a moving average analogue where a firm in each different period is treated as if it were a 'different' firm.

Here, we consider a window length of five years and four window runs where each bank's TFP growth index is evaluated 20 times with each observation shifting two periods as shown below:

Window 1	1986 1987 1988 1989 1990
Window 2	1988 1989 1990 1991 1992
Window 3	1990 1991 1992 1993 1994
Window 4	1992 1993 1994 1995 1996

As the DEAP software does not provide for an automatic window analysis based on a single data file, each window's data have to be entered as a separate run. For each bank, the average of the 20 TFP growth indices is presented in the Mean column and the standard deviation of the indices over these periods is shown in the Var column. The results are tabulated in Table 6.3.

The structure of Table 6.3 portrays the underlying framework of the analysis. For example, when Cho Hung Bank is evaluated for its first window efficiency, its performance data for years 1986–90 are included in the constraint sets along with similar performance data of the other banks in those years. The second row of data for each bank would then have two years of its data dropped and analysed in the same way. A bank can receive a different DEA productivity score for the same year in a different window as the reference sets for each window are

Table 6.3 Window analysis of TFP growth indices

	1986	1987	1988	1989	1990	1991	1992	1993	1994	1995	1996	Mean	Var
Nationwide banks													
CH	1.012	1.014	1.019	1.010	1.021							1.014	0.004
			1.009	1.016	1.017	1.018	1.016						
					1.009	1.012	1.011	1.017	1.016				
							1.014	1.013	1.015	1.011	1.009		
SP	1.096	1.087	1.086	1.088	1.091							1.081	0.006
			1.075	1.079	1.081	1.080	1.076						
					1.084	1.076	1.083	1.082	1.079				
							1.080	1.078	1.082	1.074	1.072		
CL	1.028	1.022	1.019	1.020	1.018							1.023	0.004
			1.026	1.028	1.019	1.017	1.019						
					1.026	1.024	1.021	1.027	1.026				
							1.020	1.026	1.024	1.025	1.026		
HL	1.037	1.032	1.035	1.032	1.031							1.032	0.003
			1.029	1.031	1.036	1.034	1.033						
					1.037	1.031	1.029	1.025	1.028				
							1.032	1.029	1.031	1.036	1.035		
SL	1.044	1.051	1.039	1.036	1.028							1.039	0.009
			1.027	1.029	1.037	1.045	1.057						
					1.049	1.031	1.029	1.036	1.042				
							1.043	1.048	1.021	1.038	1.041		

Table 6.3 (continued)

	1986	1987	1988	1989	1990	1991	1992	1993	1994	1995	1996	Mean	Var
Regional banks													
DG	1.011	1.013	0.978	1.002	1.013							0.997	0.028
			1.000	1.002	1.005	1.007	1.001						
					1.007	1.012	1.011	1.006	0.925				
							1.009	1.013	1.022	1.000	0.912		
PN	0.907	0.889	0.905	0.910	1.001							0.884	0.066
			0.886	0.913	0.859	0.905	0.801						
					0.894	0.799	0.804	0.922	1.000				
							0.867	0.910	0.921	0.868	0.718		
CC	0.998	1.008	0.972	1.011	0.879							0.967	0.046
			0.969	0.998	0.912	0.892	0.917						
					0.995	0.918	1.007	1.012	0.965				
							1.000	0.996	0.981	0.899	1.004		
KJ	0.926	0.892	0.876	0.961	0.802							0.909	0.053
			0.981	0.906	0.790	0.872	0.915						
					0.908	0.927	0.918	0.863	0.970				
							0.953	0.879	0.916	0.929	0.989		
CJ	0.908	0.917	0.873	0.802	0.891							0.8826	0.035
			0.891	0.789	0.901	0.912	0.891						
					0.887	0.903	0.901	0.874	0.865				
							0.912	0.853	0.872	0.902	0.908		
KK	0.884	0.918	0.922	0.906	0.900							0.904	0.024
			0.941	0.910	0.873	0.927	0.926						
					0.894	0.923	0.915	0.874	0.895				
							0.903	0.836	0.912	0.904	0.91		

Table 6.3 (continued)

	1986	1987	1988	1989	1990	1991	1992	1993	1994	1995	1996	Mean	Var
JB	0.872	0.907	0.518	0.695	0.857							0.929	0.211
			1.266	0.905	1.189	0.714	0.905						
					0.901	0.909	1.283	0.678	0.702				
							0.911	1.178	1.205	1.000	0.983		
KW	0.756	0.809	0.793	0.762	0.814							0.753	0.051
			0.803	0.785	0.807	0.763	0.744						
					0.794	0.782	0.759	0.692	0.685				
							0.749	0.684	0.692	0.682	0.657		
KN	0.985	1.007	1.002	0.985	0.712							0.9503	0.113
			1.105	1.006	0.909	1.010	0.793						
					1.006	0.796	1.016	0.973	0.958				
							1.025	1.098	0.901	0.712	1.007		
CB	1.009	1.017	1.105	1.011	0.976							1.0257	0.062
			0.982	0.991	1.016	1.014	1.024						
					0.985	0.994	1.017	1.025	1.171				
							1.008	1.013	1.201	0.974	0.981		

different. It can be seen that most banks showed stability in performance scores except for the regional banks of Kyungnam Bank and Jeon Buk Bank which had relatively wide-ranging indices as shown by the variances of 0.211 and 0.113 respectively. They also displayed quite erratic and inefficient behaviour over time. But in general, the results were considered satisfactory to lend credit to the analysis.

Although not undertaken here, the utility of the window analysis table can be extended in many ways. The greatest differences between the performance scores of banks in the same year but in different windows as well for the entire period can be calculated. Also, the best and worst banks in a relative sense, or the most stable and variable banks in terms of their five-year average DEA scores can be identified. However, standard t-tests for differences in the mean efficiency scores cannot be employed here since the sample of scores are neither independent nor normally distributed.[14]

6.4.6 Conclusion

In contrast to Gilbert and Wilson (1998), this case study showed that financial deregulation did not improve the productivity growth of nationwide and regional banks in Korea. The productivity growth of both types of banks was driven by frontier shifts given by technical change brought about by gains from the use of advanced technology and equipment. But such gains decreased over time, reflecting the increasing limits of the availability and use of new technology in services. It was also found that none of the Korean banks were producing at potential output and all but two were operating at the most productive scale of output. Thus, much needs to be achieved in getting banks to scale their operations appropriately to produce at the optimum scale of output as well as to acquire the knowledge to use inputs and technology efficiently in the provision of bank services.

Although the empirical evidence shows that deregulation efforts did not improve productivity growth, it seems somewhat harsh to assess the effectiveness of the deregulation measures without due consideration of the possible influences of other factors. This chapter suggests that the effect of the Korean deregulation efforts on bank efficiency depends on macroeconomic factors, government political objectives and policies, the extent and type of deregulation measures undertaken, as well as on other aspects of the financial market such as the development of an equity market. Perhaps one of the lessons of this exercise is to suggest that an alternative or a better way of assessing the effectiveness of deregulation efforts on bank performance is to match measurable outcomes with the intended objectives of liberalization of the government and banks.

However, the attempt to obtain efficiency gains via financial deregulation should not be undertaken at the expense of surveillance measures which are necessary to maintain the soundness and safety of the banking sector. This is especially important given the trends in the new world of banking whereby the consolidation of institutions, globalization of operations and development of new technologies pose big challenges to reaching an optimal mix of supervision and deregulation in the financial sector. The method and application in this case study has, however, been useful for flagging discussions related to the Korean banking scene with two caveats in mind. One is that more conclusive evidence on the factors affecting these efficiency indices has not been undertaken in this exercise.

The other caveat is that the rapid decline in prices of information technology products, the widespread application of computers and telecommunications technology in banks as well as the range of banking services such as Internet banking and brokerage services make it notoriously difficult to measure output and productivity growth in the banking sector. Stiroh (2001), on the other hand, is more hopeful as he states that it may be just a matter of time before computers fundamentally change the production process and usher in a period of faster productivity growth.

NOTES

1. See Charnes et al. (1994), Färe and Grosskopf (1996) and Thanassoulis (2001).
2. The caveat is that too many restrictions can handicap the optimization process of DEA.
3. See Grosskopf (1993) for a definition of the input-oriented Malmquist TFP index and Fried et al. (1993) for applications using the input-oriented measure.
4. Distance functions are representations of multiple-output, multiple-input technology which require data only on input and output quantities and do not need the specification of behavioural objectives such as cost minimization or profit maximization.
5. The Farrell technical efficiency measure gives an indication of the amount by which output can be increased without requiring extra inputs.
6. See Fried et al. (1993) for various applications considering slacks. Coelli's (1996b) DEAP software program has options for estimating with and without slacks in various DEA models.
7. See page 25 in Chapter 2 for a short discussion on bootstrapping procedures.
8. Information on access to all these software packages can be obtained from http://www.DEAZone.com.
9. This joint piece of work was undertaken with Professor Sangho Kim of Hongnam University.
10. Leightner and Lovell (1998) provide a brief summary of such studies.
11. These include Sherman and Gold (1985), Rangan et al. (1988), Ferrier and Lovell (1990), Fukuyama (1993), Miller and Nuoulas (1996) and Leightner and Lovell (1998), among many others.
12. It is interesting to note that although Gilbert and Wilson (1998) used an unbalanced panel, the productivity indexes reported and analysed for deregulation effects in Tables 3 to 7 in their paper are only for a balanced panel, similar to this study. Although their results are questionable as the unbalanced panel would yield different sample compositions, their use of the bootstrap procedure lends some credibility to their results.

13. Euh and Baker (1990) explain that internal liberalization refers to deregulation of interest rates and financial instrument innovations while external liberalization takes the form of opening domestic financial markets to financial flows, removal of foreign exchange controls and elimination of restrictions on entry of foreign banks.
14. For this, a bootstrap procedure should be used.

APPENDIX 6.1 THE CHOICE OF BANKS IN OUR DATA SET

The omitted banks in our data set as opposed to Gilbert and Wilson (1998) are the following ten nationwide banks: Seo Shin, KorEx, Shin Han, Han Mi, Dong Wha, Dong Nam, Dae Dong, Hana, Boram and Pyung Wha.

1. Seo Shin and KorEx are excluded in our data set because these banks are devoted to special mission or businesses narrowly specified by the Korean government. Thus, these banks are termed as 'Special Banks' in Korea. Soe Shin's banking activities are mostly restricted to trustee businesses that are off limits to other commercial banks before deregulation prior to 1997. KorEx's business are mostly confined to foreign exchange related business before deregulation. Thus, including those two banks will bias the production frontier because their activities are different from other commercial banks.

2. Han Mi and Shin Han banks were established in 1983 and 1982 respectively with consortium capitals. The former bank was a consortium between domestic conglomerates and Bank of America, and the latter between domestic capital and Japanese capital. These two banks are different from nationwide banks as they are not controlled by the government. On the other hand, our data set contains banks heavily controlled by the government which is the largest shareholder. Thus, from the start, these two banks did not operate under the same conditions as the other banks did in our data set. Furthermore, these two banks are very small in size and their business was restricted to the Seoul area until recently, compared with other nationwide banks.

3. Dong Nam, Dong Dae Dong, Dong Hwa, Hana, Boram and Pyung Hwa were all established in the early 1990s when the government's restriction on the formation of new banks was lifted in 1990. Although these banks are classified as nationwide banks, they are small in size just like the regional banks and their business is confined to the Seoul area. Thus, these second-tier nationwide banks are more like regional banks than nationwide banks. Also, as these banks were established in the deregulation period, they were not controlled by the government before and there is little merit in including them in a study such as this.

PART III

Some Extensions on Productivity Analysis

7 How technically efficient are Singapore's manufacturing industries?

7.1 INTRODUCTION

This chapter attempts to understand technical efficiency performance, that is, how well resources and given technology are being used in 28 manufacturing industries in Singapore from 1975 to 1994 using the parallel shifting production frontier model that allows for time varying technical efficiency effects. The estimates of the models are first used to calculate technical efficiency and then the investigation into the causes of technical inefficiency is analysed before appropriate policy measures are drawn. The rest of the chapter is organized as follows. The next section motivates the case study while section 7.3 provides a critique of previous studies on Singapore's technical efficiency estimates. Section 7.4 reviews the literature underlying the factors affecting technical efficiency. Section 7.5 describes the data sources and model used. Section 7.6 presents the empirical evidence and section 7.7 concludes.

7.2 MOTIVATION OF CASE STUDY

Although many studies have shown that output growth in Singapore's aggregate economy is input-driven, few studies apart from Tsao (1985), Wong and Tok (1994) and Leung (1997) have used industry-level data to find that output growth in Singapore's manufacturing sector in particular, has been input-driven. In the face of the labour shortage situation in Singapore, as well as the limits to the access of newer and more advanced technology, merely increasing the use of labour and capital inputs is clearly a suboptimal strategy. In this context, a relevant and important question is: how efficiently have the resources and given technology been used in the manufacturing industries? For instance, much of the capital in the manufacturing sector is imported, but how well is the foreign technology being adopted and used such that maximum possible output is produced? If resources and given technology are used inefficiently, this would result in firms operating within the production frontier and below their potential output level. Thus, the degree to which the industry approaches its potential, otherwise called technical efficiency, is of interest for policy formulation. Reliable estimates of technical efficiency are important from a policy perspective as they play a vital role in production economics and here, an improved version of the stochastic frontier model is estimated to overcome the drawbacks in the estimation methodology of earlier studies. Lastly, the issue of whether foreign-dominated industries are more efficient than those dominated by local firms, given the significant amount of FDI in Singapore, is also examined. This discussion adds to the debate on the benefits of FDI to the host country and the possible spillover effects to the domestic firms.

7.3 PREVIOUS STUDIES ON SINGAPORE'S TECHNICAL EFFICIENCY ESTIMATES

There are many estimation problems in the approach used by previous studies on Singapore's manufacturing industries' technical efficiency performance. The first study, Tay (1992), used the corrected ordinary least square (COLS) estimation on a Cobb-Douglas production function with data on 11 major manufacturing industries from 1987 to 1989. As the standard error of the error components of the disturbance term must be non-negative, it is unreasonable that the variance of some of the industries in Tay's (1992) study was negative and this raises doubt on the technical efficiency estimates and the attempt to investigate the determinants of technical efficiency.

The second study by Cao (1995) estimated technical efficiency using Coelli's (1995) stochastic frontier model and obtained maximum likelihood estimates with data for 30 manufacturing industries from 1981 to 1992. As discussed earlier in Chapter 3, first, this model has a rigid assumption that the variation of technical efficiency is monotone throughout time and that one rate of change applies to all industries. Second, there was inconsistency in the use of data by Cao, where the value added figures for 1991 and 1992 were those of net value added while those for the other years were census value added. The former figure is a refinement as it deducts other operating costs from the latter.

The third study, Wong and Gan (1995), used a similar stochastic frontier model of Coelli's (1995) and thus suffers from the same rigid assumption in the technical efficiency effects. However, they used a time trend in their model but this does not allow for inter-industry differences within the manufacturing sector. If technological progress differs according to industries, this time trend will bias the residual of the production function and thus bias technical efficiency in the following way. In the case of industries with greater than average technological progress in applying new technology, technical efficiency will then include the residual effect of technological progress which the time trend failed to reflect. These industries would then appear to be more efficient than they actually are because the time trend represents an average trend which is uniform to all industries. Conversely, industries with less than average technical efficiency would appear less efficient than they actually are because the time trend has captured more than it should. Lastly, the study tested both the export-orientation and majority-owned foreign ownership variables together in a regression on the determinants of technical efficiency and this is likely to have led to multicollinearity given that foreign-owned firms in Singapore are often export-oriented.

In all these studies, neither the appropriateness of the functional form nor the assumed half-normal distribution of the industry-specific stochastic error disturbance was tested. Second, the technical efficiency level which is bound between 0 and 1 was used as a regressand but this does not comply with standard normal assumptions of the error term in a multiple regression equation. Thus the dependent variable, technical efficiency, has to be transformed appropriately before use. Hence, conclusions from earlier studies must be noted with caution.

More recently, Leung (1998) used the data envelopment analysis method to study Singapore's manufacturing industries and concluded that efficiency change in these industries is consistently poor. Being non-parametric, this approach is deterministic in that no statistical tests can be carried out to validate the significance of the results obtained. This method is also known to be extremely sensitive to outliers in the sample.

7.4 LITERATURE REVIEW ON FACTORS AFFECTING TECHNICAL EFFICIENCY

Technical inefficiency arises due to one or more of the following factors affecting an industry's production performance: unequal access to information among industries, structural rigidities (for example, pattern of ownership), time lags inherent in learning technology, differential incentive systems, and organizational factors such as X-efficiency and human capital related variables such as lack of incentive for improvement or lack of skills to increase efficiency. Thus in reality, industries often produce at a level below their potential level of output which is the maximum possible output given the production environment faced by the industries.

Many empirical studies examining technical efficiency in the manufacturing industries of various countries can be categorized into two broad views. One argues that technical inefficiency is a long-run problem which depends on non-price factors affecting managerial decisions such as economies of scale, market structure, cyclical demand for output and insufficient supply of complementary inputs. Winston (1971) and Baily (1974) developed their models in line with this argument. The other view is that technical inefficiency is a short-run problem which is concerned with the determinants of profitability. Increases in profitability would lead to technical efficiency but this does not include non-price elements (such as market structure and size of firm) as explanatory variables of technical efficiency. Both Winston and McCoy's (1974) and Betancourt and Clague's (1975) models were based on this view.

Winston (1974) offers two other explanations for the underutilization of resources. One is that rational entrepreneurs may anticipate future events but unintended or stochastic factors prevent them from fully utilizing resources. The second is that intended excess capacity arises from some form of non-profit maximization behaviour such as lack of information, risk aversion or government control while unintended underutilization of resources exists due to demand fluctuations, input shortages, technological failures or managerial errors.

While Goldar and Renganathan (1989) argue that resource underutilization among firms can be analysed through the well-known structure–conduct–performance, Schydlowsky (1973, 1976) offered a number of reasons for inter-firm differences in resource utilization: factor intensities, relative factor prices, economies of scale, the elasticity of substitution between inputs, the elasticity of demand and the availability of working capital.

The recently developed endogenous growth theory, on the other hand, emphasizes the role of human capital on a firm's productive performance. First, management skills are said to strongly influence the firm's ability to produce maximum possible output by fully utilizing resources. The utilization rate increases through the implementation of activities such as maintenance, design and modification, and quality control. More skilled workers can be expected to raise technical efficiency, as was shown by the empirical evidence from Klotz et al. (1980) and Campbell (1984). They argue that higher skill levels among workers contribute effectively to acquisition and combination of productive resources, and the workers are more receptive to new approaches to production and management. Second, expenditure on R&D is said to improve human capital and thereby enable more efficient use of resources.

It has been further hypothesized that industries with higher capital intensities are likely to use resources more efficiently because they cannot afford the rental cost of unused capital and thus have the incentive to economize on the cost of capital as much as possible. Empirical studies such as Winston (1971), Lecraw (1978), Lim (1981) and Sheehan (1997) support this hypothesis, while empirical findings of Islam (1978), Morawetz (1981) and Srinivasan (1992) show otherwise. The latter findings are based on the possibility that, if the cost of capital becomes relatively cheap due to subsidized credit at low interest rates, then industries may accumulate more capital than is required and underutilize it.

FDI is another important determinant of technical efficiency. Dunning (1988) explains that FDI often stems from ownership advantages like specific knowledge on the use of resources due to R&D experience and/or exposure to international competition. However, Diokno (1974), Morawetz (1981), Pasha and Qureshi (1984) and Caves (1992) provide mixed empirical evidence of foreign ownership on the efficient use of resources in the host country.

The size of the firm as a measure of economies of scale has often been found to have an effect on technical efficiency. Sheehan (1997) explains that with economies of scale, firms will be able to take advantage of the relative savings of inputs that can be achieved from operating at or close to the minimum efficient scale. Pitt and Lee (1981) suggest that larger firms have higher efficiency due to economies of scale with respect to organization and technical knowledge, and perhaps due to firms' growth resulting from past efficiency. Their empirical results and those of Tyler (1979) and Sheehan (1997) support this hypothesis. But those of Millan (1975), Betancourt and Clague (1977) and Pasha and Qureshi (1984) provide evidence of a negative relationship between firm size and technical efficiency. They argue that small firms adopt more appropriate technology, are more flexible in responding to changes in technology, product lines and markets, and foster more competitive factor and product markets, and thus are able to use resources more efficiently.

The number of firms in each industry can also be used as a proxy to identify the type of market structure which encourages better use of resources. In the standard industrial organization paradigm, Scherer (1986) and Caves and Barton (1990) explain that a high concentration ratio (alternatively, the smaller the firm number) is expected to diminish competitive rivalry among industries with the likelihood of under utilizing the production capacity of resources. This is empirically supported by Esposito and Esposito (1974), Thoumi (1981) and Srinivasan (1992) among others.

On the other hand, Merhav (1970), Winston (1971), Goldschmid et al. (1974) and Goldar and Renganathan (1989) provide empirical evidence of a positive relationship between high concentration ratio and technical efficiency. They reason that a high concentration ratio brings about sufficient greater innovation and technological change to offset the adverse effects of high concentration, and that concentrated industries suffer less uncertainty of demand than other firms and can plan better for higher utilization of productive capacities.

Other factors that have been found to affect technical efficiency include age of the firm, advertising expenditure, trade liberalization, import substitution and export orientation. Not surprisingly, there are mixed views and empirical evidence on the nature of these effects as well.

7.5 DATA AND MODEL USED

7.5.1 Data Sources

The panel data of the manufacturing sector consists of 28, 3-digit manufacturing industries (Table 7.2 provides more details) from 1975 to 1994. Most of the data used in this study were from the annual publications of *Report on the Census of Industrial Production*. The GDP deflator for the manufacturing sector and gross domestic fixed capital formation price deflators are obtained from the *Singapore Yearbook of Statistics*. Appendix 7.1 explains how the variables were constructed for use.

7.5.2 Model Used

Here, an improved version of the stochastic frontier model is adopted to measure technical efficiency. Unlike previous studies, the rigid assumption of the models is relaxed to allow the technical efficiency of the manufacturing industries to vary unconditionally over time. Second, unlike earlier data sets, the panel data used here has ten additional years of observations and this is likely to lead to more reliable results. Third, time and industry-specific dummies were used to allow the technological progress experienced in the industries to vary across time and across industries.

The stochastic production function model is given as:

$$\text{Log } Y_{it} = \left(\sum_{j=1}^{S} \lambda_j \beta\right) \text{Log } L_{it} + \left(\sum_{j=1}^{S} \lambda_j \alpha\right) \text{Log } K_{it} + \delta_t + \sum_{j=1}^{S} \lambda_j - u_{it} + v_{it} \qquad (7.1)$$

where $i =$ 1, 2, ..., 28 (no. of industries);

t = 1, 2, ..., 20 (no. of years);
j = 1, 2, …, 8 (no. of dummies representing 2-digit manufacturing industry codes 31, 32, 33, 34, 35, 36, 37 and 38);
Y = value added output deflated using 1985 prices in Singapore dollars (S$);
L = number of workers;
K = capital used deflated using 1985 prices in S$;
δ = time dummies representing time periods;
λ = group industry dummies;
u_{it} = the combined effects of non-price and organizational factors that constrain firms from achieving their maximum possible output from the given set of inputs and technology at time t; and
v_{it} = statistical random disturbance terms.

In this specification, $(-u_{it})$ measures in logarithms how far the realized output is from the frontier output. Exponential $(-u_{it})$ which varies between 0 and 1 is a measure of the technical efficiency of the ith industry in the tth period. Also, u_{it} is assumed to follow a half-normal distribution. Unlike the estimations followed by Wong and Tok (1994) and Cao (1995), our procedure does not impose a uniform pattern of change on the technical efficiency of the industries over time through u_{it}. The estimation method is similar to the parallel shifting frontier model set out in Chapter 5 and the same Fortran program TEALEC was used to obtain the estimates of the frontier coefficients. Using the estimates of the above model, technical efficiency is then given by exponential $(-u_i)$ or the ratio of Y_i/Y^* where Y_i represents the actual observable output and Y^* represents the frontier or maximum attainable output. This ratio varies between 0 and 1. If industries achieve their maximum output, then they would be technically efficient and this means that $u_i = 0$.

7.5.3 Analytical Model to Investigate the Sources of Technical Inefficiency

Drawing on the existing theoretical and empirical literature on the determinants of technical efficiency, the following three variables (constrained by data availability) were chosen to study their effect on technical efficiency (TE) in Singapore's manufacturing industries.

First, the capital–labour ratio (K/L) measuring the capital intensity of the industry is given by the ratio of capital expenditure to the number of workers employed in the industry. Second, given that Singapore has had a long history since the early 1970s as a major recipient of FDI, the effect of foreign ownership on the use of resources and given technology is investigated. A dummy variable (*OWND*) is used for industries which have more than 45 per cent of the total number of firms in that industry wholly foreign or joint ventures which are less than half-locally owned. Third, the size of the industry measured by industry sales (*SALES*) was used to test for the significance of the scale effect on technical efficiency. In theory, industries with large sales are often capital intensive. However, the correlation coefficient between the two variables of 0.23 was considered low so that any multicollinearity effects arising from the inclusion of both these variables in the regression are minimal and would not produce spurious results.

The regression equation was then estimated in logarithms to measure changes in technical efficiency. Since technical efficiency levels are bounded between the value of 0 and 1, in order to comply with the standard normal assumptions of the error term in a multiple regression equation, the technical efficiency values were transformed to log *TE* - log (1- *TE*). Due to this transformation, the regression coefficients have no direct interpretation but it is possible to calculate the elasticity value from the estimated coefficient.[1]

7.6 EMPIRICAL RESULTS AND ANALYSIS

The model estimates are reported in Table 7.1. At the outset, the explanatory power of the frontier model given by γ was 0.78 and found to be statistically significant. This means that the ratio of industry-specific variance to that of total variance is significant, implying that realized outputs differ from potential outputs significantly and these differences are due to differences in industry-specific technical efficiencies and not due to any random chance factors. As expected of manufacturing industries, the labour coefficient is lower than the capital coefficient and it can be seen that the time and industry-specific dummies are also significant.

7.6.1 Technical Efficiency (TE) Estimates

Table 7.2 provides an overview of the technical efficiency performance of the manufacturing industries over time calculated using the estimates from Table 7.1. It was found that 50 per cent of the industries in the manufacturing sector operated at least 25 per cent below their potential output level. The lack of technical efficiency was also noted by Leung (1998) who used the non-

Table 7.1 Maximum likelihood estimates of the stochastic production frontier

Variables	Parameter	Parameter estimates
Constant	α_0	-0.8765 (0.1745)
Industry dummies (7)	α_I	5 out of 7 are significant at the 5% level
Time dummies (19)	δ_k	11 out of 19 are significant at the 5% level
Labour (industry 31)	β	0.3612 (0.1745)**
Labour slope dummy (32)	β_1	0.0204 (0.0093)**
Labour slope dummy (33)	β_2	0.0056 (0.0088)
Labour slope dummy (34)	β_3	0.0024 (0.0036)
Labour slope dummy (35)	β_4	0.0315 (0.0145)**
Labour slope dummy (36)	β_5	0.0385 (0.0172)**
Labour slope dummy (37)	β_6	-0.0018 (0.0008)**
Labour slope dummy (38)	β_7	-0.0012 (0.0005)**
Capital (industry 31)	λ	0.6353 (0.3105)**
Capital slope dummy (32)	λ_1	0.0102 (0.0045)**
Capital slope dummy (33)	λ_2	-0.0028 (0.0013)**
Capital slope dummy (34)	λ_3	-0.0032 (0.0048)
Capital slope dummy (35)	λ_4	-0.0106 (0.0043)**
Capital slope dummy (36)	λ_5	0.0042 (0.0058)
Capital slope dummy (37)	λ_6	0.0108 (0.0046)**
Capital slope dummy (38)	λ_7	0.0125 (0.0052)**
Ratio of industry-specific variation to total variation	γ	0.7820 (0.1276)*

Notes: Figures in parenthesis are asymptotic standard errors.
* means that the coefficient is significant at the 1 per cent level of significance.
** means that the coefficient is significant at the 5 per cent level of significance.

parametric Malmquist index of measuring efficiency. Table 7.2 also shows that while industries like tobacco products, leather and leather products, and paints, pharmaceutical and other chemical products have high technical efficiency levels levels of 90 per cent or more, industries like food, rubber products and jelutong processing plastic products, and pottery and glass products have very low

Table 7.2 Technical efficiency estimates of Singapore's manufacturing industries

Manufacturing industries (3-digit industry code in brackets)	Average technical efficiency	1976	1982	1988	1994
(311/2) Food	0.522	0.493	0.473	0.555	0.472
(313) Beverage	0.773	0.858	0.913	0.920	0.643
(314) Tobacco products	0.939	0.970	0.983	0.920	0.971
(321) Textiles	0.607	0.533	0.433	0.752	0.725
(322) Wearing apparel	0.852	0.842	0.850	0.971	0.668
(323) Leather and leather products	0.901	0.983	0.880	0.970	0.832
(324) Footwear	0.627	0.902	0.453	0.466	0.696
(331) Timber products (except furniture)	0.701	0.760	0.544	0.721	0.801
(332) Furniture and fixtures	0.821	0.956	0.771	0.725	0.775
(341) Paper and paper products	0.679	0.567	0.441	0.788	0.683
(342) Printing and publishing	0.836	0.926	0.731	0.800	0.896
(351) Industrial chemicals and gases	0.710	0.557	0.467	0.982	0.622
(352) Paints, pharmaceutical and other chemical products	0.975	0.973	0.971	0.984	0.984
(353/4) Petroleum products	0.907	0.975	0.973	0.856	0.720
(355/6) Rubber products and jelutong processing	0.416	0.509	0.370	0.365	0.419
(357) Plastic products	0.417	0.351	0.358	0.451	0.460
(361/2) Pottery and glass products	0.484	0.741	0.352	0.208	0.573
(363) Structural clay products	0.521	0.424	0.602	0.331	0.789
(364) Cement	0.844	0.981	0.980	0.459	0.986
(365) Concrete products	0.831	0.996	0.974	0.479	0.683

Table 7.2 (continued)

Manufacturing industries (3-digit industry code in brackets)	Average technical efficiency	1976	1982	1988	1994
(369) Non-metallic mineral products	0.775	0.862	0.970	0.603	0.814
(371) Iron and steel	0.849	0.773	0.971	0.978	0.473
(372) Non-ferrous products	0.627	0.539	0.509	0.830	0.464
(381) Fabricated metal products	0.702	0.780	0.718	0.722	0.364
(382) Industrial machinery	0.800	0.972	0.909	0.662	0.698
(383) Electrical machinery	0.666	0.585	0.604	0.702	0.667
(384) Electronic products	0.889	0.850	0.692	0.972	0.974
(385) Transport equipment	0.717	0.218	0.944	0.971	0.872

low technical efficiency levels ranging between 40 per cent and 50 per cent. Some industries which showed high levels of technical efficiency in one period did not consistently achieve those levels in other periods, such as the footwear, industrial chemicals and gases, pottery and glass products, structural clay products, cement, concrete products and transport equipment industries. Thus there were fairly wide variations in the technical efficiency estimates within the same industry and across industries over time. However, there was no distinct pattern in the behaviour of the industries' technical efficiency over time except for the petroleum industry whose technical efficiency estimates had a declining trend. The excess capacity in this industry could have resulted because of the emerging petroleum refineries in the region especially in Indonesia, as well as due to an over-investment in this capital intensive industry in the late 1980s. The electronic products industry which is a key player in the manufacturing sector registered an average technical efficiency of 89 per cent indicating the existence of 11 per cent of unrealized productive capacity.

7.6.2 Estimates from Analytical Model

$$\text{Ln } TE = -1.36^{*} - 0.26^{*}\text{Ln}\left(\frac{K}{L}\right) + 0.28^{*}\text{Ln}(SALES) - 0.26 \ OWND \quad (7.2)$$
$$(0.524) \qquad (0.056) \qquad (0.043) \qquad (0.209)$$

Standard errors are given in parenthesis and * indicates significance of the estimated coefficient at 5 per cent level of significance. The diagnostics tests (not reported here) showed no misspecification or problems with heteroscedasticity. The above equation was, however, corrected for autocorrelation. The $\bar{R}^2$ of 0.69 showed that the estimation is quite satisfactory as the factors identified (or rather for which proxies could be obtained) are able to explain 69 per cent of the variation in technical efficiency. Unfortunately, there were no consistent time-series data on other important factors such as R&D expenditure, advertising expenditure, proportion of skilled workers to unskilled workers, or any information about product differentiation, to improve the analysis on the determinants of technical efficiency.

The empirical results show that the *K*/*L* ratio is negative and significant. This can be explained by the following two reasons. First, the rapid rate of transformation in the economy from labour-intensive to capital-intensive manufacturing operations (as evidenced in Chowdhury and Islam 1993 and Young 1992) enabled the use of embodied technology to increase output significantly, leading to sufficient profits such that there was little incentive for industries to use the technology efficiently. Also, in order to qualify for various incentives from the government, many industries accumulated capital (Goh and Low 1996) which they did not have sufficient knowledge to use efficiently.

Second, labour as well as skill deepening did not commensurate with capital deepening. Shortage of labour has been a problem since the early 1980s when the government implemented the foreign worker policy restricting the number of foreign workers in Singapore. The *World Competitiveness Report* (1990) found that worker turnover was highest in Singapore compared with the other newly industrializing economies (NIEs). This is reinforced by the 1992 Singapore Manufactures Futures Survey which reports that 85 per cent of the firms which responded considered labour turnover a significant concern. The job-hopping tendency among workers is a deterrent for managers to invest in worker training which can then help improve technical efficiency. The survey also indicated that 74 per cent and 83 per cent of the firms raised the availability of unskilled labour[2] and skilled labour, respectively. The lack of skill-deepening is further supported by the National Productivity Board's (1994) evidence that despite improvements,

Singapore's present educational level is still relatively low compared with other NIEs, Japan and the US.

Thus gains from the use of high value added capital could not be realized due to a lack in the quantity and quality of the labour force and hence improvements in technical efficiency did not occur. The government's current efforts to improve the situation include Singapore's attempt to attract skilled foreign labour and relax the foreign worker policy; the call to Singaporeans abroad to return home; the removal of restrictions on skilled women's foreign spouses' work opportunities and permanent residency. The education system is also revamped with emphasis on broad education with creative thinking as a subject and there are plans for a fourth fully-fledged university. In fact, Maynes et al. (1997) found that the government expenditure on education is not a significant factor determining Singapore's GDP growth.

The foreign ownership variable, on the other hand, is found to be an insignificant factor in improving technical efficiency.[3] It must be noted that this insignificance could reflect the use of the dummy variable as a poor proxy and different results can be expected if firm-level data on foreign ownership in various manufacturing industries are made available.

However, Athukorala and Chand's (2000) study show that majority-owned US foreign manufacturing affiliates in Singapore obtained TFP growth of only 2.43 per cent over 1982–92 which was low compared to US operations in Hong Kong, Taiwan, South Korea, Belgium and Denmark. As explained earlier, due to the poor competition from local firms and the strong encouragement and various concessions from the government, multinational companies may have used overly capital-intensive production to sustain profits, thereby using inefficient factor proportions. Furthermore, Kholdy (1997) provides evidence for Singapore where FDI in manufacturing Granger-causes capital formation but does not cause labour productivity. This also lends support to the negative K/L ratio result.

Leung (1997) on the other hand, found that foreign ownership had a positive and significant influence on TFP growth. His results are, however, not surprising since foreign capital which has embodied capital would have had an overwhelmingly positive effect on technological progress even if it caused a deterioration in technical efficiency, such that the overall effect on TFP growth was positive and significant.[4] Also, in Leung's study, both the ratio of exports to total sales variable and the foreign ownership variable were used together in the regression analysis. This would have resulted in inaccurate results as the estimation is likely to have suffered from multicollinearity since almost all foreign-owned firms in Singapore are export oriented.

Along the same lines, Shimada (1996) provides evidence of more efficient use of capital and labour by foreign capital. He computes partial measures of efficiency using capital and labour used per unit of value added. However, in the above case study, technical efficiency is a total or overall measure and this is a far better measure given that capital and labour are jointly used to produce output. Importantly, Shimada's (1996) anxiety 'about the stagnant TFP growth in foreign companies since 1989' supports our case that foreign firms may not necessarily be more efficient than local firms. This is because the limits in technological progress arising from foreign capital are being reached and now, the technical inefficiency aspects of foreign firms' performance are beginning to show up, thereby affecting TFP growth.

A related point is that with foreign direct investment (FDI), there was a high level of importation of more complex technologies. Evidently, R&D becomes a crucial means of keeping pace with and absorbing these technologies. A growing R&D base enables a quicker and more efficient diffusion of technical expertise within the economy, lowers the cost of transfers, and captures more of the spillovers generated by the operation of foreign firms. Most importantly, it permits the industrial sector greater flexibility, allows it to diversify, and grants it greater autonomy by creating a 'technology culture'. In this regard, Singapore's technological base is weak and lags behind the efforts of developed countries, let alone the other NIEs. This is shown by the low share of R&D expenditure to GDP of Singapore relative to other countries (see Table 7.3).

Table 7.3 Share of R&D expenditure to GDP

	1981	1985	1990	1995
Singapore	0.26	0.54	0.84	1.35**
Taiwan	0.94	1.01	1.66	1.81
South Korea	0.67	1.48	1.95	2.61
US	2.43	2.08	2.81	2.58*
Japan	2.38	2.48	2.79	2.59

Note: * refers to 1994 value and ** refers to 1996 value.
R&D statistics in Hong Kong are hard to come by.

Source: Economic Survey of Singapore, Ministry of Trade and Industry, Singapore.
Taiwan Statistical Databook, Council for Economic Planning and Development, Taiwan.

Thus, Singapore is not in a good position to cultivate the habit of innovation as such an environment is largely missing. Athough a free-riding strategy of not investing in R&D might well be optimal (given the huge sunk costs and the delay in returns to research), the ability to absorb appropriate knowledge still depends on one's own research capability. Although Singapore has consciously and successfully raised the R&D expenditure to GDP ratio over the years, it still pales in comparison with the others and has only lately reached the target of 2 per cent set for 1995. Not only is the nation's R&D manpower ratio of 41 research scientists and engineers per 10 000 workers far below that of Japan's ratio of 81, United States' ratio of 75, Taiwan's ratio of 54 and South Korea's 47, but Singapore was estimated to require 13 000 research scientists and engineers by the year 2000 and this has yet to be realized.

Finally, the last determinant, *SALES*, is positive and significant. This indicates that resources are used more efficiently with economies of scale. However, being large and more capital intensive may not lead to improvements in technical efficiency if labour deepening in terms of quantity and quality does not take off. Thus there is a need for the formulation of policies to work hand in hand and complement one another.

7.6.3 Limitations of Study

First, as discussed in Chapter 3, there are limitations of the two-stage estimation procedure whereby technical efficiency is first estimated and then regressed on a host of factors. Second, industries may not be homogenous enough to justify such analysis for the broad sector, and if possible, each industry should be studied separately using firm-level data. Nevertheless, these results can be interpreted as the mean efficiency measures of firms within the industries. Third, Caves (1992) points out that estimation depends only on the shape of the empirical distribution of output and thus cannot detect industries consisting of uniformly inefficient firms. These points set the boundaries within which we propose hypotheses and interpret the results.

Another caveat highlighted by Caves (1992) is that in dealing with microeconomic data (firm level) in a steady-state framework, inefficiency optimally measured could be attributed only to managerial slack. In a dynamic, fairly aggregate setting (industry level) where the production frontier shifts up over time, an additional source of efficiency arises in the lag of adjustment to new technological conditions. This lag partly explains why factors like R&D that push the frontier upward can involve an apparent loss in efficiency.

7.7 CONCLUSION

Using an improved version of the stochastic production function, the empirical results showed that manufacturing industries in Singapore were not using resources and technology efficiently and thus were operating at 73 per cent of their potential output level on average. This means that more output can be obtained by improving technical efficiency. If substantial improvements in technical efficiency can be gained, then this knowledge of using resources and technology efficiently could motivate and set the stage for innovation, thereby leading to technological progress as well.

While most studies have investigated the causes of low TFP growth, this study's objective was to identify some sources of technical inefficiency (since Mahadevan and Kalirajan (2000) found technical inefficiency to be the cause of low TFP growth in Singapore's manufacturing industries) to formulate appropriate policies. This is an important difference since policy actions intended to improve total factor productivity growth would be badly misdirected if there is a lack of understanding of the interaction between the concepts of improvements in technical efficiency and technological progress, the sum of which constitutes total factor productivity growth.

It was found that, for improvements in technical efficiency, increases in capital intensity must be accompanied by increases in the growth and quality of the labour force. More efforts to relax the supply restrictions on labour such as reducing or even abolishing the levy on skilled workers should be considered. The national goal of 4 per cent of payroll on formal training is insufficient and more government funds should be used to train workers.

In addition, expanding output allowed manufacturing industries to reap economies of scale and thus have the ability and the incentive to hire better-skilled workers to use resources efficiently. The government's policy to grow and groom local, small and medium-sized enterprises into large enterprises by providing incentives and grants through the Economic Development Board can be expected to lead to improvements in technical efficiency in those industries.

Empirical evidence also showed that MNCs failed to provide sufficient spillover effects and were themselves not more efficient than local firms. Thus MNCs should be carefully selected to provide opportunities for training workers and imparting knowledge.

NOTES

1. Equating *TE*/1-*TE* to the antilog of the estimated coefficient value and solving for *TE* gives the elasticity value of the variable's effect on changes in *TE*.
2. Singaporeans are known to shun blue-collar jobs and although the Singapore government has allowed the use of foreign unskilled labour, this is limited given the heavy levies and penalties imposed on firms' overuse of unskilled foreign labour.
3. As FDI-intensive industries also tend to be capital intensive, there might be multicollinearity problems. Hence the correlation coefficient between *OWND* and *K/L* was checked and it was found to be low at 0.31.
4. It has been shown in the literature that TFP growth is made up of technological progress and changes in technical efficiency.

APPENDIX 7.1 VARIABLES USED

The value added output for each manufacturing industry was obtained from published data and was deflated using the GDP deflator of the manufacturing sector.

Expenditure on capital assets (which are basically composed of land, buildings and structures, machinery equipment, office equipment, and transport equipment) was taken as an aggregate value due to the varying categorization of capital assets over time. For example, from 1974 to 1990, capital assets were given in four categories and in 1991, it was revised to two assets groups. Capital expenditure for the entire period was taken at gross value as data on capital assets sold were not available since 1993. The gross capital expenditure was then deflated by the average of the gross domestic capital formation price deflators of the various types of capital. To depreciate gross capital expenditure, an average of the depreciation rates for various types of capital given by Jorgenson (1990) was used. The capital stock series was then calculated using the perpetual inventory method with the net value of fixed assets for 1974 as the initial capital stock.

The number of workers employed in each industry was used for labour.

8 Trade liberalization and productivity growth in Australia's manufacturing industries

8.1 INTRODUCTION

This chapter adds to the revival of interest in the trade–growth nexus as the impact of trade liberalization on productivity gains remains empirical, given the ambiguity in the literature on this issue. The conventional wisdom that trade liberalization leads to productivity gains has found support from earlier studies as well as recent studies such as Dowrick (1994), Rodrik (1995), Harrison (1996) and Edwards (1998). Proponents of trade liberalization argue that returns to entrepreneurial effort increase with exposure to foreign competition. However, Harvrylshyn (1990), Grossman and Helpman (1991), Rodrik (1992a and 1992b) and Tybout (1992) have questioned the importance of these supposed productivity gains. This scepticism stems from the view that trade liberalization might retard productivity growth by shrinking domestic firms' sales, which would in turn reduce the incentive for these firms to invest in technological efforts. Most sceptical of all are Rodriguez and Rodrik (1999) who voice serious doubts as to the very existence of an identifiable relationship between trade liberalization and productivity growth.

In the light of this debate, this chapter attempts to address Rodrik's (1995) lament on the 'cross-country measurement of distortions' by focusing on the effect of trade liberalization on a small open economy, Australia. Australia is a suitable case study because of its long history of protecting its domestic manufacturing sector. However, the post-1973 unilateral tariff reductions allowed Australia to show a reformed face with respect to trade liberalization.[1] Most inter-temporal studies on Australian trade reform such as Dixon and McDonald (1991), Chand (1999), Oczkowski and Sharma (2001) and Jayanthakumaran (1999) conclude that the impact of this trade liberalization on productivity gains is positive, although some of the studies only show a weak relationship.

The case study here differs from the above-mentioned studies by making two significant contributions. The first is in the measurement of productivity growth. While Dixon and McDonald (1991) and Jayanthakumaran (1999) used the partial labour productivity growth measure, Chand (1999) and Oczkowski and Sharma (2001) measured total factor productivity (TFP) growth using the non-frontier approach. Here, TFP growth is estimated using the frontier approach to overcome some drawbacks of the partial and non-frontier measures. The partial measure has long been criticized for not measuring overall changes in efficiency changes since it is affected by changes in the composition of inputs. TFP growth, on the other hand, allows for the impact of factor substitution as it considers the joint use of both capital and labour in production, but the non-frontier approach to TFP growth has two major problems. First, the residual TFP growth calculated using the growth accounting method in the non-frontier approach explains little as it includes 'everything and anything' of output growth not accounted for by input growth.

The second problem with the non-frontier approach is that it assumes the presence of technical efficiency (Atkinson and Cornwall 1998). Thus its TFP growth measure is inaccurate as it is synonymous with technological progress. But the literature on productivity growth has shown that TFP growth is composed of both technological progress and improvements in technical efficiency. Technological progress results from the advanced technology embodied in capital and is represented by the outward shifts in the production frontier over time. Increased technical efficiency, on the other hand, results from the more efficient use of technology and inputs (due to the accumulation of knowledge in the learning-by-doing process, diffusion of new technology, improved managerial practice and so on) and is represented by movements towards the best-practice frontier. Hence by assuming technical efficiency, the non-frontier TFP growth is measured by frontier shifts only. In linking trade and productivity, Tybout (1992) states that it is a mistake to think of productivity growth as an orderly shift in the production function. Thus, the frontier approach which identifies both the roles of technical efficiency and technological progress in industry performance is used to obtain accurate TFP growth measures in this study.

The second contribution of this chapter stems from the separate measures of technological progress and technical efficiency that constitute TFP growth. This allows the separate investigation of the impact of trade liberalization on each of these components of TFP growth and so enhances the analysis of policy implications. As technological progress and technical efficiency are analytically different concepts and could well move in opposing directions, there is no reason to expect trade liberalization to have a similar effect on both these components. Studies such as Pitt and Lee (1981), Nishimizu and Page (1991), Page (1984), Condon et al. (1985), Moran (1987) and Havrylyshyn (1991) which used the efficiency-frontier methodology to investigate the impact trade liberalization did so using only the technical efficiency measure and ignored technological progress. The ignored interactions between these components of TFP growth may provide a consensus on the productivity effects of trade liberalization in studies of different countries. Table 8.1 illustrates the importance of considering the effects of trade liberalization separately on the components of TFP growth as this may help us understand and formulate better policies with regards to trade liberalization.

Table 8.1 Possible effects of trade liberalization on productivity growth

Impact of trade liberalization			
Technological progress	Strength of effect	Technical efficiency change	TFP growth
↑		↑	↑
↑	>	↓	↑
↑	<	↓	↓

The table shows that the overall effect of trade liberalization depends on the nature and strength of the separate impact of trade liberalization on technological progress and technical efficiency. One should also note that if the impacts are different but insignificant, then the effect on TFP growth would be different from that indicated in Table 8.1. Thus various permutations of the above impacts can be established. The effect of trade liberalization on an economy's productivity growth could then take on a U-curve or an inverted U-curve relationship over time, if there are offsetting effects of trade liberalization on technological progress and technical efficiency that change over time.

The rest of the chapter is as follows. The next section provides a brief summary of the type of assistance provided to the Australian manufacturing sector over time. Section 8.3 sets out the theoretical framework of the stochastic frontier model and section 8.4 discusses the data sources. Section 8.5 presents the estimated production frontier and the measures of technological progress and technical efficiency. Section 8.6 provides an empirical analysis of the effect of trade liberalization and other factors on both the efficiency components of TFP growth for policy formulation. The last section concludes.

8.2 ASSISTANCE TO THE AUSTRALIAN MANUFACTURING SECTOR

In the past, Australia's resource-intensive exports to many of the major markets of the world and her particular geographical difficulties seemed to warrant a programme of protection and support for manufacturing to redress the balance (Mayes et al. 1994). Thus, government assistance was provided to allow the establishment of a viable domestic manufacturing sector by sheltering it from competition arising from world trade. At the end of 1960s, Australia's tariffs on imports were higher than that of every other country except New Zealand. However, by the early 1970s, it was increasingly accepted that without substantial liberalization in trade and industrial policy, Australia's standard of living would fall behind many OECD countries. Thus began the gradual process of the removal of protection. Chand (1999) explains that the changes in assistance have included a 25 per cent cut across the tariff rate in July 1973; the introduction of quota assistance due to downturn in economic activity in 1974; tariff reductions in January 1977; announcements in the May 1988 economic statement; and the programme of tariff reductions since then. The falling effective rate of assistance (ERA) and nominal rate of assistance (NRA) for the manufacturing sector over time is depicted in Figure 8.1.

The figure shows that by the mid-1990s, the average ERA to manufacturing fell to 7 per cent from about 20 per cent in 1985/86 and 35 per cent in the early 1970s. The assistance reduction was by no means uniform across the manufacturing industries. While reforms in the transport equipment industry began during 1978/79 to 1982/83, those in the textile, clothing, footwear and leather industry started only from the mid-1980s. These two sectors have been the recipients of higher levels of protection compared to the manufacturing average. The current average level of assistance is still higher than the level of assistance of about 5 per cent that is offered in industrialized nations, indicating further scope for trade liberalization in Australia.

8.3 DATA AND MODELS USED

8.3.1 The Stochastic Frontier Model

Based on the non-neutral shifting production frontier, the model for this exercise is given by:

$$Ln\,Y = a_o + a_1 T + (\beta_o + \sum_{m=1}^{7} \beta_m D_m)\,Ln\,L_{it} + (\alpha_o + \sum_{m=1}^{7} \alpha_m D_m)\,Ln\,K_{it} + u_{it} + v_{it} \tag{8.1}$$

where Y = value added output;
T = time trend;
D_m = industry slope dummies;
L = labour; and
K = capital.

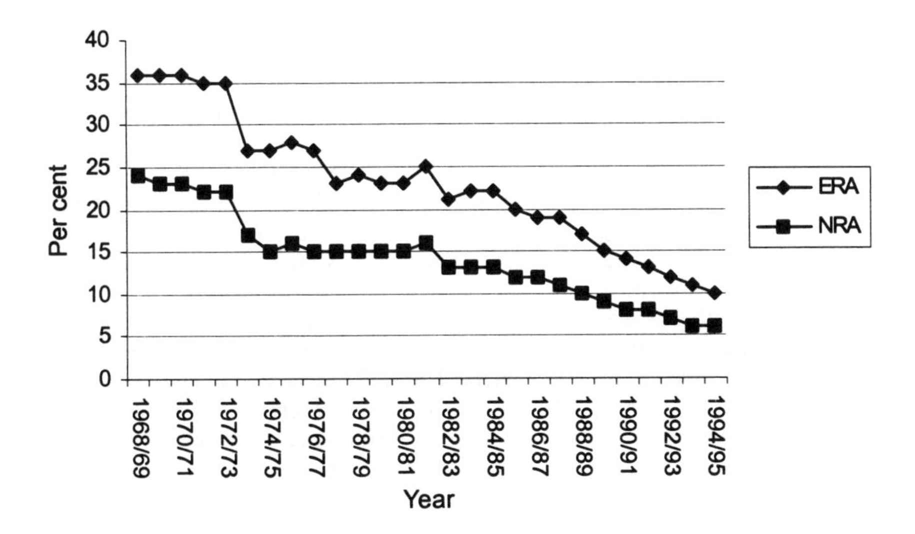

Figure 8.1 ERA and NRA in total manufacturing

Source: Figure 1 from Chand (1999).

Notes: ERA – effective rate of assistance.
NRA – nominal rate of assistance.
See Table 8.5 for definitions of ERA and NRA.

The input shares of the manufacturing industries given by α and β are allowed to vary by the use of seven industry slope dummies. The time trend, on the other hand, captures all variations that affect industries' output over time.

8.3.2 Data Sources

Data were drawn from the Industry Commission database and the Australian Bureau of Statistics (ABS) publications for the eight two-digit manufacturing industries from 1968/69 to 1994/95 (see Appendix 8.1). The data up to 1992–93 is detailed in terms of the sources and methods used in Industry Commission (1995). It was then updated using data from the Industry Commission database as well as ABS publications such as *Manufacturing Establishments: Details of Operations* and *Manufacturing Industry*. These include data for domestic research and development, public infrastructure (both of which are in 1989/90 prices), number of establishments in the industry, and sales of all goods produced by industry. As there were no consistent industry-specific time-series data to deflate the sales variable, the All Manufacturing Index which represents price movements of goods produced by establishments in manufacturing, was used instead. Table 8.5 provides a brief description of all these variables.

For output, the 'unassisted' value added measure in 1989–90 prices was obtained by deflating value added in domestic prices by ERA. This follows Chand's (1999) demonstration that output should be revalued on an unassisted basis when attempting to analyse the impact of border assistance on growth. Employment is measured by the number of persons employed in each industry weighted by the index of number of hours worked. Capital input on the other hand is distinguished between machinery and equipment, and non-residential construction. Gretton and Fisher's (1997) measure of capital capacity derived using the perpetual inventory method on ABS data was used to construct the capital stock series. Gretton and Fisher also incorporated various asset age structures in their calculation and found their capital stock measure in constant 1989–90 prices to be robust when sensitivity tests using other approaches were carried out.

8.4 THE ESTIMATED PRODUCTION FRONTIER AND EFFICIENCY MEASURES

The coefficients obtained from the maximum likelihood estimation of the stochastic frontier model are summarized in Table 8.2. It can be seen that the input shares are not identical across the majority of the industries as is shown by the significance of the slope dummies. Initially, the more general translog model was estimated but as the second-order conditions were not found to be

Table 8.2: Stochastic frontier estimates of the model

Variables	Parameter	Parameter estimates
Constant	a_0	1.93 (0.7701)*
Time trend	a_1	1.04 (0.042)*
Labour (Industry 1)	β_o	0.5078 (0.0143)*
Labour dummy (Industry 2)	β_1	0.0316 (0.0072)*
Labour dummy (Industry 3)	β_2	0.0045 (0.0165)
Labour dummy (Industry 4)	β_3	-0.0014 (0.0028)
Labour dummy (Industry 5)	β_4	0.0031 (0.0008)*
Labour dummy (Industry 6)	β_5	0.0025 (0.0006)*
Labour dummy (Industry 7)	β_6	-0.0016 (0.0054)
Labour dummy (Industry 8)	β_7	0.0059 (0.0007)*
Capital (Industry1)	α_o	0.4613 (0.0103)*
Capital dummy (Industry 2)	α_1	-0.0034 (0.0062)*
Capital dummy (Industry 3)	α_2	0.0172 (0.0011)*
Capital dummy (Industry 4)	α_3	0.0141 (0.0482)
Capital dummy (Industry 5)	α_4	0.0028 (0.0012)*
Capital dummy (Industry 6)	α_5	0.0145 (0.0058)*
Capital dummy (Industry 7)	α_6	0.0137 (0.0036)*
Capital dummy (Industry 8)	α_7	-0.0161 (0.0412)

Notes: See Appendix 8.1 for industry codes.
Figures in parenthesis are asymptotic standard errors.
* means that the coefficient is significant at the 5 per cent level of significance.

significant, the Cobb-Douglas model was considered the better model to fit the data. While Narasimham et al. (1988) demonstrated that the Cobb-Douglas functional form is less restrictive when all of the coefficients are allowed to vary, Tybout (1990) explains that the Cobb-Douglas functional form allows maximum flexibility in dealing with secondary data.

Using the estimates in Table 8.2 and the framework set out in Figure 5.1 of Chapter 5, technological progress and gains in technical efficiency are calculated for all eight industries and tabulated in Tables 8.3 and 8.4. The tables show a distinct pattern for some industries for which discussion follows. The food, beverage and tobacco industry is not only one of the largest industries (accounting for about 20 per cent of all Australian manufacturing production) but is also a major exporting industry. This clearly reflects Australia's large

Table 8.3 Annual average technological progress (%)

Industries	1969/70 to 1973/74	1974/75 to 1979/80	1980/81 to 1984/85	1985/86 to 1989/90	1990/91 to 1994/95
Food, beverage and tobacco	0.78	0.86	3.16	3.19	3.39
Textile, clothing, footwear and leather	0.82	0.18	1.2	0.72	1.42
Printing, publishing and recorded media	0.73	1.67	3.25	3.27	3.58
Petroleum, coal, chemicals and associated products	0.76	0.98	3.08	3.09	3.67
Basic metal products	0.74	1.9	2.15	1.77	1.91
Structural metal products	0.57	0.59	3.43	3.31	3.47
Transport equipment	0.67	1.18	3.23	3.28	3.63
Other manufacturing industries	0.69	0.83	3.24	3.29	3.32

agricultural sector and, being resource-based, this industry is the least labour-intensive. TFP growth in this industry hinges on the efficiency of the agricultural sector where Australia has a comparative advantage. But this dependency on a thriving agricultural sector could partly be the reason for the inefficient use of technology and the inputs as seen from the poor gains from technical efficiency over time. Being capital-intensive in nature, the gains from technological progress were however quite substantial (see Table 8.4).

The capital-intensive feature is also characteristic of the basic metal products industry which is another key industry that exploits Australia's strong resource base. This industry has been the largest export earner in the past decade and seems to have thrived due to Asia's lack of resources. Interestingly, this was the only industry which registered improvements in technical efficiency over time.

Table 8.4 Annual average technical efficiency gains (%)

Industries	1969/70 to 1973/74	1974/75 to 1979/80	1980/81 to 1984/85	1985/86 to 1989/90	1990/91 to 1994/95
Food, beverage and tobacco	0.06	1.05	-0.8	-0.97	-1.1
Textile, clothing, footwear and leather	0.09	1.02	-0.22	0.41	-0.46
Printing, publishing and recorded media	0.03	0.09	-0.84	-1.29	-1.4
Petroleum, coal, chemicals and associated products	0.11	1.01	-0.86	-1.33	-1.52
Basic metal products	0.07	0.08	0.08	0.11	0.21
Structural metal products	0.07	1.03	-1.11	-1.25	-1.36
Transport equipment	0.06	0.93	-0.98	-1.35	-1.30
Other manufacturing industries	0.08	0.96	-1.20	-1.41	-1.45

The textile, clothing, footwear and leather industry in contrast, is the most labour-intensive with the lowest wage rates (Clark et al. 1996) and in general, has the lowest technological progress and TFP growth compared to the other industries. This industry has had to face very severe competition from labour-abundant low wage producers from Asia and thus remains heavily protected despite significant falls in ERA since 1984/85. The continued protection could well be hindering improvements in productivity. The case is quite similar with the transport equipment industry which enjoys heavy protection with respect to motor vehicles. Such protection was initiated by a desire for a national car industry on prestige and security grounds. However, technological progress in the transport industry was higher than that of the textile industry as there are more opportunities for the use of better technology in the transport industry.

The petroleum, coal and chemical industries are the most capital-intensive of the manufacturing industries but have yet to gain from technical efficiency. This could be because these industries face minimal competitive imports and are (with the exception of the coal industry) not strongly trade oriented and cater mainly to domestic demand. Also, the coal industry has had a historical record of high levels of industrial disputation, while the petroleum refineries are unable to operate at full capacity due to the need to undertake routine maintenance and the high cost of coastal shipping in Australia (Clark et al. 1996).

8.5 IMPACT OF TRADE LIBERALIZATION AND OTHER FACTORS ON TFP GROWTH, TECHNOLOGICAL PROGRESS AND GAINS IN TECHNICAL EFFICENCY

Besides trade liberalization, many other factors affecting productivity growth have been identified in the literature but the choice of factors in this exercise is heavily dictated by the availability of data. They are described in Table 8.5.

Table 8.5 Inter-industry determinants of productivity growth

Variable	Symbol	Description
Capital-labour ratio	*K/L*	Stock of physical capital per unit of person employed
Domestic research and development	*R&D*	Measured as the aggregate stock of public and private R&D available for use in production
Public infrastructure	*G*	General government stock of net public capital for non-dwelling construction
Effective rate of assistance	*ERA*	Encompasses effective rate of protection as well as non-border interventions such as protection subsidies, input taxes and subsidies, tax provisions etc
Nominal rate of assistance	*NRA*	Includes tariffs and import quotas but ignores input distortions in the form of any benefits and penalties
Number of firms	*FIRMNO*	Number of establishments in the industry
Sales	*SALES*	Sales of all goods produced by industry

Note: ERA and NRA are alternative measures of trade liberalization.

In addition to this and as suggested by Parham and Makin (2000), macroeconomic variables such as inflation rate and exchange rates[2] were also used but as these were insignificant in their effects on technological progress and gains in technical efficiency, they were dropped. Various estimations using some of the variables in Table 8.5 to reduce the potential for multicollinearity were carried out. Although some of the data were only available for selected years, the smallest sample size for any one estimation was quite large at 64.

With all of the efficiency measures, a semilogarithmic equation was estimated by logging only the independent variables. The estimation results are summarized in Table 8.6. Although a battery of diagnostics tests did not reveal any problems, the $\bar{R}^2$ of most of the equations were not that high, similar to Chand (1999).

Table 8.6 Regression results for determinants of gains in technical efficiency

Variable	(i)	(ii)	(iii)	(iv)
Constant	1.02 *	1.31 *	0.89 *	1.13 *
	(0.512)	(0.648)	(0.44)	(0.526)
K/L			0.266*	0.18*
			(0.127)	(0.082)
R&D	0.06	0.09		
	(0.037)	(0.071)		
G	0.16	0.084	0.049	0.031
	(0.099)	(0.061)	(0.031)	(0.027)
ERA	- 0.17		- 0.192	- 0.08
	(0.104)		(0.118)	(0.066)
NRA		- 0.062		
		(0.042)		
FIRMNO				0.512
				(0.434)
SALES	0.39 *	0.46 *	0.31 *	
	(0.199)	(0.221)	(0.148)	
$\bar{R}^2$	0.36	0.31	0.62	0.45

Notes: Figures in parenthesis are standard errors.
* indicates that the estimated coefficient is significant at the 5 per cent of significance.

It can be seen from Table 8.6 that the decline in the ERA did not affect gains in technical efficiency as it was found to be insignificant in all the equations.[3] No significant effect was observed when the alternative measure of assistance rate, NRA, was used. But this may not be surprising as Australia implemented a made-to-measure tariff during the protective regime (Anderson 1987). Karmel and Brunt (1966) and Hunter (1965) explain that such a tariff rate was set with the aim of allowing only efficient firms to survive. Thus, although the aim of the tariff was to protect the industries and to nurture them, it was also to prevent technically inefficient firms from operating. If so, given that the existing firms in the industry are already fairly technically efficient, then it can be expected that any gains in technical efficiency due to a fall in ERA would be rather small.

Equations (ii) and (iii) in Table 8.7 show that the reduction in ERA significantly improved technological progress. Thus, it appears that with trade liberalization, the incentive to use better technology increased in order to compete efficiently but there was a lack of enhanced understanding of the efficient use of the technology and inputs.

With TFP growth, Table 8.8 shows that the effect of *ERA* was still positive (since technological progress was found to be overwhelming larger than the negative gains in technical efficiency) but has weakened compared to its effect on technological progress as it is only significant at the 10 per cent level. This finding is important as it shows that studies using the non-frontier approach (whose TFP growth is essentially measured by technological progress) may find strong evidence favouring trade liberalization,[4] unlike studies adopting the frontier approach where technological progress and technical efficiency move in opposite directions as in the Australian case.

Two attempts were made to check the robustness of the results obtained following Edwards (1998). First, to consider the possibility of a non-linear relationship between trade liberalization and technological progress and technical efficiency, a quadratic term of *ERA* and *NRA* was included in the regressions. As the quadratic coefficient was insignificant, there was little need to worry about non-linearities underlying the trade effect. Second, the regressions were run for a few subsets of time periods to check if the trade effect was period-specific, but no evidence of that was apparent, given that the results did not change significantly.

With R&D, it was found not to affect gains in technical efficiency significantly but it had some positive effect on technological progress and TFP growth.[5] With increasing levels of R&D, the availability of better technology or modifying existing technology presents itself clearly but this does not translate to more effective use of the technology unless there is sufficient training for workers to acquire the knowledge and expertise in dealing with the technology in place.

Table 8.7 Regression results for determinants of technological progress

Variable	(i)	(ii)	(iii)	(iv)
Constant	1.23 (1.12)	1.62* (0.816)	2.08* (0.75)	2.14 (1.36)
K/L			0.32 * (0.15)	0.11 * (0.046)
R&D	0.18** (0.109)	0.45 ** (0.27)		
G	0.22 (0.146)	0.19 (0.136)	0.41 (0.26)	-0.53 (0.325)
ERA		- 0.27 * (0.125)	- 0.34 * (0.171)	
NRA	- 0.33 (0.471)			- 0.38 ** (0.218)
FIRMNO		- 0.58 ** (0.337)	- 0.56 * (0.283)	
SALES	0.46 (0.29)			0.61 (0.402)
$\bar{R}^2$	0.44	0.71	0.78	0.56

Notes: Figures in parenthesis are standard errors.
* and * * indicates that the estimated coefficient is significant at the 5 per cent and 10 per cent level of significance respectively.

In fact, when faced with technical innovation over time, industries may adopt such innovations in a sluggish manner and this form of rigidity may prevent the optimal use of inputs in each period, due the inability to adjust instantly.

The only statistically significant factor that increased TFP growth, technological progress and technical efficiency is the *K/L* ratio which is a measure of an industry's capital intensity. Industries with higher capital intensities are likely to economize on the cost of capital because they cannot use the best technology available. However, if capital deepening is not accompanied by increasing skill levels of workers, then the overall positive effect on productivity growth may be minimal.

Table 8.8 Regression results for determinants of TFP growth

Variable	(i)	(ii)	(iii)	(iv)
Constant	1.31 *	1.82 *	1.93 *	2.05 *
	(0.663)	(0.915)	(0.821)	(0.951)
K/L			0.41*	0.34*
			(0.197)	(0.156)
R&D	0.11**	0.32*		
	(0.067)	(0.101)		
G	0.31	0.19	0.22	0.18
	(0.204)	(0.121)	(0.173)	(0.113)
ERA		- 0.13 **	- 0.26 **	
		(0.077)	(0.146)	
NRA	- 0.01			- 0.26
	(0.007)			(0.161)
FIRMNO		-0.48 *	-0.49 *	
		(0.203)	(0.196)	
SALES	0.11 **			0.13
	(0.067)			(0.089)
$\bar{R}^2$	0.39	0.59	0.67	0.33

Notes: Figures in parenthesis are standard errors.
* and ** indicates that the estimated coefficient is significant at the 5 per cent and 10 per cent level of significance respectively.

Unlike the study of Nishimizu and Page (1991), government expenditure in this analysis had no influence on either component of TFP growth. But the degree and type of government intervention is an important issue that is not sufficiently considered here due to lack of data. This prevents any strong conclusion on the impact of government expenditure on productivity growth in the Australian manufacturing sector.

The effect of market structure on productivity was captured with the use of number of firms and sales of an industry. It was found that economies of scale represented by an increase in sales, improved technical efficiency as it allowed industries to take advantage of the relative savings of inputs that can be achieved from operating at or close to the minimum efficient scale (Sheehnan 1997). With technological progress, a high concentration of firms in the industry represented by a small number of firms was seen to have some effect (although not a strong one). The firms can be expected to have the capacity and incentive to invest in better technology as they cater to a large share of the industry's demand and face less competition.

8.5.1 Implications for Australia

The empirical results show that trade liberalization has led to improved technological progress but has had an insignificant effect on gains in technical efficiency. Given that Australia's manufacturing industries are not at the high end of the technology ladder, this offers the continued possibility of technological progress from the use of better and more advanced technology with further trade liberalization. However, it must be ensured that with the adoption of better technology, technological mastery follows in the way of improved technical efficiency as trade liberalization does not seem to provide sufficient incentive for training and improving the quality of the labour force. Hence, in order to enjoy the full benefits of trade liberalization on productivity gains, the pace of adopting better technology needs to be right to allow a better understanding and application of the technology. That is, maximizing technological progress at the expense of technical efficiency is not an optimal strategy.

In the long run, technological progress would decline due to the limited possibilities of obtaining newer and more advanced technology. Thus, gains from technical efficiency simply cannot be ignored or this may result in Australia experiencing an inverted U effect of trade liberalization on productivity gains over time.

8.5.2 Limitations of This Study

Having drawn some implications for Australia based on the empirical evidence, it is necessary to discuss the limitations of the study.

First is the issue of robustness of the results. The efficiency measures obtained would be different if different model specifications underlying the estimated production frontier were used or if a cost frontier was estimated or a non-parametric methodology was used. Thus caution needs to be exercised when interpreting econometric results presented above. Second, much more can be learned from micro-econometric analysis of firm-level data (but this is not available for Australia) as this constitutes a rich source of uncovering the ways in which trade policy affects productivity growth. The effects can be expected to be different across industries within the same economy, perhaps highlighting the need for industry-specific trade policy measures.

Third is the issue of causality effects highlighted by Rodriguez and Rodrik (1999). There is little evidence from Bernard and Jensen (1995, 1998) and Aw et al. (2000) that firms derive technological or other benefits from exporting per se; the common pattern is that efficient producers self-select into export markets. This aspect has not been investigated or related to trade liberalization policy for the Australian economy. Fourth, the empirical results have not clearly distinguished between the effects of other parts of the policy package that accompanied the trade reform process in Australia. There was some attempt to include inflation rate (to reflect the inflation targeting policy of the 1990s) and exchange rate (to reflect the free float of the Australian dollar since 1983) in the regressions but it was not econometrically possible to tease out the interaction between trade liberalization and the macroeconomic policy regime and thereby their effect on productivity growth.

Fifth, the timing and type of trade liberalization policy also have an important bearing on the result (Sachs and Warner 1995). For example, how effectively do ERA and NRA capture the range of the trade liberalization tools used in the Australian economy? There is always the question of accuracy in the trade measures used. With the matter of timing, the question of whether there was a parallel process of liberalization underway in Australia's trade partners is crucial for considering the full benefits of trade liberalization in Australia. Thus the process of assessing trade effects more accurately is a demanding and complex task and it must be acknowledged that this study and most previous studies have a long way to go in that respect.

8.6 CONCLUSION

Unlike earlier studies on Australia, here, TFP growth is first decomposed into technological progress and gains in technical efficiency and the effect of trade liberalization is then investigated separately on TFP growth as well as on each of the components of TFP growth. The empirical findings suggests that some of the ambiguity in the literature may be resolved by such separate investigation.

This is done by highlighting the importance of not only the frontier approach adopted here but also of the possible pitfalls of considering TFP growth as a single entity. This line of analysis is especially relevant for economies which experience technological progress and gains in technical efficiency that move in opposite directions. Clearly, as Rodiguez and Rodrik (1999) point out, the trade relationship would still remain contingent as it depends on a host of country and external characteristics, but the decompositional analysis underlying TFP growth adds another dimension to the evaluation of trade liberalization policies and narrows the range on uncertainties surrounding this debate. It would be interesting to compare and contrast similar analyses that consider other possible decompositions or sources of TFP growth. Finally, instead of being lost in the pursuit of a single answer, let us allow the complexity of the relationship of trade liberalization and productivity growth to challenge and encourage us to improve our efforts towards a better understanding of the issue.

NOTES

1. See Freedman and Stonecash (1997) for a survey on Australian manufacturing industry policy.
2. Dollar's (1992) concern that misalignment of real exchange rate would affect the effect of trade liberalization on productivity growth is less of a problem for Australia given Chand's (2001) study which shows that any such misalignment is very modest.
3. This result is similar to Moran (1987) but other efficiency studies such as Pitt and Lee (1981), Nishimizu and Page (1991), Page (1984), Condon et al. (1985) and Havrylyshyn (1991) found a positive effect for this relationship.
4. Both Chand (1999) and Oczkowski and Sharma (2001) show evidence of positive effects of trade liberalization.
5. Atella and Quintieri (2001) show that Coe and Helpman's (1995) result that domestic R&D is an important determinant of TFP growth is far from conclusive as the link between TFP and R&D strongly depends on the way in which TFP is measured.

APPENDIX 8.1 AUSTRALIA'S MANUFACTURING INDUSTRIES

1. Food, beverage and tobacco
2. Textile, clothing, footwear and leather
3. Printing, publishing and recorded media
4. Petroleum, coal, chemicals and associated products
5. Basic metal products
6. Structural metal products
7. Transport equipment
8. Other manufacturing industries

9 Looking beyond obtaining the 'real' TFP growth for Malaysia's manufacturing sector

9.1 INTRODUCTION

The objective of this chapter is threefold. First, as an empirical exercise, the case study throws light on the productivity performance of Malaysia's manufacturing sector. Second, in terms of methodology, both the parametric (non-parallel shifting stochastic production frontier) and non-parametric (DEA) frontier models are used to obtain TFP growth rates. Third, based on the empirical results, policy implications are drawn and what constitutes a real TFP growth measure is briefly discussed. The chapter is organized as follows.

After a brief discussion of the Malaysian economy and a review of the TFP studies done on Malaysia, the frontier models are specified and data sources explained. This is followed by the estimation results and analysis. The last section concludes.

9.2 THE MALAYSIAN ECONOMY

The Malaysian economy has been one of the best performers in the developing world over the past 25 years until the onset of the 1997 Asian financial currency crisis. Malaysia grew at an average rate of 7.8 per cent in the decade of the 1970s and at 8.8 per cent during 1987 to 1996. This rapid economic growth was partly due to changes in the structure of the economy. Manufacturing which contributed only 16.4 per cent of the GDP of a predominantly agricultural and primary goods producing country in 1975, accounted for 34.2 per cent of the economy's 1996 output. This was made possible by the significant amount of FDI that went into the manufacturing sector since the amendment of the Investment Act in 1986 which liberalized foreign sector ownership and provided incentives for FDI.

The composition of the Malaysian manufacturing sector (see Table 9.1) has also changed considerably over time. It can be seen that while the food, beverage and tobacco as well as the textiles, clothing and footwear industries have experienced falling value added shares, that of machinery, metal products, electrical machinery and transport equipment have increased their shares. Other manufactured products with a moderate increase in value added share include optical and scientific equipment, toys and sporting goods, and other manufactures over the 1981–96 period.

Table 9.1 Value added shares of key industries in the Malaysian manufacturing sector (%)

Industries	1975	1985	1990	1996
Food, beverage and tobacco	27.2	14.7	9.7	8.8
Textiles, clothing and footwear and leather products	7.6	4.9	6.5	4.6
Wood products and furniture	8.9	6.2	7.2	6.8
Paper and printing	5.3	5.2	4.6	4.3
Chemicals	6.4	15.8	10.8	7.8
Petroleum and coal	2.9	3.2	2.6	2.5
Rubber	11.0	3.4	4.7	4.0
Non-metallic mineral products	3.6	6.1	4.9	4.1
Metal products	3.7	3.0	3.5	3.5
Machinery	3.1	2.0	3.9	5.6
Electrical machinery	11.1	15.1	21.5	30.5
Transport equipment	3.0	4.3	5.5	6.3

Source: *Annual Survey of Manufacturing Industries*, Department of Statistics, Malaysia.

Table 9.2 provides summary statistics on the manufacturing industries. In terms of value added, the large industries are the electrical machinery, industrial chemicals and food industries. Industries which are relatively labour intensive as measured by low capital labour ratios include furniture and fixtures, machinery and electrical machinery industries.

Table 9.2 Summary statistics on the manufacturing industries (mean value over 1981–96)

Industries	Value added (RM$'000)	Capital (RM$'000)	Labour (No. of workers)
Food	1568808.3	2452629.7	75026
Beverage	228698.2	295005.4	5168
Tobacco	281521.4	298072.1	5070
Textiles	513740.3	291536.3	5423
Wearing apparel	367105.6	285289.8	5804
Leather	14206.5	277919.4	5773
Footwear	13195.3	274569.5	5650
Wood	979142.7	269383.0	5590
Furniture and fixtures	173898.7	218368.1	19280
Paper	254842.3	265175.3	5532
Printing, publishing	473599.4	260431.3	5492
Industrial chemicals	1302360.7	253062.4	5422
Other chemicals	404209.4	245839.9	5512
Petroleum refineries	373251.7	235040.4	5538
Miscellaneous products of petroleum and coal	56215.6	223074.4	5573
Rubber	838472.6	211217.6	5657
Plastic	498355.5	200400.5	5688
Pottery, china and earthenware	52441.4	182298.5	5706
Glass	121824.9	167767.4	6446
Non-metallic mineral	761137.3	173701.5	6898
Iron and steel	415155.4	175672.8	6580
Non-ferrous metal	129492.7	171727.6	6245
Fabricated metal	615366.3	194384.5	8357
Machinery	681538.1	210722.6	10308
Electrical machinery	3929556.7	4275996.5	200405
Transport equipment	785669.8	1122952.2	28036
Professional, scientific and measuring controlling equipment	168015.4	216641.7	12260
Other manufacturing	158145.8	254686.2	15127

Source: *Annual Survey of Manufacturing Industries*, Department of Statistics, Malaysia.

In the late 1990s, Malaysia embarked on a plan to enter the league of developed industrial nations by 2020.[1] The *Second Industrial Master Plan 1996–2005* states that this is to be achieved by promoting a shift in the national development strategy, from one that used to be input-driven towards one that is productivity-driven. In addition, the manufacturing sector has been identified as a key growth engine in this transformation process. Hence, it is imperative and timely to analyse the productivity growth performance of this sector but first let us take a look at the TFP studies that have been done on Malaysia so far.

9.3 REVIEW OF TFP GROWTH STUDIES ON MALAYSIA

Table 9.3 shows a summary of the main TFP growth studies on Malaysia. As expected, the TFP growth estimates are wide ranging due to the use of different data and time periods as well as differences in methodology and models specified. Although TFP growth estimates varied widely among the cross-country studies, in general, these studies showed that Malaysia's TFP growth is low and output growth is input-driven. Most of these studies also used economy-wide data and thus the results have very broad implications for each of the sectors of the economy. Since the economy is a weighted sum of the agricultural, manufacturing and services sectors, any shift in labour from a less productive sector to a more productive sector would result in an increase in overall TFP growth without any real change in TFP growth rates of either sector. This is especially important for Malaysia which has had quite a substantial change in the composition of its economy – the agricultural sector experienced a decline of 15 per cent of its GDP share of output from 1975 to 1996; the manufacturing sector, on the other hand, saw an increase in its share from 16.4 per cent to 34.2 per cent during that time while the services sector registered a fall of about 7 per cent. With services, the emphasis on TFP growth is noted in the Seventh Malaysian Plan but as in most other economies, this issue has generated little research interest as Abdullah (1999) is the only study that provides some discussion on various service industries' TFP growth using Malaysian Productivity Reports.

A point to note is that, while most of the cross-country studies used the parametric approach to estimate a Cobb-Douglas production function, that of the inter-temporal studies (with the exception of Gan and Soon 1996) used the non-parametric approach of the translog-divisia index to estimate TFP growth.

This study adds to the existing empirical literature in three ways. First, previous studies on Malaysian manufacturing have only considered the non-frontier measure using the translog divisia index approach.

Table 9.3 TFP growth estimates for Malaysia

Source	Time period	Aggregate economy	Manufacturing sector	Services sector
Alavi (1996)	1979–89		1	
Cheong and Hew (2000)	1987–97	2.2		
	1985–96		3.2	
National Productivity Corporation of Malaysia as reported in Abdullah (1999)	1987–91			5.5
	1992–96			2.4
Collins and Bosworth (1996)	1960–73	1.0		
	1973–84	0.4		
	1984–94	1.4		
Drysdale and Huang (1997)	1950–90	-0.5		
National Productivity Corporation of Malaysia as reported in Hoon and Muhamad (1996)	1986–89	0.6		
	1990–95	0.54		
Gan and Soon (1996)	1974–78	2.0		
	1979–83	0.5		
	1984–89	1.6		
	1990–95	2.2		
Kawai (1994)	1970–80	2.5		
	1980–90	0.7		

Table 9.3 (continued)

Source	Time period	Aggregate economy	Manufacturing sector	Services sector
Lewis and Taylor (2001)	1963–98	3.3		
Maison and Arshad (1992) as reported in Cheong and Hew (2000)	1973–89		Negative	
Maisom, Mohd and Nor Aini (1994)	1974–89		8.13	
Nadiri and Son (1999)	1969–90	1.6		
Nehru and Dhareshwar (1994)	1960–90	0.96[a] 0.09[b]		
Okamoto (1994)	1982–85 1986–90		-1.9 0.3	
Sarel (1997)	1978–96 1991–96	2.0 2.0		
Economic Planning Unit (1996)	1970–90 1991–95	1.2 2.5		
Syrquin (1991) as reported in Toh and Lim (1992)	1960–70 1970–82 1980–89	3.0 3.0 0.5		
Tham (1995)	1971–75 1976–80 1981–87	-1.42 0.26 -2.68		

Table 9.3 (continued)

Source	Time period	Aggregate economy	Manufacturing sector	Services sector
Tham (1996)	1986–93		0.1	
Tham (1997)	1986–91		0.3	
World Bank (1989)	1975–79 1981–84		3.8 -1.9	
World Bank (1993)	1960–89	1.1[c] -1.34[d]		
Thomas and Wang (1992)	1960–87	1.95		

Source: Updated from Mahadevan (2002a).

Notes: [a] Using first-differenced model.
[b] Using error-correction model.
[c] Using the full sample of 87 countries.
[d] Using a sample of high-income countries.

Using the non-frontier approach, while World Bank (1989), Okamoato (1994) and Maison and Arshad (1992) show low and negative TFP growth for the Malaysian manufacturing sector from the late 1970s to the decade of the 1980s, Tham (1996, 1997) and *The National Productivity Corporation* (1999) provide evidence of declining TFP growth for this sector in the 1990s. Somewhat puzzling and hard to explain is the unusually high TFP growth estimates of Maisom et al. (1994) for the manufacturing sector. How would these results compare with the use of the frontier approach? Will the frontier models also provide low TFP growth measures?

The second difference in this study is that empirical robustness is ensured by the use of both the parametric and non-parametric frontier approaches to calculate TFP growth. Under the parametric approach, two stochastic production frontier models (one with industry-specific input shares and the other with non-industry-specific input shares) incorporating non-parallel shifts were estimated. With the non-parametric approach, the data envelope analysis (DEA) technique was used. Using a panel data set of 28 manufacturing industries (see Appendix 9.1) from 1981 to 1996, a measure of TFP growth is first obtained and then decomposed to technical change and change in technical efficiency for all three models. The results are then compared to previous studies with a focus on the Malaysian manufacturing sector as TFP growth studies on the aggregate economy may have broad implications that are not necessarily reflective of TFP growth performance of specific sectors in the economy.

The third motivation behind this chapter is that the comparative performance of the results from alternative methodologies would add to similar work by Bjurek and Hjalmarsson (1990), Coelli and Perelman (1999) and Kumbhakar et al. (1999) which provide mixed evidence of the similarities in the results from the use of various models. Often, the choice of the method is said to depend on a range of factors. For instance, if the researcher simply wants to know if output growth is TFP or input-driven growth, then either approach would suffice. But to answer questions on maximum productive or best practice output levels, the stochastic frontier can be used to understand the industries' catching up behaviour with respect to its own maximum potential while DEA allows for the study of the performance of each industry relative to efficient industries in the sample. In the empirical literature, both the parametric and non-parametric methods of the frontier approach have been widely used to analyse the manufacturing sector.

9.4 FRONTIER MODELS AND DATA SOURCES

9.4.1 The Parametric Approach

Unlike the conventional stochastic frontier approach, the frontier models used here are based on the non-neutral shifting production technology framework. Furthermore, as this model relies on the generalized least squares estimation technique, it does not require the imposition of an ad hoc assumption on the distribution of technical efficiency which is purely based on the attractiveness of the statistical properties of the assumed distributions without any theoretical justification.[2]

The generalized version of the model and the estimation procedures have been detailed in Chapter 5. Here, the following models underlying the Cobb-Douglas production technology are adopted.

$$Ln\ Y = a_o + a_1 T + (\beta_o + \sum_{m=1}^{8} \beta_m D_m)\ Ln\ L_{it} + (\alpha_o + \sum_{m=1}^{8} \alpha_m D_m)\ Ln\ K_{it} \qquad (9.1)$$

$$Ln\ Y = a_o + \sum_{t=1}^{15} \delta_t + \sum_{m=1}^{8} \lambda_m + \beta\ Ln\ L_{it} + \alpha\ Ln\ K_{it} \tag{9.2}$$

where Y = value added output measured in 1978 prices;
T = time trend;
D_m, λ_m= industry dummies grouped at the 2-digit level;
δ_t = time dummies representing each year;
L = labour measured by number of workers employed; and
K = capital expenditure measured in 1978 prices.

Both models were estimated using the Fortran program TERAN. In model (1), a time trend is used to capture all variations over time that affect industries' output and the data are pooled for estimation with dummy variables being used to provide different input shares for different industries. In model (2), the input shares are assumed to be the same for all manufacturing industries but industry-specific and time-specific dummies have been used to provide different intercepts for different industries in various years. Using the parameter estimates (shown in Tables 9.4 and 9.5), TFP growth, technical efficiency change and technical change is first calculated for each industry using the decompositional framework set out in Figure 5.1 in Chapter 5. Then these measures are calculated for the manufacturing sector using a weighted share approach of each of the manufacturing industry's value added.

9.4.2 The Non-Parametric Approach

Here, the Malmquist TFP growth index is defined using distance functions and DEA as detailed in Chapter 6. Following Färe et al. (1994), the output-oriented Malmquist TFP change index can be decomposed into:

$$\text{TFP growth} = \underset{\text{(catching up effect)}}{\text{Technical efficiency change}} \times \underset{\text{(frontier effect)}}{\text{Technical change}} \tag{9.3}$$

The constant returns to scale technology was imposed on the distance functions to make the model comparable with the Cobb-Douglas parametric models given by equations (9.1) and (9.2).[3] Using Coelli's (1996b) DEAP program, four linear programs must be solved for each industry and for this sample consisting of 16 years, 46 linear programs were solved for each industry.

9.4.3 Data Sources[4]

Data on value added, capital and labour from 1981 to 1996 for 28 manufacturing industries were compiled from the *Annual Survey of Manufacturing Industries* published by the Department of Statistics, Malaysia. As data on capital expenditure was not published, fixed capital stock was used instead. The disadvantage in using such 'lumpy' capital data is that in some years it would seem that very large investment in capital has taken place and in other years, this figure would appear small, thereby underestimating or overestimating the amount of capital expenditure. With labour, the number of workers employed was used due to the lack of data on man-hours. The value added variable was deflated by the GDP deflator for the manufacturing sector and the capital variable was deflated using the gross domestic fixed capital formation deflator. Both deflators with 1978 as the base year were obtained from the *Yearbook of Statistics* published by the Department of Statistics, Malaysia.

9.5 EMPIRICAL RESULTS AND ANALYSIS

Table 9.4 shows the parameter estimates of the parametric model 1. At the outset, it must be noted that the ratio of the variance of u_{it} to that of $(u_{it} + v_{it})$ was found to be 0.62 with a likelihood ratio test statistic of 3.19. As this ratio is statistically significant based on the chi-square distribution, it indicates that the adopted model is valid for interpretation.

As expected of the manufacturing sector, the capital share given by the αs is higher than the labour share given by the βs. Most of the industries' input shares are statistically significant and the sum of the input shares is close to one reflecting the adopted Cobb-Douglas production technology. The model also satisfied various diagnostic tests (not reported here) on functional form, autocorrelation and homoscedasticity. Table 9.5, on the other hand, shows the estimates from the parametric model 2. The diagnostics tests (not reported here) did not reveal problems on misspecification, heteroscedasticity or autocorrelation. The capital share of 0.72 and the labour share of 0.26 are not far off from those obtained from model 1.

With the non-parametric model, as no standard errors are directly obtainable (except if bootstrapping procedure was used), it was not possible to test the statistical differences of the industries' performance over time. However, as an alternative, in order to check if the TFP growth estimates were sensitive to the presence of outliers, the procedure by Resti (1997) was followed.

Table 9.4 Parameter estimates of the stochastic production frontier model 1

Variables	Parameter	Estimates
Constant	a_0	1.77 (0.901)*
Time trend	a_1	1.21 (0.513)*
Labour (Industry 31)	β_o	0.32 (0.097)*
Labour (Industry 32)	β_1	-0.0034 (0.0062)*
Labour (Industry 33)	β_2	0.0172 (0.0011)*
Labour (Industry 34)	β_3	0.0141 (0.0482)
Labour (Industry 35)	β_4	0.0028 (0.0012)*
Labour (Industry 36)	β_5	0.0145 (0.0058)*
Labour (Industry 37)	β_6	0.0137 (0.0036)*
Labour (Industry 38)	β_7	-0.0161 (0.0412)
Labour (Industry 39)	β_8	0.0019 (0.0002)*
Capital (Industry31)	α_o	0.67 (0.0811)*
Capital (Industry 32)	α_1	0.0316 (0.0072)*
Capital (Industry 33)	α_2	0.0059 (0.0007)*
Capital (Industry 34)	α_3	0.0048 (0.0021)*
Capital (Industry 35)	α_4	0.0045 (0.0165)
Capital (Industry 36)	α_5	-0.0014 (0.0028)
Capital (Industry 37)	α_6	0.0031 (0.0008)*
Capital (Industry 38)	α_7	0.0025 (0.0006)*
Capital (Industry 39)	α_8	-0.0016 (0.0054)

Note: See Appendix 9.1 for industry codes.
Figures in parenthesis are asymptotic standard errors.
* means that the coefficient is significant at the 5 per cent level of significance.

After solving the DEA problem using all the observations composing the sample, four industries which had an index of unity were deleted and the DEA problems were solved once more on the new sample. The correlation between the indices obtained from the original sample and the reduced sample was 0.87 and the Spearman rank correlation was 0.84. These results were reassuring for the robustness of the indices.

Table 9.6 compares the TFP growth rates of the non-parametric model and the two parametric models to previous studies It can also be seen that the parametric

Table 9.5 Parameter estimates of the stochastic production frontier model 2

Variables	Parameter	Estimates
Constant	a_0	1.438 (0.709)*
Capital share	α	0.72 (0.341)*
Labour share	β	0.26 (0.118)*
Time dummies	δ_t	13 of the 15 dummies were significant
Industry dummies	λ_m	All 8 dummies were significant

Note: Figures in parenthesis are asymptotic standard errors.
* means that the coefficient is significant at the 5 per cent level of significance.

Table 9.6 Comparison of TFP growth rates for the manufacturing sector

	This study			Okamoto (1994)	*Productivity Report 1999*	Tham (1996 and 1997)	World Bank (1989)
	Para. Models 1	2	Non-para. model				
1981–84	-0.82	0.11	0.40				-1.9
1980–89	-1.06		0.44		2.79		
1986–90	-0.57	-0.02	0.35	0.3			
1986–91	-0.63		0.38			0.3	
1986–93	-1.18		0.27			0.1	
1990–96	-1.54	0.01	0.26		1.6		

Note: Para stands for parametric and Non-para stands for non-parametric.

models give fairly different results as they are based on different functional forms. While model 1 shows a deterioration of TFP growth over 1981–84, 1986–90 and 1990–96, model 2's TFP growth rate does not exhibit a clear pattern.

Nevertheless, it can be said that on average, both parametric models show very low TFP growth rates for Malaysia's manufacturing sector. This is also true of the non-parametric model whose TFP growth rates, although positive,[5] show a consistent declining trend over time similar to the parametric model 1. These results not only conform to the findings of Tham (1996, 1997) and the *Productivity Report* 1999 but are also comparable in terms of low TFP figures to

Okamato (1994) and the World Bank (1989) although the latter studies included intermediate materials as one of the inputs.

To further compare the sources of productivity growth, the decompositional analysis is undertaken and tabulated for all three models in Table 9.7. For the non-parametric model, information on output and input growth are not provided as the DEA technique unlike the parametric models only decomposes the Malmquist TFP growth index and not the output growth.

Table 9.7 Sources of output growth and TFP growth in Malaysia's manufacturing sector (%)

	1981–84	1986–90	1990–96
Parametric model 1			
Output growth	1.66	1.69	0.98
Input growth	2.43	2.26	2.52
TFP growth	-0.82	-0.57	-1.54
Technical change	0.25	0.31	0.43
Change in technical efficiency	-1.07	-0.88	-1.97
Parametric model 2			
Output growth	1.66	1.69	0.98
Input growth	1.57	1.71	0.97
TFP growth	0.11	-0.02	0.01
Technical change	0.08	0.13	0.22
Change in technical efficiency	0.03	-0.15	-0.21
Non-parametric model			
Output growth	N.A.	N.A.	N.A.
Input growth	N.A.	N.A.	N.A.
TFP growth	0.40	0.35	0.26
Technical change	0.10	0.18	0.24
Change in technical efficiency	0.30	0.17	0.02

Note: N.A. means not applicable.

It can be seen that similar to previous studies, the parametric models show that output growth is input-driven rather than TFP growth-driven. Also, both the parametric models show positive and increasing technical change but the increasingly negative gains from technical efficiency is overwhelming, resulting in low TFP growth rates. The non-parametric model also showed positive and increasing gains from technical change, but the gains from technical efficiency although positive, declined over time. Thus, the source of some TFP growth as shown by all the models is technical change while technical inefficiency is clearly a major concern causing poor TFP growth. How can this be explained?

First, domestic R&D in Malaysia has barely increased beyond 1 per cent of its GDP. In fact, the government which had originally set an R&D target of 2 per cent of the GDP by 2000 had to reduce this ratio to 1.5 per cent. Lall (2001) notes that the 'R&D gap is a crucial problem for Malaysia' given that the Malaysian industrial and export structure is as 'advanced' as South Korea and Taiwan in the technological spectrum.

On the other hand, while Athukorala and Menon (1999) document the significant flow of FDI into Malaysia, the comprehensive MASTIC (Malaysian Science and Technology Information Centre, 1994) survey shows that multinational companies (MNCs) rather than the local producers or government are leading the industrial research effort in Malaysia.

Thus, the gains from technical change can be attributed to the use of more advanced imported technology brought about by the promotion and significant flow of FDI into Malaysian manufacturing since 1986. Furthermore, Ghani and Suri (1999) explain that the boom in bank lending also made rapid rates of capital accumulation possible. However, technological mastery did not follow the pace of technology adoption as seen by the declining gains in technical efficiency which means that the industries were not able to acquire or use appropriate technical knowledge to ensure maximum output from the use of the advanced technology. This is especially evident with declining technical efficiency from 1981–84 to 1986–90.

The manufacturing operations of the late 1980s were not very different from that of the early 1980s as evidenced by Guyton (1995) and Menon (1998) where FDI was engaged in low-skilled, assembly, inspection and testing activities. Thus with more experience and better knowledge over time, the industries can be expected to enjoy technical efficiency but clearly that did not take place.

This lack in technological mastery is also supported by Lall's (2001) observation that 'Malaysia's educational structure lacks the ability to meet the technical needs of the industry'. He further notes the industries' complaints on the high turnover rates for middle-level employees. This could affect managers' incentive to provide training to improve workers' skills. In fact, the World Bank (1995) reports on the failure of the government's late 1980s Double Deduction Incentive for Training scheme and Lall (1996) comments that the various government schemes simply did not take off, reflecting weakness in their design and delivery and the lack of capability on the part of enterprises.

The launching of the National Action Plan for industrial technology and development in 1990 saw a more serious commitment from the public sector to motivate industrial research and technological upgrading of the small and medium-sized enterprises and aid the development of linkages. Narayanan and Wah (2000) provide a range of references on the series of schemes that have come on stream. It is, however, too early to judge the success of these improved efforts in the schemes.

With FDI, the Malaysian government could benefit greatly in the long term if it is selective in the type of FDI sought. The MNCs should be made to provide substantial training to workers to impart knowledge regarding the use of technology. In fact, Nadiri and Son (1999) show that foreign capital only contributed 0.95 per cent to aggregate Malaysian TFP growth while Mahadevan (2002a) showed negative TFP growth emanating from the FDI that goes into Malaysia's manufacturing. This is further supported by Narayanan and Wah (2000) who find that MNCs have been slow in transferring R&D expertise in the electronics and electrical sector. According to Rasiah (1995), it is important to continue to attract FDI but this should be done at high levels of skill and technical sophistication and it is necessary to raise domestic contributions to production and technological activity so as to provide the supplier and service structure that MNCs need for value added production. There is also little evidence of backward linkage effects as a low level of procurement from MNCs to local firms by way of intermediate products or exploiting outsourcing opportunities is seen to exist (Narayanan and Wah 2000). For instance, the import of intermediate inputs has increased about threefold from 1980 to 1990 and this has more than doubled in 1993 at about RM$90 000 and again in 1996 at a staggering RM$182 000.[6]

The government should also be mindful of the growing pool of foreign unskilled workers from Indonesia and Thailand who serve as cheap labour that discourage the MNCs from the use of better technology. Also, Tham (1997) explains that the increase in the demand for skilled workers has forced wages to increase more rapidly. Thus the government could be more selective in its import of foreign labour by adopting similar policies to Singapore and Hong Kong which have been very successful in attracting highly skilled workers from around the world. Unfortunately, the shortage of skilled workers highlighted by the World Bank (1989) and Lall (2001) remains unsolved. Enrolment rates for tertiary education increased only marginally from less than 2 per cent in 1960 to about 6 per cent in 1992 (Asian Development Bank 1998). Tham (1997) explains that the emergence of 'twinning degree programmes' in the 1990s has helped but has not absorbed the demand for skilled labour. And it has been only since 1996 that the private sector has been allowed to grant university degrees (Cheong and Hew 2000). The liberalization of the education sector to allow foreign institutions to offer educational programmes in Malaysia as well as in collaboration with local bodies is a fairly recent trend which might take some time to bear fruit.[7]

In sum, the decompositional analysis on productivity growth has served to highlight the following. The rising trend of technical change shows that there is still room to gain from the use of advanced technology and this is possible as Malaysia's manufacturing industries are yet to mature given that their operations are currently at the middle level of the technology ladder. This means that there is greater scope for adopting new technology only if Malaysia moves on to higher value added manufacturing activities. Jomo et al. (1999) argue that the current level of technological activity in Malaysia cannot be sustained indefinitely into the future although the technology gap has to some extent been compensated by the MNCs.

Although the limits in the availability of continuously advanced technology may constrain the gains from technical change, Sakellaris and Wilson (2002) along with Greenwood et al. (1997, 2000) show how the underestimation of technical change has undermined the importance of investment-specific inputs embodying technical advance. They suggest an important role for capital investment in spurring productivity growth above and beyond its traditional role of capital deepening.

9.6 CONCLUSION

Although it is comforting that the empirical evidence from the three models broadly conform, the evidence on the relative significance of the various components of output growth is less clear cut. It then appears sensible to say that no one measure of TFP growth from any one model should be taken to represent the 'right' value given the advantages and disadvantages of the approaches to productivity measurement as discussed in Chapter 2. However, as in time series literature, one may consider constructing averages of the growth rates that may be potentially better than any one value from one method. But the applicability of this idea is yet to be investigated and this could possibly involve Monte Carlo experiments (Coelli and Perelman 1999).

Nevertheless, as policy formulation is often the ultimate objective in productivity analysis, the trends in TFP growth should be of greater interest and considered far more reliable than the magnitude of TFP growth per se. Also, as TFP growth measures a whole range of things, it is best to decompose TFP growth appropriately to allow an understanding of the sources of productivity growth for policy implementation. The trends of the sources of productivity growth then pave the path for the important exercise (which is beyond the scope of this chapter) of empirically investigating the significance of various factors before drawing specific policy options to address each of the low efficiency components of the TFP growth measure.

Previous studies on Malaysia often undertook a regression analysis of possible factors influencing TFP growth as a single measure without recognizing that different efficiency components of TFP growth are at play. This would lead to spurious results as policy options intended to improve TFP growth would be badly misdirected given that the concepts of technical change and technical efficiency are analytically different. This is especially important for Malaysia given that technical change and gains from technical efficiency were seen to move in opposite directions.

More specifically, for the Malaysian manufacturing sector, technical change was positive and increasing while gains from technical efficiency declined. Has openness to FDI coupled with an export-oriented strategy led to increases in output growth and, in the event, caused technical change to be excessive, resulting in technical inefficiency? If so, this calls for an evaluation of management practices, training incentives, government policies related to foreign direct investment, and educational and industrial policies. This is not to say that such policies are necessarily misplaced, but more effort is needed in such endeavours to ensure that the policies work hand in hand to maximize TFP growth and minimize any trade-offs in the efficiency components of TFP growth as evidenced above. For instance, capital deepening must be complemented with labour-deepening, as merely accelerating the shift towards higher value added activities without corresponding upward shifts in skill level would not necessarily result in positive TFP growth and even if it did, it would be possible only in the short run and not be sustainable in the long run.

In conclusion, there may be little to quibble over obtaining a so-called accurate or real value of TFP growth measure for Malaysia or for any other economy for that matter, but the concept of TFP is too important to be dismissed lightly. The possibility of the emergence of empirical regularities and/or irregularities as more empirical work is done with different methods on the same data cannot be ruled out completely. At the same time, given the various advancements in TFP measurement techniques, TFP estimation and decomposition should be seen to offer a *T*ruly *F*ruitful *P*ossibility if used and interpreted appropriately.

NOTES

1. This was envisaged by the Malaysian Prime Minister, Dr Mohammed Mahathir, as Vision 2020.
2. Most stochastic frontier models assume that technical efficiency follows a half-normal or truncated normal distribution.
3. The constant returns to scale technology was relaxed in Mahadevan (2002c) which provides details on the technical and scale efficiency results for the Malaysian industries.
4. A special thanks to Dorairaju Suppaiyah of the Statistics Department in Kuala Lumpur who patiently answered my queries and efficiently provided the necessary data.
5. The TFP growth estimates under DEA are likely to be lower than those from the stochastic frontier since any measurement error is considered as technical inefficiency in the DEA approach.
6. These figures were obtained from the annual reports of Bank Negara, Malaysia.
7. While Monash University established a campus in 1998, the University of Nottingham did so in 2000 and currently, there are plans for Curtin University of Technology to establish itself in Sarawak.

APPENDIX 9.1 THE MALAYSIAN MANUFACTURING SECTOR

3-digit industry codes	Manufacturing industries
311–312	Food
313	Beverage
314	Tobacco
321	Textiles
322	Wearing apparel
323	Leather
324	Footwear
331	Wood
332	Furniture and fixtures
341	Paper
342	Printing, publishing
351	Industrial chemicals
352	Other chemicals
353	Petroleum refineries
354	Miscellaneous products of petroleum and coal
355	Rubber
356	Plastic
361	Pottery, china and earthenware
362	Glass
369	Non-metallic mineral
371	Iron and steel
372	Non-ferrous metal
381	Fabricated metal
382	Machinery
383	Electrical machinery
384	Transport equipment
385	Professional and scientific and measuring controlling equipment
390	Other manufacturing

References

Abdullah, M.L. (1999), 'Measurement of Total Factor Productivity of the Service Sector and Sources of Productivity Growth', *Asian Productivity Journal,* Summer: 72–87.

Abramovitz, M. (1956), 'Resource and Output Trends in the US Since 1870', *American Economic Review*, vol. 46, no. 2: 5–23.

— (1962) 'Economic Growth in the United States', *American Economic Review*, vol. 52, no. 4: 762–782.

Afriat, S. (1972), 'Efficiency Estimation of Production Functions', *International Economic Review*, vol. 13, no. 3: 568–598.

Ahn, S.C., Good, D.H. and Sickles, R.C. (2000), 'Estimation of Long-Run Inefficiency Levels: A Dynamic Frontier Approach', *Econometric Reviews*, vol. 19, no.4: 461–492.

Aigner, D.J. and Chu, S.F. (1968), 'On Estimating the Industry Production Function', *American Economic Review*, vol. 58: 826–839.

Aigner, D.J., Lovell, C.A.K. and Schmidt, P. (1977), 'Formulation and Estimation of Stochastic Production Function Models', *Journal of Econometrics*, vol. 6, no. 1: 21–37.

Akamatsu, K. (1962), 'A Historical Pattern of Economic Growth in Developing Countries', *Developing Countries*, vol. 1, no. 1: 3–25.

Alavi, R. (1996), *Industrialisation in Malaysia: Import Substitution and Infant Industry Performance*, Routledge, London and New York.

An, J., Bae, S.K. and Ratti, R. (2001), 'Ownership Restrictions and Economic Performance: The Case of Korean Banks', Paper presented at the Allied Economic Association Conference in Seoul.

Anderson, K. (1987), 'Tariffs and the Manufacturing Sector', in Maddock, R. and McLean, I. (eds) (1987), *The Australian Economy in the Long Run*, Cambridge University Press, Cambridge.

Ark, B.V. (1996), 'Issues on International Comparison of Productivity: Theory and Measurement', in *Industry Productivity: International Comparison and Measurement Issues*, OECD Proceedings, OECD, Paris.

Arrow, K. (1962), 'The Economic Implications of Learning By Doing', *Review of Economic Studies*, vol. 29, no. 3: 155–173.

Asian Development Bank (1998), *Asian Development Outlook*, Oxford University Press, Hong Kong.

— *Key Indicators,* Oxford University Press, New York.

Atella, V. and Quintieri, B. (2001), 'Do R&D Expenditures Really Matter for TFP?', *Applied Economics*, vol. 33, no. 11: 1385–1389.

Athukorala, P. and Chand, S. (2000), 'Trade Orientation and Productivity Gains from International Production: A Study of Overseas Operations of US Multinationals', *Transnational Corporations*, vol. 9, no. 2:1–29.

Athukorala, P. and Menon, J. (1999), 'Outward Orientation and Economic Development in Malaysia', *World Economy*, vol. 22, no. 8: 119–39.

Atkinson, S.E. and Cornwall, C. (1998), 'Estimating Radial Measures of Productivity Growth: Frontier vs Non-Frontier Approaches', *Journal of Productivity Analysis*, vol. 10: 35–46.

Aw, B.Y., Chang, S. and Roberts, M. (2000), 'Productivity and Turnover in the Export Market: Evidence from Taiwan and South Korea', *World Bank Economic Review*, vol. 14, no. 1: 65–90.

Baily, M.D. (1974), *Capital Utilization in Kenya Manufacturing Industry*, Unpublished PhD dissertation, University of Cambridge.

Baily, M.N. and Gordon, R.J. (1988), 'Measurement Issues, the Productivity Slowdown, and the Explosion of Computer Power', *Brookings Papers on Economic Activity 2*: 347–420.

Banker, R.D. (1993), 'Maximum Likelihood, Consistency and Data Envelopment Analysis: A Statistical Foundation', *Management Science*, vol. 39, no. 10: 1265–73.

Battese, G.E. and Coelli, T.J. (1992), 'Frontier Production Functions and Technical Efficiency: A Survey of Empirical Applications in Agricultural Economics', *Agricultural Economics* vol. 7 nos. 3/4: 185–208.

— (1995), 'A Model for Technical Inefficiency Effects in a Stochastic Frontier Production Function and Panel Data', *Empirical Economics*, vol. 20: 325–399.

Bauer, P.W. (1990), 'Recent Developments in the Econometric Estimation of Frontiers', *Journal of Econometrics*, vol. 46, no. 1/2: 39–56.

Berger, S. and Lester, R.K. (1997), *Made by Hong Kong*, Oxford University Press, Hong Kong.

Bernard, A.B. and Jensen, J.B. (1995), 'Exports, Jobs and Ages in U.S. Manufacturing 1976–1987', *Brookings Papers on Economic Activity: Microeconomics*: 67–112.

— (1998), 'Exporting and Productivity', Paper presented at the 1998 Summer Institute, NBER, Cambridge, MA, August.

Berndt, E.R. and Christensen, L.R. (1973), 'The Translog Function and the Substitution of Equipment, Structures, and Labour in US Manufacturing, 1929-68', *Journal of Econometrics*, vol. 1, no. l: 81–113.

Berndt, E.R. and Fuss, M.A. (1986), 'Productivity Measurement with Adjustments for Variations in Capacity Utilization, and Other Forms of Temporary Equilibrium', *Journal of Econometrics*, vol. 33, no. 1/2: 7–30.

Bernolak, I. (1980), 'The Measurement of Output and Capital Inputs' in Bailey, D. and Hubert, T. (eds), *Productivity Measurement*, Gower, London.

Betancourt, R. and Clague, C.K. (1977), 'The Theory of Capital Utilization in Labor-Managed Enterprises', *Quarterly Journal of Economics*, vol. 91, no. 3: 453–67.

Bjurek, H. and Hjalmarsson, L. (1990), 'Deterministic Parametric and Nonparametric Estimation of Efficiency in Service Production', *Journal of Econometrics*, vol. 46: 213–27.

Blejer, M.I. and Sagari, S.B. (1988), 'Sequencing the Liberalization of Financial Markets', *Finance and Development*, vol. 25, no. 1: 18–20.

Bloch, H. and Tang, S.H.K. (1999), 'Technical Change and Total Factor Productivity Growth: A Study of Singapore's Manufacturing Industries', *Applied Economics Letters*, vol. 6: 697–701.

Breusch, T. and Pagan, A.R. (1979), 'A Simple Test for Heteroscedasticity and Random Coefficient Variation', *Econometrica*, vol. 47: 1287–94.

Broeck, J.V.D., Koop, G., Osiewalski, J. and Steel, M.F.J. (1994), 'Stochastic Frontier Models: A Bayesian Perspective', Journal of Econometrics, vol. 61: 273–303.

Brown, M. (1968), *On the Theory and Measurement of Technological Change*, Cambridge University Press, Cambridge.

Bumgarner, M. and Prime, P.B. (2000), 'Capital Mobility and Investor Confidence: The Case of Hong Kong's Reversion to China's Sovereignty', *Pacific Economic Review*, vol. 5, no. 2: 263–78.

Burgess, J.F. and Wilson, P.W. (1993), 'Technical Efficiency in Veterans Administration Hospitals', in Fried, H.O., Lovell, C.A.K and Schmidt, S.S. (eds), *The Measurement of Productive Efficiency*, Oxford University Press, New York.

Campbell, C. (1984), 'Correlates of Residual Growth in New Zealand Manufacturing Industries, 1952–73', Paper presented to the Economics Section ANZAAS, Canberra.

Cao, Y. (1995), 'Assessing Technical Efficiency of Manufacturing Industries in a Small Open Economy: Singapore', Working Paper Series 23–95, Nanyang Business School, Nanyang Technological University, Singapore.

Cargill, T. (1999), 'The Political Economy of Financial Liberalization in Korea: Lessons from Japan and the United States', *Economic Papers* (Bank of Korea), vol.1, no. 2: 219– 41.

Caves, R.E. (ed.) (1992), *Industrial Efficiency in Six Nations*, MIT Press, Cambridge.

Caves, R.E. and Barton, D.R. (1990), *Efficiency in US Manufacturing Industries,* MIT Press, Cambridge, MA.

Caves, R.E., Christensen, L.R. and W.E. Diewert (1982), 'The Economic Theory of Index Numbers and the Measurement of Input, Output and Productivity', *Econometrica*, vol. 50, no. 6: 1393–1414.

Caves, R.E., Christensen, L.R., Tretheway, M.W. and Windle, R.J. (1987), 'An Assessment of the Efficiency Effects of the US Airline Deregulation via an International Comparison', in Bailey, E.E. (ed.), *Public Regulation: New Perspectives on Institutions and Policies,* MIT Press, Cambridge.

Chamberlain, G. (1980), 'Analysis of Covariance With Qualitative Data', *Review of Economic Studies*, vol. 47: 225–38.

Chan, S.K. (1996), 'Value-Added Productivity: A Hong Kong Example', *APO Productivity Journal*, Asian Productivity Organisation, Tokyo.

Chand, S. (1999), 'Trade Liberalization and Productivity Growth: Time Series Evidence from Australian Manufacturing', *Economic Record*, vol. 75, no. 228: 28–36.

— (2001), 'How Misaligned is the Australian Real Exchange Rate?', Paper presented at the Research School of Pacific and Asian Studies, Australian National University.

Charnes, A., Cooper, W.W., Lewin, A.Y. and Seiford, L.M. (eds.) (1994), *Data Envelopment Analysis: Theory, Methodology and Applications*, Kluwer Academic Publishers, Boston.

Charnes, A., Cooper, W.W. and Rhodes, E., (1978), 'Measuring the Efficiency of Decision Making Units', *Journal of Operational Research*, vol. 2: 429–44.

Chen, E.K.Y. (1977), 'Factor Inputs, Total Factor Productivity, and Economic Growth: The Asian Case', *Developing Economies*, vol. 15, no. 2: 121–43.

— (1997), 'The Total Factor Productivity Growth Debate: Determinants of Economic Growth in East Asia', *Asia Pacific Economic Literature*, vol. 11, no. 1: 18–38.

Cheong, O.H. and Hew, Wei-Yen (2000), 'Malaysia', in *Productivity Growth and Industrial Structure in the Pacific Region*, Japan Committee for Pacific Economic Outlook and Pacific Economic Cooperation Council.

Cho, Y.J. (1986), 'Inefficiencies from Financial Liberalization in the Absence of Well-Functioning Equity Markets', *Journal of Money, Credit, and Banking*, vol. 18, no. 2: 191–9.

Chowdhury, A. and Islam, I. (1993), *The Newly Industrialising Economies of East Asia*, Routledge, London.

Clark, C., Geer, T. and Underhill, B., (1996), *The Changing of Australian Manufacturing*, Staff Information Paper, Industry Commission, Australia.

Coe, D.T. and Helpman, E. (1995), 'International R&D Spillovers', *European Economic Review*, vol. 39: 859–88.

Coelli, T. (1995), 'Estimators and Hypothesis Tests for a Stochastic Frontier Function: A Monte Carlo Analysis', *Journal of Productivity Analysis Economic Studies*, vol. 6: 247–68.

— (1996a), 'A Guide to FRONTIER Version 4.1: A Computer Program for Frontier Production Function Estimation', Centre for Efficiency and Productivity Analysis Working Paper 96/07, Department of Econometrics, University of New England, Armidale.

— (1996b), 'A Guide to DEAP Version 2.1: A Data Envelopment Analysis (Computer) Program', Centre for Efficiency and Productivity Analysis Working Paper 96/08, Department of Econometrics, University of New England, Armidale.

Coelli, T. and Perelman, S. (1999), 'A Comparison of Parametric and Non-parametric Distance Functions: With Application to European Railways', *European Journal of Operations Research*, vol. 117: 326–39.

Coelli, T. and Rao, P. (2001), 'Implicit Value Shares in Malmquist TFP Index Numbers', Centre for Efficiency and Productivity Analysis Working Paper 4/2001, School of Economics, University of New England, Armidale.

Collins, S.M. and Bosworth, B.P. (1996), 'Economic Growth in East Asia: Accumulation versus Assimilation', *Brookings Papers on Economic Activity 2*: 135–203.

Condon, T., Corbo, V. and De Melo, J. (1985), 'Productivity Growth, External Shocks and Capital Inflow in Chile 1977–81: A General Equilibrium Analysis', *Journal of Policy Modeling* vol. 7, no. 3: 329–406.

Cooper, W.W., L.M. Seiford and K. Tone (1999), *Data Envelopment Analysis: A Comprehensive Text with Models, Applications, References, and DEA-Solver Software*, Kluwer Academic Publishers, Boston.

Cornwell, C., Schmidt, P. and Sickles, R.C. (1990), 'Production Frontiers With Cross-Sectional and Time-Series Variation in Efficiency Levels', *Journal of Econometrics*, vol. 46: 185–200.

Creamer, D. (1972), 'Measuring Capital Input for Total Factor Productivity Analysis: Comments by a Sometime Estimator', *Review of Income and Wealth*, vol. 18, no. 1: 55–78.

Deardorff, A.V. (1994), 'Growth and International Investment with Diverging Populations', *Oxford Economic Papers*, vol. 46: 477–91.

Debreu, G. (1951), 'The Coefficient of Resource Utilization', *Econometrica*, vol. 19, no. 3: 273–92.

Dension, E.W. (1962), *The Sources of Economic Growth in the United States and the Alternatives Before Us*, Supplementary Paper No. 13, Committee for Economic Development, New York.

— (1972a), 'Some Major Issues in Productivity Analysis: An Examination of Estimates by Jorgenson and Griliches', *Survey of Current Business*, vol. 52, no. 5: 37–64.

— (1972b), 'Final Comments', *Survey of Current Business*, vol. 52, no. 5: 95–110.

Department of Statistics, Singapore, Census of Services, 1994.

— *Economic Survey Series: Wholesale and Retail, Hotels and Catering, and Transport and Communication, Financial and Business*, various issues.

— *Report on the Survey of Services, 1974–1989.*

— *Singapore Yearbook of Statistics.*

— *Singapore, The Service Sector 1990–1993.*

— *Singapore National Accounts 1987.*

— *Singapore Report on the Census of Industrial Production*, annual issues until 1986.

— (1997) 'Multifactor Productivity Growth in Singapore: Concept, Methodology and Trends', Occasional Paper Series.

Deprins, D., Simar, L. and Tulkens, H. (1984), 'Measuring Labour Efficiency in Post Services', in Marchand, M., Pestieau, P. and Tulkens, H. (eds) *The Performance of Public Enterprises, Concepts and Measurements*, North Holland, Amsterdam.

Diewert, E. (2000), 'The Challenge of Total Factor Productivity Measurement', *International Productivity Monitor*, no. 1: 45–52.

Diewert, E. and Nakamura, A.O. (1993), *Essays in Index Number Theory Volume 1*, North Holland, Amsterdam.

Diokno, B. (1974), 'Capacity Utilization in Government 'Favoured' Export-Oriented Firms', *Philippine Economic Journal*, vol. 13, no. 2: 149–88.

Dixon, P.B. and MacDonald, D. (1991), 'Labor Productivity in Australia', in Adams, P.D., Dixon, P.B. and Parmenter, B.R. (eds), *Sources and Effects of Productivity Growth*, Canberra: Economic Planning Advisory Council, Background Paper No. 29.

Dodsworth, J. and Mihaljek, D. (1997), *Hong Kong, China Growth, Structural Change and Economic Stability During the Transition*, IMF Occasional Paper 152.

Dollar, D. (1986), 'Technological Innovation, Capital Mobility, and the Product Cycle in North–South Trade', *American Economic Review*, vol. 76, no. 1: 177–90.

— (1992), 'Outward-Oriented Developing Economies Really Do Grow More Rapidly: Evidence from 95 LDCs, 1976–1985', *Economic Development and Cultural Change*, vol. 40, no. 3: 523–44.

Domar, E.D. (1961), 'On the Measurement of Technological Change', *Economic Journal*, vol. 71: 709–29.

Dowrick, S. (1994), 'Openness and Growth', in *Proceedings of Conference of Reserve Bank of Australia*, Reserve Bank of Australia: 10–41.

Drake, L. (2001), 'Efficiency and Productivity Change in UK Banking', *Applied Financial Economics*, vol. 11, no. 5: 557–71.

Drysdale, P. and Huang, Y. (1997), 'Technological Catch-up and Economic Growth in East Asia and the Pacific', *Economic Record*, vol. 73, no. 222: 201–11.

Dunning, J.H. (1988), *Multinationals, Technology and Competitiveness*, Allen & Unwin, London.

Economic Development Board of Singapore, *Report on the Census of Industrial Production*, Annual Issues since 1987.

Economic Planning Unit (1996), *The South Malaysian Plan 1996–2000*, Prime Minister's Department, Kuala Lumpur, National Printing.

Edwards, S. (1998), 'Openness, Productivity and Growth: What Do We Really Know?', *Economic Journal*, vol. 108: 383–98.

Eleto, O. and Koves, P. (1964), 'On a Problem of Index Number Computation Relating to International Comparison', *Statisztikai Szemle*, vol. 42: 507–18.

Enright, M.J., Scott, E.E. and Dodwell, D. (1997), *The Hong Kong Advantage*, Oxford University Press, Hong Kong.

Esposito, F.F. and Esposito, L. (1974), 'Excess Capacity and Market Structure', *Review of Economics and Statistics*, vol. 56, no. 2: 188–94.

Euh, Y.D. and Baker, J.C. (1990), *The Korean Banking System and Foreign Influence*, Routledge, London and New York.

Färe, R. (1988), *Fundamentals of Production Theory: Lecture Notes in Economics, and Mathematical Systems*, Springer-Verlag, Heidelberg.

Färe, R. and Grosskopf, S. (1996), *Intertemporal Production Frontiers: With Dynamic DEA*, Kluwer Academic Publishers, Boston, MA.

— (1997), 'Efficiency and Productivity in Rich and Poor Countries', in Jensen, B.S. and Wong, K.Y. (eds) *Dynamics, Economic Growth, and International Trade*, University of Michigan Press, Ann Arbor, MI.

Färe, R. Grosskopf, S., Lovell, C.A.K. and Yaisawarng, S. (1993), 'Derivation of Shadow Prices for Undesirable Outputs: A Distance Function Approach', *Review of Economics and Statistics*, vol. 75, no. 2: 374–80.

Färe, R., Grosskopf, S. and M. Norris (1997), 'Productivity Growth, Technical Progress, and Efficiency Changes in Industrialized Countries: Reply', *American Economic Review*, vol. 87, no. 5: 1040–43.

Färe, R., Grosskopf, S., Norris, M. and Zhang, Z. (1994), 'Productivity Growth, Technical Progress, and Efficiency Changes in Industrialised Countries', *American Economic Review*, vol. 84: 66–83.

Farrell, M.J. (1957), 'The Measurement of Productive Efficiency', *Journal of Royal Statistical Society A,* 120: 253–81.

Felipe, J. (1999), 'Total Factor Productivity Growth in East Asia: A Critical Survey', *Journal of Development Studies*, vol. 35, no. 4: 1–41.

Felipe, J. and McCombie, J.S.L. (2003), 'Methodological Problems with the Neoclassical Analysis of the East Asian Miracle', *Cambridge Journal of Economics,* vol. 27, no. 5: 695-721.

Ferrier, G.D. and C.A.K. Lovell (1990), 'Measuring Cost Efficiency in Banking: Econometric and Linear Programming Evidence', *Journal of Econometrics*, vol. 46, no. 1/2: 229–45.

Fisher, F.M. (1965), 'Embodied Technical Change and the Existence of an Aggregate Capital Stock', *Review of Economic Studies*, vol. 32, no. 4: 263–88.

Fraumeni, B.M. and Jorgenson, D.W. (1981), 'Capital Formation and US Productivity Growth, 1948–1976', in Dogramaci, A. (ed.), *Productivity Analysis: A Range of Perspectives*, Martinus Nijhoff Publishers, Boston, MA.

Freedman, C. and Stonecash, R. (1997), 'A Survey of Manufacturing Industry Policy: From the Tariff Board to the Productivity Commission', *Economic Record*, vol. 73, no. 221: 169–83.

Fried, H.O., Lovell, C.A.K. and Schmidt, S.S. (eds) (1993), *The Measurement of Productive Efficiency: Techniques and Applications*, Oxford University Press, New York.

Fry, M.J., (1990), 'Current Macroeconomic Policy Issues in Taiwan', *Tamkang Chair Lectures Series*, vol. 80, Taipei.

Fukuyama, H. (1993), 'Technical and Scale Efficiency in Japanese Commercial Banks: A Non-Parametric Approach', *Applied Economics*, vol. 25, no. 8: 1101–1112.

Fuss, M. and McFadden, D. (1978), *Production Economics: A Dual Approach to Theory and Applications Volume 1*, North-Holland, Amsterdam.

Gan, W.B. and Soon, Y.L (1996), 'Input vs Productivity Driven Growth', Paper presented at the 7th Malaysian Plan National Convention, Kuala Lumpur.

Gapinski, J.H. and Western, D.L. (1999), 'A Tiger in the Land of Panda: Growth Prospects for Hong Kong under Reversion to China', in Fu, T.T., Huang, C.J. and Lovell, C.A.K. *Economic Efficiency and Productivity Growth in the Asia-Pacific Region*, Edward Elgar, Cheltenham.

Ghani, E. and Suri, V. (1999), 'Productivity Growth, Capital Accumulation and the Banking Sector: Some Lessons from Malaysia', *World Bank Policy Research Working Paper* 2252.

Gilbert, A. and P.W. Wilson (1998), 'Effects of Deregulation on the Productivity of Korean Banks', *Journal of Economics and Business*, vol. 50, no. 2: 133–55.

Goh, K.S. and Low, L. (1996), 'Beyond "Miracles" and Total Factor Productivity', *ASEAN Economic Bulletin*, vol. 13, no. 1:1–13.

Goldar, B. and Renganathan, V.S. (1989), 'Capacity Utilization in Indian Industries', *Indian Economic Journal*, vol. 39: 82–92.

Goldschmid, H., Mann, M. and Weston, J.F. (1974), *Industrial Concentration: The New Learning*, Little Brown, Boston, MA.

Gong, B.H. and Sickles, R.C. (1992), 'Finite Sample Evidence on the Performance of Stochastic Frontiers and Data Envelopment Analysis Using Panel Data', *Journal of Econometrics*, vol. 51: 259–84.

Gordon, R. J. (1990), *The Measurement of Durable Goods Prices*, University of Chicago Press, Chicago, IL.

Greene, W.H. (1990), 'A Gamma-Distributed Stochastic Frontier Model', *Journal of Econometrics*, vol. 46, no. 1/2: 141–64.

Greenwood, J., Hercowitz, Z. and Krusell, P. (1997), 'Long-Run Implications of Investment-Specific Technological Change', *American Economic Review*, vol. 87, no. 3: 342–62.

— (2000), 'The Role of Investment-Specific Technological Change in the Business Cycles', *European Economic Review*, vol. 44, no. 2: 91–115.

Gregory, R.G. and James, D.W. (1973), 'Do New Factories Embody Best Practice Technology?', *Economic Journal*, vol. 83: 1133–55.

Gretton, P. and Fisher, B. (1997), *Productivity Growth and Australian Manufacturing Industry*, Staff Research Paper, AGPS, Canberra.

Griffiths, W.E. (1972), 'Estimation of Actual Response Coefficients in the Hildredth-Houck Random Coefficient Model', *Journal of The American Statistical Association*, vol. 67: 633–35.

Griliches, Z. and Jorgenson, J. (1966), 'Sources of Measured Productivity Change: Capital Input', *American Economic Review*, vol. 56, no. 2: 50–61.

— (1988), *Education and Productivity*, Basil Blackwell, Oxford.

— (ed.) (1992), *Output Measurement in the Service Sectors*, National Bureau of Economic Research, Conference on Research in Income and Wealth, University of Chicago Press, Chicago, IL.

Griliches, Z. and Mairesse, J. (1997), *Production Functions: The Search for Identification*, NBER Working Paper No. 5067.

Griliches, Z. and Regev, H. (1995), 'Firm Productivity in Israeli Industry 1979–88', *Journal of Econometrics*, vol. 65, no. 1: 175–204.

Grosskopf, S. (1993), 'Efficiency and Productivity', in Fried, H.O., Lovell, C.A.K., and Schmidt, S.S. (eds) (1993), *The Measurement of Productive Efficiency: Techniques and Applications*, Oxford University Press, New York.

— (1996), 'Statistical Inference and Nonparametric Efficiency: A Selective Survey', *Journal of Productivity Analysis*, vol. 7: 161–76.

Grossman, G.M. and Helpman, E. (1991), *Trade Innovation and Growth in the Global Economy*, MIT Press, Cambridge, MA.

Gunst, R.F. and Mason, R.L. (1980), *Regression Analysis and Its Applications*, Marcel Dekker, New York.

Guyton, L.E. (1995), 'Japanese FDI and Transfer of Japanese Consumer Electronics Production to Malaysia', *Journal of Far Eastern Business*, vol. 1, no. 4: 63–97.

Hamilton, C. (1989), 'The Irrelevance of Economic Liberalization in the Third World', *World Development* vol. 17, no. 10: 1523–30.

Harrison, A. (1996), 'Openness and Growth: Time Series, Cross-Country Analysis of Developing Countries', *Journal of Development Economics*, vol. 48: 419–47.

Havrylyshyn, O. (1990), 'Trade Policy and Productivity Gains in Developing Countries: A Survey of the Literature', *World Bank Research Observer*, vol. 5, no. 1: 53–73.

— (1991), 'Liberalising Foreign Trade: Yugoslavia' in Papageorgiou, D., Michaely, M. and Choksi, A.M. (eds), *Liberalising Foreign Trade Volume 3: The Experience of Israel and Yugoslavia*, Blackwell Publishers, Oxford.

Hausman, J.A. and Taylor, W.E. (1981), 'Panel Data and Unobservable Individual Effects', *Econometrica*, vol. 49: 1377– 99.

Hicks, J.R. (1981), *Wealth and Welfare: Collected Essays in Econometric Theory*, Harvard University Press, Cambridge, MA.

Hildredth, C. and Houck, J.K. (1968), 'Some Estimators for Linear Model with Random Coefficients', *Journal of The American Statistical Association*, vol. 63: 764–68.

Hoon, L.S. and Muhamad, A.W. (1996), 'Sustaining Productivity-Driven Growth in Malaysia', *Asian Productivity Journal,* Summer: 38–57.

Hsieh, C.T. (1997), 'What Explains the Industrial Revolution in East Asia? Evidence from Factor Markets', (Mimeo) Princeton University Discussion Papers no. 196.

Huang, C.J. and Liu, T. (1994), 'Estimation of a Non-Neutral Stochastic Frontier Production Function', *Journal of Productivity Analysis*, vol. 5: 171–80.

Hulten, C.R. (1992), 'Growth Accounting When Technical Change is Embodied in Capital', *American Economic Review,* vol. 82, no. 4: 964–80.

— (2001) 'Total Factor Productivity: A Short Biography', *NBER Working Paper* No.7471.

Hulten, C.R. and Wykoff, F.C. (1981), 'The Measurement of Economic Depreciation', in Hulten, C.R. (ed.) *Depreciation, Inflation and the Taxation of Income, Capital*, Urbana University Press, Washington, DC.

Hunter, A., (ed) (1965), *The Economics of Australian Industry*, Cambridge University Press, London.

Industry Commission (1995), 'Australian Manufacturing Industry and International Trade Date 1968–69 to 1992–93', Information Paper, AGPS, Canberra.

Islam, R. (1978), 'Reasons for Idle Capital: The Case of Bangladesh Manufacturing', *Bangladesh Development Studies*, vol. 6, no. 1: 27–54.

Jayanthakumaran, K. (1999), 'Trade Reforms and Manufacturing Performance', Paper presented at the Pacific Rim Allied Economic Organizations Conference held in Sydney, Australia.

Jomo, K.M., Felkar, G. and Rasiah, R. (eds) (1999) *Industrial Technology Development in Malaysia: Industry and Firm Studies*, Routledge, London.

Jondrow, J., Lovell, C.A.K., Materove, I.S. and Schmidt, P. (1982), 'On the Estimation of Technical Inefficiency in the Stochastic Frontier Production Model', *Journal of Econometrics*, vol. 19: 233–8.

Jorgenson, D.W. (1966), 'The Embodiment Hypothesis', *Journal of Political Economy*, vol. 74, no. 1: 1–17.

Jorgenson, D.W. and Fraumeni, B. (1989), 'The Accumulation of Human and Nonhuman Capital 1948–84', in Lipsey, R.E. and Tice, H.S., *The Measurement of Savings, Investment, and Wealth*, University of Chicago Press, Chicago.

Jorgenson, D.W., Gollop, F. and Fraumeni, B. (1987), *Productivity and the U.S. Economic Growth*, North Holland, Amsterdam.

Jorgenson, D.W. and Griliches, Z. (1967), 'The Explanation of Productivity Change', *Review of Economic Studies*, vol. 34: 349–83.

— (1972a), 'Issues in Growth Accounting: A Reply to Edward F. Denison', *Survey of Current Business*, vol. 52, no. 5: 65–94.

— (1972b), 'Final Reply', *Survey of Current Business*, vol. 52, no. 5: 95-110.

Jorgenson, D.W. and Yun, K.Y. (1990), *Tax Policy and the Cost of Capital*, Oxford University Press, New York.
Kaldor, N. (1957), 'A Model of Economic Growth', *Economic Journal*, vol. 67: 591–624.
Kalirajan, K.P. and Flinn, C.J. (1983), 'The Measurement of Farm-Specific Technical Efficiency', *Pakistan Journal of Applied Economics*, vol. 2: 67–180.
Kalirajan, K.P. and Shand, R. (1985), 'Types of Education and Agricultural Productivity: A Quantitative Analysis of Tamil Nadu Rice Farming', *Journal of Development Studies*, vol. 21: 222–43.
— (1994), *Economics in Disequilibrium: An Approach from the Frontier*, Macmillan, New Delhi, India.
Karmel, P.H. and Brunt, M. (1966), *The Structure of the Australian Economy*, F.W. Cheshire, Melbourne.
Kawai, H. (1994), 'International Comparative Analysis of Economic Growth: Trade Liberalization and Productivity', *Developing Economies*, vol. 32, no. 4: 373–97.
Kendrick, J.W. (1991), 'An Overview', in *Technology and Productivity: The Challenge for Economic Policy*, OECD, Paris.
Kennedy, C. and Thirlwall, A.P. (1972), 'Surveys in Applied Economics: Technical Progress', *Economic Journal*, vol. 82, no. 1: 11–72.
Kholdy, S. (1997), 'Causality between Foreign Investment and Spillover Efficiency', *Applied Economics*, vol. 27, no. 8: 745–9.
Kim, J. and Lau, L. (1994), 'The Sources of Economic Growth of the East Asian Newly Industrialised Countries', *Journal of Japanese and International Economy*, vol. 8, no. 3: 235–71.
Kim, Y. and Schmidt, P. (2000), 'A Review and Empirical Comparison of Bayesian and Classical Approaches to Inference on Efficiency Levels in Stochastic Frontier Models with Panel Data', *Journal of Productivity Analysis*, vol. 14: 91–118.
Klotz, B., Madoo, R. and Hanson, R. (1980), 'A Study of High Low Labour Productivity Establishments in Manufacturing', in Kendrick, J.W. and Vaccara B.N. (eds), *New Developments in Productivity Measurement and Analysis*, University of Chicago Press, Chicago, IL.
Kodde D.A. and Palm, F.C. (1986), 'Wald Criteria for Jointly Testing Equality and Inequality Restrictions', *Econometrica*, vol. 54: 1243–8.
Koop, G. (2001), 'Cross-Sectoral Patterns of Efficiency and Technical Change in Manufacturing', *International Economic Review*, vol. 42, no. 1: 73–103.
Koop, G., Osiewalski, J. and Steel, M. (1999), 'The Components of Output Growth: A Stochastic Frontier Analysis', *Oxford Bulletin of Economics and Statistics*, vol. 61, no. 4: 455–87.

— (2000), 'Modeling the Sources of Output Growth in a Panel of Countries', *Journal of Business and Economics Statistics*, vol. 18, no. 3: 284–99.

Koopmans, T.C. (1951), *Activity Analysis of Production and Allocation*, Cowles Commission for Research in Economics, Monograph No. 13, Wiley, New York.

Kopp, R.J. and Smith, V.K. (1980), 'Frontier Production Function Estimates for Steam Electric Generation: A Comparative Analysis', *Southern Economic Journal*, vol. 46, no. 4: 1049–59.

Krugman, P. (1979), 'A Model of Innovation, Technology Transfer, and the World Distribution Income', *Journal of Political Economy,* vol. 87, no. 2 : 235–66.

— (1990a), *The Age of Diminished Expectation*, MIT Press, Cambridge, MA.

— (1990b), *Rethinking International Trade*, Cambridge, MIT Press, Cambridge, and London.

— (1994), 'The Myth of Asia's Miracle', *Foreign Affairs*, vol. 73 no. 6: 62–78.

Kumbhakar, S.C. (1987), 'The Specification of Technical and Allocative Inefficiency in Stochastic Production and Profit Frontiers', *Journal of Econometrics*, vol. 34, no. 3: 335–48.

— (1990), 'Production Frontiers, Panel Data and Time Varying Technical Inefficiency', *Journal of Econometrics*, vol. 46: 201–11.

Kumbhakar, S.C., Gosh, S.C. and McGuckin, J.T. (1991), 'A Generalised Production Frontier Approach for Estimating Determinants of Inefficiency in US Dairy Farms', *Journal of Business and Economic Statistics,* vol. 9, no. 3: 279–86.

Kumbhakar, S.C., Heshmati, A. and Hjalmarsson, L. (1999), 'Parametric Approaches to Productivity Measurement: A Comparison Among Alternative Models', *Scandinavian Journal of Economics*, vol. 101, no. 3: 405–24.

Kumbhakar, S.C. and Lovell, C.A.K. (2000), *Stochastic Frontier Analysis*, Cambridge University Press, New York.

Kwong, K.S., (2000), 'Sectoral Decomposition of TFP Growth: The Case of Hong Kong', Paper presented at the East Asian Economic Association Conference, Singapore.

Kwong, K.S., Lau, L.J. and Lin, T.B. (2000), 'The Impact of Relocation on the Total Factor Productivity of Hong Kong Manufacturing', *Pacific Economic Review*, vol. 5, no. 2: 171–91.

Lall, S., (1996), *Learning from the Asian Tigers: Studies in Technology and Industrial Policy*, St Martin's Press, New York.

— (2001), *Competitiveness, Technology and Skills*, Edward Elgar, Cheltenham.

Land, K.C., Lovell, C.A.K. and Thore, S. (1993), 'Chance-Constrained Data Envelopment Analysis', *Managerial and Decision Economics*, vol. 14: 541–54.

Lecraw, D. (1978), 'Determinants of Capacity Utilization by Firms in Less Developed Countries', *Journal of Development Economics*, vol. 5, no. 2: 139–53.

Lee, C.H., Lee, Keun and Lee, Kangkoo (2000), 'Chaebol, Financial Liberalization and Economic Crisis: Transformation of Quasi-Internal Organization in Korea', Working Paper, Seoul National University.

Lee, C.Y. and Lee, Y.S. (2001), 'On the Estimation of the Productivity of Korean Commercial Banks', *Economic Papers* (The Bank of Korea), vol. 4: 40–67.

Lee, Y.H. and Schmidt, P. (1993), 'A Production Frontier with Flexible Temporal Variation in Technical Inefficiency', in Fried et al. (eds), *The Measurement of Productive Efficiency: Techniques and Applications*, Oxford University Press, New York: 237–55.

Leibenstein, H. (1966), 'Allocative Efficiency vs X-Inefficiency', *American Economic Review*, vol. 56: 392–415.

Leibenstein, H. and Maital, S. (1992), 'Empirical Estimation and Partitioning of X-Inefficiency: A Data-Envelopment Approach', *American Economic Review*, vol. 82, no. 2: 428–33.

Leightner, J.E. and C.A.K. Lovell (1998), 'The Impact of Financial Liberalization on the Performance of Thai Banks', *Journal of Economics and Business*, vol. 50, no. 2: 115–32.

Leung, H.M. (1997), 'Total Factor Productivity Growth in Singapore's Manufacturing Industries', *Applied Economics Letters*, vol. 4, no. 8: 525–8.

— (1998), 'Productivity of Singapore's Manufacturing Sector: An Industry Level Non-Parametric Study', *Asia Pacific Journal of Management*, vol. 15, no. 1: 19–31.

Levitan, S.A. (1985), 'Services and Long-Term Structural Change', *Economic Impact* no. 52: 29–32.

Lewis, P. and J. Taylor (2001), 'The Effects of International Trade and Human Capital Development on Total Factor Productivity and Economic Growth in Malaysia', Paper presented at the Conference for Economists in Perth, September.

Li, S.X. (1998), 'Stochastic Models and Variable returns to Scales in Data Envelopment Analysis', *European Journal of Operational Research*, vol. 104: 523–48.

Lim, D. (1981), 'Malaysia: Country Study', in Bautista, R., Hughes, H., Lim, D., Morawetz, D. and F.E. Thoumi (eds), *Capital Utilization in Manufacturing*, Oxford University Press, New York.

Lucas, R.E., Jr (1988), 'On the Mechanics of Economic Development', *Journal of Monetary Economics*, vol. 22, no. 1: 3–42.

Mahadevan, R. (2002a), 'What Is and Is Not Measured by the Total Factor Productivity Growth Studies in Malaysia?', *Malaysian Journal of Economic Studies*, vol. 39, no. 1 (forthcoming).

— (2002b), 'The Tale of Two Cities Revisited: Total Factor Productivity Growth in the Manufacturing Sector of Hong Kong and Singapore' (Mimeo).

— (2002c), 'A DEA Approach to Understanding the Productivity Growth of Malaysia's Manufacturing Industries', *Asia Pacific Journal of Management,* vol. 19, no. 4: 587-600.

Mahadevan, R. and Kalirajan, K.P. (1999), 'On Measuring Total Factor Productivity Growth in Singapore's Manufacturing Industries', *Applied Economics Letters*, vol. 6: 295–8.

— (2000), 'Singapore's Manufacturing Sector's TFP Growth: A Decomposition Analysis', *Journal of Comparative Economics*, vol. 28: 828–39.

Maisom, A. and Arshad, M. (1992), 'Patterns of Total Factor Productivity Growth in Malaysian Manufacturing Industries 1973–1989,' Paper presented at the HIID-ISIS Seminar, Kuala Lumpur, Institute of Strategic and International Studies, Malaysia.

Maison, A., Mohd, A.H. and Nor Aini, Amdzah (1994), 'Productivity and Efficiency in Malaysian Manufacturing Sector: A Time Series Analysis', in Semundram, M. and Yap, M. (eds), *Proceedings of the First Malaysian Econometric Conference*, Malaysian Institute of Economic Research, Kuala Lumpur.

Malaysian Science and Technology Information Centre (1994), *1992 National Survey of Research and Development,* Kuala Lumpur: Ministry of Science, Technology and Environment.

Malmquist, S. (1953), 'Index Numbers and Indifference Curves', *Trabajos de Estatistica*, vol. 4, no. 1: 209–42.

Marschak, J. and Andrew, W. (1944), 'Random Simultaneous Equations and the Theory of Production', *Econometrica*, vol. 12, no. 3/4: 143–205.

Mayes, D., Harris, C. and Lansbury, M. (1994), *Inefficiency In Industry*, Harvester Wheatsheaf, London.

Maynes, G., Brooks, R. and Davidson, S. (1997), 'Education, Human Capital Accumulation, and Economic Growth: The Singapore Experience 1974–96', Paper presented at the International Australia–Singapore Forum held at the University of Western Sydney, MacArthur.

Meeusen, W., and J. Van Den Broeck (1977), 'Efficiency Estimations from Cobb Douglas Production Functions With Composed Error', *International Economic Review*, vol. 18, no. 2: 435–44.

Menon, J. (1998), 'Total Factor Productivity Growth in Foreign and Domestic Firms in Malaysian Manufacturing', *Journal of Asian Economics*, vol. 9, no. 2: 251–80.

Merhav, M. (1970), 'Excess Capacity-Measurement, Causes and Uses: A Case Study of Industry in Israel', *Industrialization and Productivity Bulletin*, vol. 15, United Nations International Development Organisation, New York.

Millan, P. (1975), 'The Intensive Use of Capital in Industrial Plants: Multiple Shifts as an Economic Option', Ph. D dissertation, Harvard University.

Miller, S.M. and A.G. Noulas (1996), 'The Technical Efficiency of Large Bank Production', *Journal of Banking and Finance*, vol. 20, no. 3: 495–509.

Moran, C. (1987), 'Aggregate Production Functions, Technical Efficiency, and Trade Orientation in Developing Countries', World Bank Working Paper 1987-3, International Economic Analysis and Prospects Division, International Economics Department, Washington, DC.

Morawetz, D. (1981), 'Israel: Country Study', in Bautista, R. et al., (eds), *Capital Utilization in Manufacturing,* Oxford University Press, New York.

Morrison, C.J. (1986), 'Productivity Measurement with Non-Static Expectations and Varying Capacity Utilization: An Integrated Approach', *Journal of Econometrics*, vol. 33, no. 1/2: 51–74.

Mundlak, Y. (1978), 'On the Pooling of Time-Series and Cross-Section Data', *Econometrica*, vol. 4, no. 1: 69–86.

Nadiri, M.I., (1972), 'International Studies of Factor Inputs and Total Factor Productivity: a Brief Survey', *Review of Income and Wealth*, vol. 18, no. 2: 129–54.

Nadiri, M.I. and Son, W. (1999), 'Sources of Growth in East Asian Economies', in Fu, T.T., Huang, C.J. and Lovell, C.A.K. (1999), *Economic Efficiency and Productivity Growth in the Asia-Pacific Region,* Edward Elgar, Cheltenham.

Narasimham, G.V.L., Swamy, P.A.V.B. and Reed, R.C. (1988), 'Productivity Analysis of US Manufacturing Using a Stochastic-Coefficient Production Function', *Journal of Business and Economic Statistics*, vol. 6, no. 3: 339–49.

Narayanan, S. and Wah, L.Y. (2000), 'Technological Maturity and Development Without Research: The Challenge for Malaysian Manufacturing', *Development and Change*, vol. 31, no. 2: 435–57.

Nataf, André (1948), 'Sur La Possibilité de Construction de Certains Macromodéles', *Econometrica*, vol. 16, no. 3: 232–44.

National Productivity Board (1994), *Productivity and Quality Statement 1994*, Magenta Colorprinters, Singapore.

National Productivity Corporation of Malaysia, *The Productivity Report* 1999.

Nehru, V. and Dhareshwar, A. (1994), 'New Estimates of Total Factor Productivity Growth for Developing and Industrial Countries', World Bank Policy Research Paper No. 1313.

Nelson, R. (1981), 'Research on Productivity Growth and Productivity Differences: Dead Ends and New Departures', *Journal of Economic Literature*, vol. 19: 1029–64.

Nerlove, M. (1965), *Estimation and Identification of Cobb-Douglas Productions*, Rand McNally, Chicago, IL.

Nishimizu, M. and Page, J. (1982), 'Total Factor Productivity Growth, Technological Progress and Technical Efficiency Change: Yugoslavia 1965–78', *The Economic Journal*, vol. 92, no. 368: 920–36.

— (1991), 'Trade Policy, Market Orientation and Productivity Change in Industry', in J. de Melo and Sapir, A. (eds), *Trade Theory and Economic Reforms: Essays in Honour of Bela Balassa*, Blackwell Publishers, Massachusetts.

Norsworthy, J.R. and Jang S.L. (1992), *Empirical Measurement and Analysis of Productivity and Technological Change*, Elsevier Science Publishers, North Holland.

Norsworthy, J.R., Jang S.L. and Lu, W.Y. (1988), *Annual Depreciation Rates by Industry*, Working Paper.

Norsworthy, J.R. and Malmquist, J.R., David, H. (1983), 'Input Measurement and Productivity Growth in Japanese and US Manufacturing', *American Economic Review*, vol. 73, no. 5: 947–67.

Ockowski, E. and Sharma, K. (2001), 'Imperfect Competition, Returns to Scale and Productivity Growth in Australia Manufacturing: A Smooth Transition Approach to Trade Liberalization', *International Economic Journal*, vol. 15, no. 2: 99–113.

Okamoto, Y. (1994), 'Impact of Trade and FDI Liberalization Policies on the Malaysian Economy', *Developing Economies*, vol. 32, no. 4: 460–78.

Okun, A.M. (1962), 'Potential GNP: Its Measurements and Significance', *Proceedings of the Business and Economic Statistics Section of the American Statistical Association*: 98–104.

Olesen, O.B. and Petersen, N.C. (1995), 'Chance Constrained Efficiency Analysis', *Management Science*, vol. 41: 442–57.

Olley, S. and Pakes, A. (1992), *The Dynamics of Productivity in the Telecommunications Equipment Industry*, NBER Working Paper no. 3977.

Olson, J.A, Schmidt, P. and Waldman, D.M. (1980), 'A Monte Carlo Study of Estimators of Stochastic Production Functions', *Journal of Econometrics*, vol. 13, no. 1: 67–82.

Oulton, N. and O'Mahoney, M. (1994), *Productivity and Growth: A Study of British Industry, 1954–86*, Cambridge University Press, Cambridge.

Owyong, D. (2001), 'Singapore', in *Measuring Total Factor Productivity – Survey Report*, Asian Productivity Organisation, Tokyo.

Page, J.M. (1984), 'Firm Size and Technical Efficiency: Application of Production Frontiers to Indian Survey Data', *Journal of Development Economics*, vol. 16, no. 1/2: 129–152.

Parham, D. and Makin. (2000), 'Australia's Productivity Performance', in *Productivity Growth and Industrial Structure in the Pacific Region*, Japan Committee for Pacific Economic Outlook and Pacific Economic Cooperation Council.

Park, W.A. (1996), 'Financial Liberalization: The Korean Experience' in Ito, Taketoshi and Krueger, Anne (eds) *Financial Deregulation and Integration in East Asia*, National Bureau of Economic Research, University of Chicago Press, Chicago.

Pasha, H.A. and Qureshi, T. (1984), 'Capacity Utilization in Selected Industries in Pakistan', *Pakistan Journal of Applied Economics*, vol. 3, no. 1: 29–56.

Pitt, M.M. and Lee, L.F. (1981), 'Measurement and Sources of Technical Inefficiency in the Indonesian Weaving Industry', *Journal of Development Economics*, vol. 9: 43–64.

Ramstetter, E.D. (ed) (1999), *Recent Trends and Prospects for Major Asian Economies*, East Asian Economic Perspectives, vol. 10, Special Issue.

Rao, V.V. Bhanoji and Lee, C. (1995), 'Sources of Growth in the Singapore Economy and its Manufacturing and Service Sectors', *Singapore Economic-Review*, vol. 40, no. 1: 83–115.

Rangan, N., Hassan, Y.A., Pasurka, C. and Grabowski, R. (1988), 'The Technical Efficiency of US Banks', *Economic Letters*, vol. 28, no. 2: 169–75.

Rao, P. and Battesse, George E. (1998), *An Introduction to Efficiency and Productivity Analysis*, Kulwer Academic, Boston, MA.

Rasiah, R. (1995), *Foreign Capital and Industrialization in Malaysia*, Macmillan, London.

Ray, S.C. and Desli, E. (1997), 'Productivity Growth, Technical Progress, and Efficiency Change in Industrialized Countries: Comment', *American Economic Review*, vol. 87, no. 5: 1033–39.

Resti, A. (1997), 'Evaluating the Cost Efficiency of the Italian Banking System: What Can Learned from the Joint Application of Parametric and Non-Parametric Techniques', Journal of *Banking and Finance*, vol. 21, no. 2: 221–50.

Richmond, J. (1974), 'Estimating the Efficiency of Production', *International Economic Review*, vol. 15, no. 2: 515–21.

Robinson, J. (1970), 'Capital Theory Up To Date', *Canadian Journal of Economics*, vol. 3, no. 2: 309–17.

Rodriguez, F. and Rodrik, D. (1999), *Trade Policy and Economic Growth: A Skeptic's Guide to the Cross-National Evidence*, Centre for Economic Policy Research Working Paper 2143.

Rodrik, D. (1992a), 'The Limits of Trade Policy Reforms in Developing Countries', *Journal of Economic Perspectives*, vol 6, no. 1: 87–105.

— (1992b), 'Closing the Productivity Gap: Does Trade Liberalization Really Help?', in Helleiner, G.K. (ed.), *Trade Policy, Industrialisation and Development: New Perspectives*, Oxford University Press, Oxford.

— (1995), 'Trade and Industrial Policy Reform' in Behrman, J. and Srinivasan, T.N. (eds) *Handbook of Development Economics Volume III*, Elsevier Science, Amsterdam, New York and Oxford.

— (1997), *TFPG Controversies, Institutions, and Economic Performance in East Asia*, NBER Working Paper 5914.

Romer, P.M. (1986), 'Increasing Returns and Long-Run Growth', *Journal of Political Economy*, vol. 94, no. 5: 1002–37.

Sachs, J.D. and Warner, A.M. (1995), 'Economic Reform and the Process of Global Integration', *Brooking Papers on Economic Activity* 1: 1–118.

Sakellaris, P. and Wilson, D.J. (2002), 'Quantifying Embodied Technological Change', Paper presented at the American Economic Association Meeting, Atlanta.

Sarel, M. (1995), 'Growth in East Asia: What We Can and What We Cannot Infer', Paper Presented at the Conference on Growth and Productivity, organised by the Reserve Bank of Australia in Sydney, July, also an IMF Working Paper 95/98.

— (1997), 'Growth and Productivity in ASEAN Countries', IMF Working Paper 97/97.

Sargent, T.C. and Rodriguez, A.R. (2000), 'Labour or Total Factor Productivity: Do We Need To Choose?', *International Productivity Monitor*, no. 1: 41–4.

Scherer, F.M. (1986), Industrial Market Structure and Economic Performance, Rand McNally, Chicago.

Schmidt, P. (1976), 'On the Statistical Estimation of the Parametric Frontier Production Frontier', *Review of Economics and Statistics*, vol. 58: 238–9.

Schmidt, P. and Sickles, R.C. (1984), 'Production Frontiers and Panel Data', *Journal of Business and Economic Statistics*, vol. 2: 367–74.

— (1985/86), 'Frontier Production Functions', *Econometric Reviews* vol. 4, no. 2: 289–328.

Schultz, T.W. (1975), 'The Value of the Ability to Deal With Disequilibria', *Journal of Economic Literature*, vol. 13, no. 3: 827–46.

Schydlowsky, M.D. (1973), 'On Determining the Causality of Underutilization of Capacity', Working Note, Department of Economics, Boston University, MA (Mimeo).

— (1976), *Capital Utilization, Growth, Employment, Balance of Payments and Price Stabilization*, Discussion Paper Series No. 22, Department of Economics, Boston University.

Scott, M.F. (1989), *A New View of Economic Growth*, Oxford University Press, New York.

Seiford, L.M. and Thrall, R.M. (1990), 'Recent Developments in DEA: The Mathematical Programming Approach to Frontier Analysis', *Journal of Econometrics*, vol. 46: 7–38.

Seitz, W.D. (1970), 'The Measurement of Efficiency Relative to a Frontier Production Function', *American Journal of Agricultural Economics*, vol. 52, no. 4: 505–11.

Sengupta, J.K. (1989), *Efficiency Analysis By Production Frontier: The Nonparametric Approach*, Kluwer, Dordrecht.

— (1990), 'Transformations in Stochastic DEA Models', *Journal of Econometrics*, vol. 46, no. 1/2: 109–23.

— (1998), 'Stochastic Data Envelopment Analysis: A New Approach', *Applied Economics Letters*, vol. 5: 287–90.

Shaikh, A. (1980), 'Laws of Production and Laws of Algebra: Humbug II', in Nell, Edward J. (ed), *Growth, Profits and Property: Essays in the Revival of Political Economy*, Cambridge University Press, Cambridge: 80–95.

Shaw, G.K. (1992), 'Policy Implications of Endogenous Growth Theory', *Economic Journal*, vol. 102: 611–21.

Sheehan, M. (1997), 'The Evolution of Technical Efficiency in the North Ireland Manufacturing Sector, 1973–1985', *Scottish Journal of Political Economy*, vol. 44, no. 1: 59–81.

Shephard, R.W. (1970), *Theory of Cost and Production Functions*, Princeton University Press, Princeton, NJ.

Sherman, H.D. and F. Gold (1985), 'Bank Branch Operation Efficiency: Evaluation with Data Envelopment Analysis', *Journal of Banking and Finance*, vol. 9, no. 2: 291–315.

Shimada, H. (1996), 'Impact of DFI on the Supply Side of the Singapore Economy', *ASEAN Economic Bulletin*, vol. 12, no. 3: 369–79.

Simar, L. (1992), 'Estimating Efficiencies from Frontier Models with Panel Data: A Comparison of Parametric, Non-Parametric and Semi-Parametric Methods with Bootstrapping', *Journal of Productivity Analysis*, vol. 3: 171–203.

— (2000), 'A General Methodology for Bootstrapping in Non-Parametric Frontier Models', *Journal of Applied Statistics*, vol. 27, no. 6: 779–803.

Simar, L. and Wilson, P. (1999), 'Estimating and Bootstrapping Malmquist Indices', *European Journal of Operational Research*, vol. 115, no. 3: 459–71.

Solow, R.M. (1957), 'Technical Change and the Aggregate Production Function', *Review of Economics and Statistics*, vol. 39, no. 3: 312–20.

— (1960), 'Investment and Technical Progress', in Arrow, K.J., Karlin, S. and Suppes, P. (eds), *Mathematical Methods in the Social Sciences*, Stanford University Press, California.

Srinivasan, P.V. (1992), 'Determinants of Capacity Utilization in Indian Industries', *Journal of Quantitative Economics*, vol. 8, no. 1: 139–56.

Star, S. (1974), 'Accounting for the Growth of Output', *American Economic Review*, vol. 64, no. 1: 122–35.

Stiroh, K. (2001), 'What Drives Productivity Growth', *Economic Policy Review*, vol. 7, no. 1: 37–60.

Stolp, C. (1990), 'Strengths and Weaknesses of Data Envelopment Analysis: An Urban and Regional Perspective', *Computers, Environment and Urban Systems*, vol. 14, no. 2: 103–16.

Sung, Y.W. and Wong, K.Y. (2000), 'Growth of Hong Kong Before and After Its Reversion to China: The China Factor', *Pacific Economic Review*, vol. 5, no. 2; 201–28.

Swamy, P.A.V.B. (1970), 'Efficient Inference in a Random Coefficient Regression Model', *Econometrica*, vol. 38: 311–23.

Syrquin, M. (1986), 'Productivity Growth and Factor Reallocation', in Chenery, H.B., Robinson, S. and Syrquin, M. (1986), *Industrialisation and Growth: A Comparative Study*, Oxford University Press, New York.

Szulc, B.J. (1964), 'Indices for Multiregional Comparisons', *Prezeglad Statystyczny* (Statistical Review), vol. 3: 239–54.

Takenaka, H. (1995), 'Changing Asia-Pacific and the Japanese Economy', Keio University, Mimeo.

Tan, L.Y. and Virabhak, S. (1998), 'Total Factor Productivity Growth in Singapore's Service Industries', *Journal of Economic Studies*, vol. 25, no. 5: 392–409.

Tan, R.G.K., Lall, A. and Tan, M.C.H. (2000), 'Singapore', in *Productivity Growth and Industrial Structure in the Pacific Region*, Japan Committee for Pacific Economic Outlook and Pacific Economic Cooperation Council, Japan.

Tang, K.Y. (2000), 'Hong Kong, China', in *Productivity Growth and Industrial Structure in the Pacific Region*, Japan Committee for Pacific Economic Outlook and Pacific Economic Cooperation Council, Japan.

Tay, S.T. (1992), 'Determinants of Production Efficiency: An Econometric Analysis of the Manufacturing Industries in Singapore', Working Paper Series No:10, School of Accountancy and Business, Nanyang Technological University.

Tham, S.Y. (1995), 'Productivity, Growth and Development in Malaysia', *Singapore Economic Review,* vol. 40, no. 1: 41–63.

— (1996), 'Productivity and Competitiveness of Malaysian Manufacturing Sector', Paper presented at the National Convention of the 7th Malaysian Plan, August, Kuala Lumpur.

— (1997), 'Determinants of Productivity Growth in the Malaysian Manufacturing Sector', *ASEAN Economic Bulletin*, vol. 13, no. 3: 333–43.

Thanassoulis, E. (2001), *Introduction to the Theory and Application of Data Envelopment Analysis*, Kluwer, Norwell, Massachusetts.

Thanassoulis, E. and Emrouznejad A. (1996), *Warwick Windows DEA, User's Guide*, Warwick University, UK. See http://www.warwick.ac.uk/~bsrlu/findex.htm.

Theil, H. (1973), 'A New Index Number Formula', *Review of Economics and Statistics*, vol. 54: 552–54.

Thoumi, F.E. (1981), 'Columbia: Country Study', in Bautista, R., Hughes, H., Lim, D., Morawetz, D. and F.E. Thoumi (eds), *Capital Utilization in Manufacturing*, Oxford University Press, Oxford.

Timmer, C.P. (1971), 'Using a Probabilistic Frontier Production Function To Measure Technical Efficiency', *Journal of Political Economy*, vol. 79, no. 4: 776–94.

Tinbergen, J. (1942), 'Zur Theorie der Langfristigen Wirtschaftsentwicklung', *Weltwirtsschaftliches Archiv*, vol. 55, no. 1: 511–49; translated as 'On the Theory of Trend Movements', in Klassen, L.H., Koych, L.M. and Witteveen, H.J. (eds) (1959), *Jan Tinbergen Selected Papers*, Amsterdam, North Holland: 82–221.

Toh, K.W. and Lim, T.G. (1992), 'Industrial Restructuring and Performance in Malaysia', Report prepared for World Institute for Development Economics Research, Helsinki.

Tsao, Y. (1982), 'Growth and Productivity in Singapore: A Supply Side Analysis', PhD Dissertation, Harvard University.

— (1985), 'Growth Without Productivity', *Journal of Development Economics*, vol. 18: 25–38.

Tybout, J.R. (1990), 'Making Noisy Data Sing: Estimating Production Technologies in Developing Countries', *Journal of Econometrics*, vol. 53: 25–44.

— (1992), 'Linking Trade and Productivity: New Research Directions', *World Bank Research Observer*, vol. 6, no. 1: 234–42.

Tyler, W.G. (1979), 'Technical Efficiency in Production in a Developing Country: An Empirical Investigation of the Brazilian Plastics and Steel Industries', *Oxford Economic Papers*, vol. 31, no. 3: 477–58.

Van Eklan, R. (1995), 'Accounting for Growth in Singapore', *IMF Occasional Paper 119.*

Varian, H., (1990), 'Goodness-Of-Fit In Optimizing Models', *Journal of Econometrics*, vol. 46: 125–40.

Vernon, R. (1966), 'International Investment and International Trade in the Product Cycle', *Quarterly Journal of Economics*, vol. 80, no. 2: 190–207.

Waldman, M. (1984), 'Properties of Technical Efficiency Estimations in the Stochastic Frontier Model', *Journal of Econometrics*, vol. 25, no. 3: 353–64.

Wan, G.H. (1995), 'Technical Change in Chinese State Industries', *Journal of Comparative Economics*, vol. 21: 308–25.

Wickens, M.R. (1970) 'Estimation of the Vintage Cobb-Douglas Production Function for the United States 1900–1960', *Review of Economics and Statistics*, vol. 52, no. 2: 187–93.

Wilson, P.W. (1995), 'Detecting Influential Observations in Data Envelopment Analysis', *Journal of Productivity Analysis*, vol. 6: 27–45.

Winston, G.C. (1971), 'Capital Utilization in Economic Development', *Economic Journal*, vol. 81, no. 3: 36–60.

— (1974), 'The Theory of Capital Utilization and Idleness', *Journal of Economic Literature*, vol. 12, no. 4: 1301–20.

Winston, G.C. and McCoy, T.O. (1974), 'Investment and the Optimal Idleness of Capital', *Review of Economic Studies*, vol. 41, no. 3: 110–25.

Wong, F.C. and Gan W.B. (1994), 'Total Factor Productivity Growth in the Singapore Manufacturing Industries During the 1980s', *Journal of Asian Economics*, vol. 5, no. 2: 177–96.

Wong, F.C. and Gan W.B. (1995), 'Technical Efficiency and Productivity Growth in Singapore's Manufacturing Industries', Mimeo.

Wong, F.C. and Tok, Y.W. (1994), 'Technical Efficiency and Total Factor Productivity Growth in the Singapore Manufacturing Industries during 1980s', Paper presented at the 2nd International Conference on Asia-Pacific Economic Modelling, Sydney, 24–26 August.

Wong, R.Y.C. (1996), 'The Growth of Manufacturing and Services in Hong Kong', *HKCER Letters,* no.40.

World Bank (1989), *Malaysia: Matching Risks and Rewards in a Mixed Economy*, World Bank, Washington, DC.

— (1993), *The East Asian Miracle: Economic Growth and Public Policy*, Oxford University Press, New York.

— (1995), *Malaysia Meeting Labour Needs: More Workers and Better Skills*, World Bank, Washington, DC.

World Competitiveness Report 1990, Jointly prepared by the International Institute for Management Development and the World Economic Forum, Switzerland.

Xue, M. and Harker, P.T. (1999), 'Overcoming the Inherent Dependency of DEA Efficiency Scores: A Bootstrap Approach', Working Paper 99-17, Financial Institution Centre, Wharton School, University of Pennsylvania.

Yang, T.L. (1999), *Korea in the 21st Century*, Nova Science Publishers, New York.

You, J.K. (1976), 'Embodied and Disembodied Technical Progress in the United States, 1929–1968', *Review of Economics and Statistics*, vol. 58, no. 1: 123–27.

Young, A. (1992), 'A Tale of Two Cities: Factor Accumulation and Technical Change in Hong Kong and Singapore', *National Bureau of Economics Research*, Macroeconomics Annual 1992: 13–54.

— (1994), 'Lessons from the East Asian NICs: A Contrarian View', *European Economic Review*, vol. 38, no. 3/4: 964–73.

— (1995), 'Tyranny of Numbers: Confronting the Statistical Realities of the East Asian Growth Experience', *Quarterly Journal of Economics*, vol. 110, no. 3: 641–80.

Zellner, A.S. (1971), *An Introduction to Bayesian Inference in Econometrics*, John Wiley & Sons, New York.

Zellner, A.S., Kementa, J. and Dreze, J. (1966), 'Specification and Estimation of Cobb-Douglas Production Functions', *Econometrica*, vol. 34: 784–95.

Index